Photoshop® CS3 for Forensics Professionals

Photoshop® CS3 for Forensics Professionals

A Complete Digital Imaging Course for Investigators

George Reis

Wiley Publishing, Inc.

Acquisitions and Development Editor: Pete Gaughan
Technical Editor: Casey Caudle
Production Editor: Sarah Groff-Palermo
Copy Editor: Judy Flynn
Production Manager: Tim Tate
Vice President and Executive Group Publisher: Richard Swadley
Vice President and Executive Publisher: Joseph B. Wikert
Vice President and Publisher: Neil Edde
Media Project Supervisor: Laura Atkinson
Media Development Specialist: Kit Malone
Media Quality Assurance: Angie Denny
Book Designer: Franz Baumhackl
Compositor: Chris Gillespie, Happenstance Type-O-Rama
Proofreader: Ian Golder
Indexer: Ted Laux
Anniversary Logo Design: Richard Pacifico
Cover Designer: Ryan Sneed
Cover Image: © Pete Gardner / Digital Vision / gettyimages

Copyright © 2007 by Wiley Publishing, Inc., Indianapolis, Indiana

Published simultaneously in Canada

ISBN: 978-0-470-11454-4

No part of this publication may be reproduced, stored in a retrieval system, or transmitted in any form or by any means, electronic, mechanical, photocopying, recording, scanning, or otherwise, except as permitted under Sections 107 or 108 of the 1976 United States Copyright Act, without either the prior written permission of the Publisher, or authorization through payment of the appropriate per-copy fee to the Copyright Clearance Center, 222 Rosewood Drive, Danvers, MA 01923, (978) 750-8400, fax (978) 646-8600. Requests to the Publisher for permission should be addressed to the Legal Department, Wiley Publishing, Inc., 10475 Crosspoint Blvd., Indianapolis, IN 46256, (317) 572-3447, fax (317) 572-4355, or online at http://www.wiley.com/go/permissions.

Limit of Liability/Disclaimer of Warranty: The publisher and the author make no representations or warranties with respect to the accuracy or completeness of the contents of this work and specifically disclaim all warranties, including without limitation warranties of fitness for a particular purpose. No warranty may be created or extended by sales or promotional materials. The advice and strategies contained herein may not be suitable for every situation. This work is sold with the understanding that the publisher is not engaged in rendering legal, accounting, or other professional services. If professional assistance is required, the services of a competent professional person should be sought. Neither the publisher nor the author shall be liable for damages arising herefrom. The fact that an organization or Website is referred to in this work as a citation and/or a potential source of further information does not mean that the author or the publisher endorses the information the organization or Website may provide or recommendations it may make. Further, readers should be aware that Internet Websites listed in this work may have changed or disappeared between when this work was written and when it is read.

For general information on our other products and services or to obtain technical support, please contact our Customer Care Department within the U.S. at (800) 762-2974, outside the U.S. at (317) 572-3993, or fax (317) 572-4002.

Wiley also publishes its books in a variety of electronic formats. Some content that appears in print may not be available in electronic books.

Library of Congress Cataloging-in-Publication Data is available from the publisher.

TRADEMARKS: Wiley, the Wiley logo, and the Sybex logo are trademarks or registered trademarks of John Wiley & Sons, Inc. and/or its affiliates, in the United States and other countries, and may not be used without written permission. Photoshop is a registered trademark of Adobe Systems Incorporated. Ocean Systems, ClearID, and dPlex Pro are trademarks of Ocean Systems. All other trademarks are the property of their respective owners. Wiley Publishing, Inc., is not associated with any product or vendor mentioned in this book.

10 9 8 7 6 5 4 3 2 1

Dear Reader

Thank you for choosing *Photoshop CS3 for Forensics Professionals.* This book is part of a family of premium quality Sybex graphics books, all written by outstanding authors who combine practical experience with a gift for teaching.

Sybex was founded in 1976. More than thirty years later, we're still committed to producing consistently exceptional books. With each of our graphics titles we're working hard to set a new standard for the industry. From the paper we print on, to the writers and artists we work with, our goal is to bring you the best graphics books available.

I hope you see all that reflected in these pages. I'd be very interested to hear your comments and get your feedback on how we're doing. Feel free to let me know what you think about this or any other Sybex book by sending me an e-mail at nedde@wiley.com, or if you think you've found an error in this book, please visit http://wiley.custhelp.com. Customer feedback is critical to our efforts at Sybex.

Best regards,

NEIL EDDE
Vice President and Publisher
Sybex, an Imprint of Wiley

Acknowledgments

Many people have helped me to learn more about photography, digital imaging, and image processing. And, many people have contributed substantially to helping this book come into existence. I'd like to thank everyone who has contributed and name a few who have stood out.

Casey Caudle provided technical editing for me and corrected many mistakes and misstatements. Casey played a good devil's advocate when necessary and made this book much better through his contributions.

Steve Everist, Ken Jones, Joe Heppler, Steve Scarborough, and Mike French all provided early feedback that was key to the development of the material in this book.

Chris Russ and Dr. John Russ have been my "go to" experts whenever I've had questions about image processing. They have always been generous with their time and information and have helped me to understand many image processing concepts.

Pete Gaughan is my editor at Sybex. Pete is a hands-on editor who asks important questions along the way to make sure the information is accurate, consistent, and appropriate.

The Adobe Photoshop team cannot go without thanks. I've been fortunate to have had a good relationship with Adobe for several years, and the product managers and engineers are a phenomenal group. I believe Adobe is one of the few large corporations that does a great job of listening to its customers and taking action on customer feedback.

A few thousand police officers, fingerprint examiners, crime scene investigators, forensic video analysts, photographers, and imaging specialists have taken workshops from me over the years. I always learn from them. Much of the material in this book is from things I've learned from those taking my workshops.

About the Author

George Reis has 15 years of experience as a forensic photographer, fingerprint examiner, and crime scene investigator with the Newport Beach (California) Police Department. During that time, he brought digital imaging technology to the NBPD in several phases, beginning in 1992, making that agency one of the first in the world to utilize this technology in their daily workflow.

Reis is certified by the International Association for Identification (IAI) in Photography and Digital Imaging. He serves on the board of the IAI Photography and Digital Imaging certification committee.

Reis now provides training and consulting services to law enforcement through his company, Imaging Forensics, Inc. Thousands of law enforcement personnel have taken workshops from Reis since 1995. He provides workshops in forensic photography, Photoshop for forensic video analysis, Photoshop for fingerprint analysis, introduction to Photoshop in forensics, and other related topics.

Through Imaging Forensics, Reis also provides consulting and expert witness services to prosecutors and civil and defense attorneys. He has worked on cases involving video analysis, photographic analysis, image processing, and the application of Photoshop throughout the U.S. and Canada.

Reis lives with his wife, Cathy, in southern California. He enjoys organic gardening, reading the classics, listening to the blues, and attending plays, ballets, and musicals as well as smoking fine cigars and drinking a good IPA or Cabernet. His daughter, Emily, graduated from the University of Southern California and lives in New York.

Contents

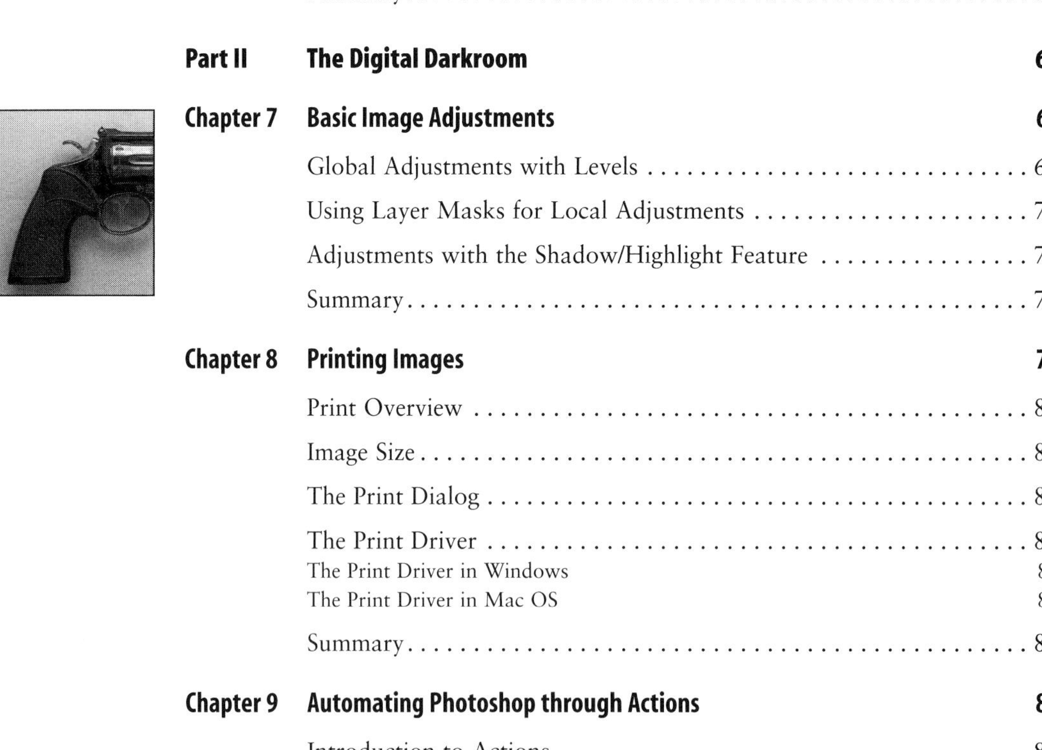

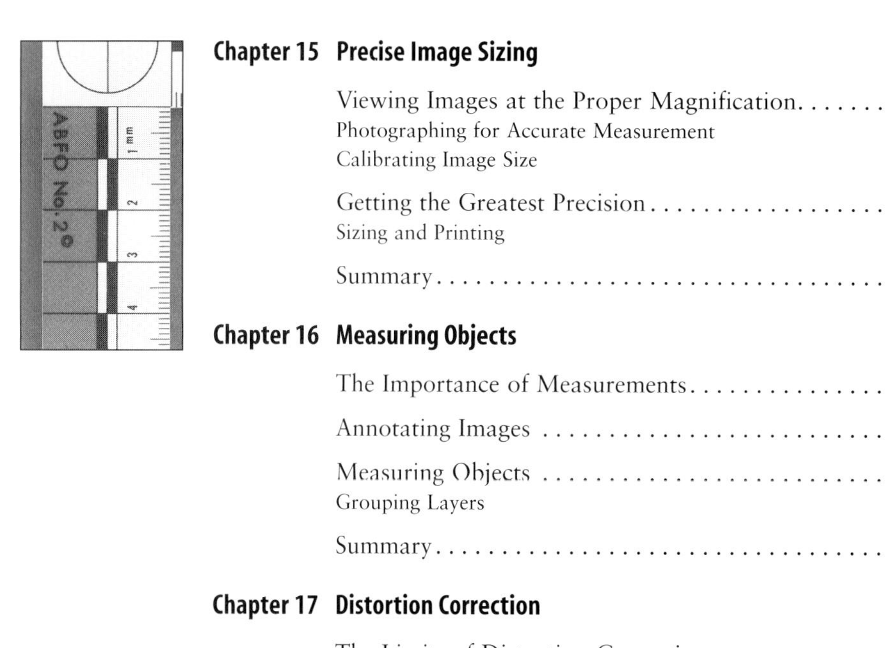

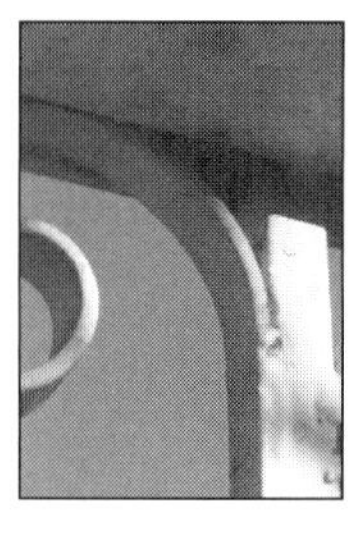

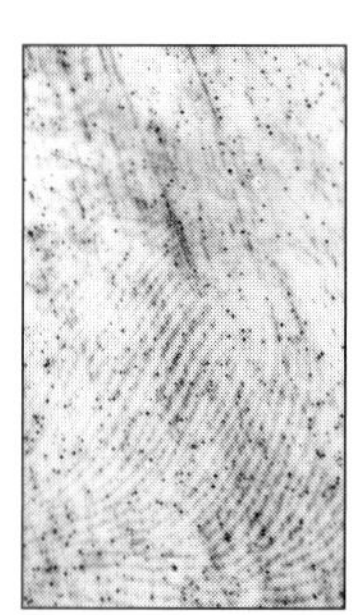

Photoshop File Edit Image
4/22/02
6 21 05P

Introduction

Today it seems like everyone has a digital camera and that digital photography has been around forever. There are hundreds of models of digital cameras available, and finding film is getting to be more and more difficult. But, this really isn't the way it always was.

In 1992, I was working at the Newport Beach Police Department. The department bought a Kodak DCS 200 digital camera that provided a whopping 1.5 million pixels and cost around $10,000. It didn't use a memory card, but it had an internal computer hard drive and a SCSI connection to download photos to the computer. All of the components in the camera were of the highest quality, and the digital photos of fingerprints and evidence actually looked incredible.

In those days, a handful of law enforcement users were experimenting with digital imaging technology. If one of us discovered something earth changing, like how to make a fingerprint 1:1, we'd all be on the phone with each other talking in excited voices. When any of us presented our images at a conference and (for example) increased the contrast on a projected image, the "oohs" and "ahhs" from the audience were comparable to what you would hear at a Doug Henning performance.

Fifteen years later, there are very few cameras available with fewer than 3 million pixels, although for under $40 you can get a 640×480 Barbie digital camera. Everyone knows how to adjust the contrast on a digital image, so there are no more "oohs" and "ahhs." Digital photography has become the norm, and yet there are very few resources for forensics users on the topics of digital photography, image processing, and using software like Adobe Photoshop. Even more surprising is that there is still a large amount of misinformation about the use of digital imaging in a law enforcement environment.

Last year I provided some training to personnel at an East Coast state law enforcement agency. They were just incorporating digital cameras. They waited until then because they were under the impression that digital images couldn't be used in court. And even after making the decision to use digital photography, they were under the impression that no adjustments could be made to their images and that they had to incorporate some sort of specialized image authentication and security software to use this technology at all! This story isn't nearly as unusual as it should be. And the misinformation comes from all levels; it comes from vendors trying to sell expensive solutions for nonexistent problems, from administrative personnel who heard this from someone at another agency—but can't remember who or where—and from end users who are afraid that technology may eliminate their job.

My hope is that this book will do two things: correct some of the misinformation and provide a resource of methods to do many of the imaging tasks in a law enforcement setting.

We can use digital cameras in a law enforcement setting, and we can make adjustments to those images. Many times, we are obligated to do so in order to present a fair representation of what we saw to the jurors in a case. We also can enhance images to see the detail better in a fingerprint, tool mark, or video from a security camera. The first section of this book deals with many of the issues that will hopefully clear up some of the misinformation that continues to circulate in the forensics community.

Providing a resource of methods to perform the imaging tasks that face us in a law enforcement setting is what the second and third sections deal with. Each chapter is a step-by-step tutorial to provide the basics for the tasks that we have at hand.

Who Should Read This Book

There are four groups that may benefit from this book:

Forensics Professionals This book is primarily intended for those working in forensics to use as a resource for imaging tasks. This includes photographers, fingerprint examiners, video analysts, tool mark and footwear examiners, crime scene investigators, and criminalists. But that list isn't complete; in many agencies a patrol officer is responsible for maintaining the photo archive and printing images for court, or this task may fall to a community services officer or a detective. Regardless of their title, this book is for those with jobs in law enforcement whose work includes taking photos, archiving photos, or working with photos in any aspect in the law enforcement workflow.

Attorneys Although this book only touches on the legal aspects of digital imaging in forensics, attorneys can use this book to see some of what can be realistically accomplished with imaging technology and whether their expert has kept within the guidelines of best practices.

Non-forensics Science and Technical Users In many technical fields, from biomedical and research to architecture, engineering, and astronomy, best practices and image content play a larger role than aesthetics. In these fields, the techniques used in this book may be helpful.

Students Any student considering any aspect of law enforcement, forensics, or any technical field in which imaging may be part of your job can benefit from the techniques in this book. The concepts of best practices, repeatability of image processing techniques, and using valid procedures will be valuable in many career paths.

What You Will Learn

The first section of this book provides the reader with the basics of using Photoshop in a forensics setting. This includes the use of best practices to exceed the requirements of court, setting up preferences in Photoshop and Bridge, and developing a workflow from archiving to courtroom testimony.

It is recommended that you read and understand the first section of this book before continuing with the rest. All remaining chapters stand on their own and do not need to be read in any particular order.

The second two sections of the book provide the reader with simple tutorials of how to do many tasks that typically arise in a forensics environment. I'll cover basic digital darkroom tasks such as correcting a color cast, printing images for court, and making contact sheets for a detective or prosecutor as well as more advanced tasks such as eliminating repeating patterns from the background of a fingerprint image and frame averaging a sequence of images to reduce image noise.

What You Need

To complete any of the tutorials in this book, you will need a recent version of Adobe Photoshop. Many of the techniques can be done with rather old versions of Photoshop, some require CS2 or newer, and a couple require CS3. In addition, some things require scripts or plug-ins that are included on the companion CD. Any technique can be used with your own images or with the images provided on the accompanying CD.

What Is Covered in This Book

Photoshop CS3 for Forensic Professionals is organized to provide you with general information about setting up a digital imaging workflow in a forensic setting, and tutorials providing step-by-step methods for many of the procedures that may be done in a forensic setting.

Part I: The Essentials. The chapters in this section are about setting up your workflow and archiving your images and provides an introduction to Adobe Photoshop and Adobe Bridge, including setting up preferences. Also covered are the concepts of best practices for writing reports and providing courtroom testimony.

Chapter 1: Best Practices. Best practice are standard operating procedures or guidelines that we follow to maintain the integrity of our images.

Chapter 2: Reports and Testimony. Any case will potentially end up in court. This chapter shows you how to prepare good quality reports and testify with confidence.

Chapter 3: Basic Imaging Settings. This chapter covers the color settings, preferences, and monitor calibration issues for a forensic imaging environment.

Chapter 4: Navigating with Bridge. Bridge is a companion product that ships with Photoshop and is an excellent tool for file navigation, downloading digital photos, and batch-processing Photoshop actions.

Chapter 5: Camera Raw. This chapter provides an introduction to the Adobe Photoshop Camera Raw plug-in. You'll learn the capabilities of this powerful tool for working with Raw formats from digital files and now for TIFF and JPEG files too.

Chapter 6: Viewing Metadata. Metadata can be important in both image analysis and in recording the history of your own image processing steps.

Part II: The Digital Darkroom. This section includes seven chapters on what traditionally has been done in the darkroom, from correcting color casts to making prints for court and creating courtroom exhibits.

Chapter 7: Basic Image Adjustments. This chapter includes information on correcting color casts and bad exposures globally (to the entire image) as well as making local adjustments.

Chapter 8: Printing Images. In this chapter, I'll show you how to set the image size, resolution, and color management policies to obtain the best-quality prints using Photoshop and your printer.

Chapter 9: Automating Photoshop through Actions. Actions are shortcuts that can increase the efficiency of using Photoshop. They can be used for batch printing, color correction, image analysis techniques, and any process that is applied to multiple images.

Chapter 10: Contact Sheets. Contact sheets are pages of thumbnail-sized images. This chapter covers the uses of the built-in Photoshop tool for making contact sheets as well as a free script that gives more capabilities.

Chapter 11: PDF Presentations. This is a tool for making multiple-page PDF files of digital images. It can also be an alternative to using PowerPoint for courtroom presentation of digital images.

Chapter 12: Preparing Court Exhibits. This chapter introduces methods for combining multiple images onto a single canvas and adding annotations.

Chapter 13: Photomerge. Photomerge provides a way to combine multiple, overlapping digital photos into a single, high-resolution image. This feature is great for photographing very large scenes as well as scenes in very confined locations such as a hallway, closet, or bathroom.

Part III: Image Analysis and Enhancement. The chapters in Part III cover techniques for clarifying images so that details can be better viewed and used for analysis or comparison.

Chapter 14: Compositing Images. Using layer modes, you can combine multiple images in Photoshop layers and blend them.

Chapter 15: Precise Image Sizing. Image sizing enables you to calibrate your images to exactly 1:1 or other ratios for fingerprints, tool marks, footwear, and so on.

Chapter 16: Measuring Objects. You can measure the length as well as the angles of objects in your images. This can be a benefit in evidence photos, crime scene and traffic collision photos, and any photo in which the size or angle of objects are important.

Chapter 17: Lens Distortion Correction. You can use a Photoshop filter to correct for the barrel distortion inherent in photographs taken with wide-angle lenses.

Chapter 18: Noise Reduction. In this chapter, I'll show you methods to reduce the amount of image noise in digital images.

Chapter 19: Deblurring and Sharpening. This chapter covers techniques for eliminating blur caused by improper focus and motion blur as well as the use of filters for increasing edge contrast to see edge detail better.

Chapter 20: Contrast Enhancement. You can use the same techniques you learned in Chapter 7 to enhance images and clarify detail. This chapter shows you how.

Chapter 21: Color Isolation. Color isolation is perhaps one of the most powerful Photoshop techniques for extracting important image data when color information is present in your images.

Chapter 22: Pattern Removal. This chapter covers a Photoshop plug-in filter as well as a free stand-alone software to remove repeating patterns from your images.

Chapter 23: Forensic Video Analysis. There are some unique aspects to forensic video analysis—such as multiplexing, interlacing, and pixel aspect ratio distortions—that can be addressed in Photoshop. This chapter covers methods for these as well as using frame averaging techniques for image noise reduction.

Chapter 24: Additional Features. Some features that aren't covered in separate chapters are discussed in this chapter.

What's on the CD

The companion CD-ROM provides sample images that you can use to practice the techniques from the book, following along with the tutorials.

I've also included some demo software and several scripts that you can install in your Photoshop folder to save time and make your work more effective:

- Ocean Systems ClearID™: Plug-in filters and scripts that include a deconvolution filter (Chapter 19), Pattern Remover (Chapter 22), and several other valuable filters. This is a demo version and more information can be obtained from Ocean Systems at www.oceansystems.com.
- Contact Sheet X: A script that adds functionality for making contact sheets in Photoshop as described in Chapter 10. I've also added two templates with the script titled "Police_Landscape.psd" and "Police_Portrait.psd."

- AdjustmentLayers: A script that automatically names Adjustment Layers with the parameters set in the layer. This script is referred to in several chapters that use Adjustment Layers.
- Field Advance: A script that enables field-level advance of video files or interlaced TIFF sequences in Photoshop as described in Chapter 23.
- Frame Average: A script that automates the process for frame averaging in Photoshop as described in Chapter 23.

How to Contact the Author

I welcome feedback from you about this book or about books you'd like to see from me in the future. You can reach me by writing to reis@imagingforensics.com. For more information about my work, please visit my website at www.imagingforensics.com.

Sybex strives to keep you supplied with the latest tools and information you need for your work. Please check the website at www.sybex.com, where we'll post additional content and updates that supplement this book if the need arises. Enter **George Reis** or **Photoshop Forensics** in the search box (or type the book's ISBN—**9780470114544**), and click Search to get to the book's update page.

The Essentials

I

This first section of six chapters covers several issues that one should be familiar with prior to working with images in an imaging forensics environment. After reviewing the rules and guidelines that govern the use and handling of images in a legal setting, we'll look at how to set up and navigate through Photoshop, Bridge, and Adobe Camera Raw.

1 Best Practices

In any aspect of evidence collection, crime scene documentation, and evidence processing, it is important to adhere to best practices in the methods used and the documentation recorded to show that the evidence presented is what it purports to be. Best practices may frequently go beyond the requirements of court so that any legitimate challenge to the procedures or the results can be met. That is, the goal isn't merely to have the evidence admitted into court; the evidence must also hold up to any legitimate challenges once it has been admitted into court.

Chapter Contents

Rules of Evidence

The use of digital images in court is determined by rules of evidence and by case law. In both of those areas (at the time of this writing), digital images are allowed as evidence in court (and have been since at least 1991). There are no requirements beyond those required of any photographic image—and that is that they depict what they purport to depict.

The significant portions of the Federal Rules of Evidence are rules 1001 to 1008 (see sidebar). These rules define what is considered an original, what is considered a duplicate, and the burden of proof should there be a challenge. Most states also have their own rules of evidence; many have adopted the wording of the Federal Rules.

Federal Rules of Evidence (Rules 1001—1008)

Rule 1001. Definitions

For purposes of this article the following definitions are applicable:

1 Writings and recordings. "Writings" and "recordings" consist of letters, words, or numbers, or their equivalent, set down by handwriting, typewriting, printing, photostating, photographing, magnetic impulse, mechanical or electronic recording, or other form of data compilation.

2 Photographs. "Photographs" include still photographs, X-ray films, video tapes, and motion pictures.

3 Original. An "original" of a writing or recording is the writing or recording itself or any counterpart intended to have the same effect by a person executing or issuing it. An "original" of a photograph includes the negative or any print therefrom. If data are stored in a computer or similar device, any printout or other output readable by sight, shown to reflect the data accurately, is an "original".

4 Duplicate. A "duplicate" is a counterpart produced by the same impression as the original, or from the same matrix, or by means of photography, including enlargements and miniatures, or by mechanical or electronic re-recording, or by chemical reproduction, or by other equivalent techniques which accurately reproduces the original.

Rule 1002. Requirement of Original

To prove the content of a writing, recording, or photograph, the original writing, recording, or photograph is required, except as otherwise provided in these rules or by Act of Congress.

Rule 1003. Admissibility of Duplicates

A duplicate is admissible to the same extent as an original unless (1) a genuine question is raised as to the authenticity of the original or (2) in the circumstances it would be unfair to admit the duplicate in lieu of the original.

Federal Rules of Evidence (Rules 1001—1008) *(Continued)*

Rule 1004. Admissibility of Other Evidence of Contents

The original is not required, and other evidence of the contents of a writing, recording, or photograph is admissible if—

1 Originals lost or destroyed. All originals are lost or have been destroyed, unless the proponent lost or destroyed them in bad faith; or

2 Original not obtainable. No original can be obtained by any available judicial process or procedure; or

3 Original in possession of opponent. At a time when an original was under the control of the party against whom offered, that party was put on notice, by the pleadings or otherwise, that the contents would be a subject of proof at the hearing, and that party does not produce the original at the hearing; or

4 Collateral matters. The writing, recording, or photograph is not closely related to a controlling issue.

Rule 1005. Public Records

The contents of an official record, or of a document authorized to be recorded or filed and actually recorded or filed, including data compilations in any form, if otherwise admissible, may be proved by copy, certified as correct in accordance with rule 902, or testified to be correct by a witness who has compared it with the original. If a copy which complies with the foregoing cannot be obtained by the exercise of reasonable diligence, then other evidence of the contents may be given.

Rule 1006. Summaries

The contents of voluminous writings, recordings, or photographs which cannot conveniently be examined in court may be presented in the form of a chart, summary, or calculation. The originals, or duplicates, shall be made available for examination or copying, or both, by other parties at reasonable time and place. The court may order that they be produced in court.

Rule 1007. Testimony or Written Admission of Party

Contents of writings, recordings, or photographs may be proved by the testimony or deposition of the party against whom offered or by that party's written admission, without accounting for the nonproduction of the original.

Rule 1008. Functions of Court and Jury

When the admissibility of other evidence of contents of writings, recordings, or photographs under these rules depends upon the fulfillment of a condition of fact, the question whether the condition has been fulfilled is ordinarily for the court to determine in accordance with the provisions of rule 104.

Continues

Federal Rules of Evidence (Rules 1001—1008) *(Continued)*

However, when an issue is raised (a) whether the asserted writing ever existed, or (b) whether another writing, recording, or photograph produced at the trial is the original, or (c) whether other evidence of contents correctly reflects the contents, the issue is for the trier of fact to determine as in the case of other issues of fact.

House Committee on the Judiciary, *Federal Rules of Evidence*, 108th Cong., 2nd sess., 2004. Committee Print 8.

Case Law

Case law includes Frye and Daubert challenges, appellate cases, and the plethora of non-challenged cases.

Frye or Daubert hearings may be held as a pretrial hearing to determine the admissibility of scientific evidence in court. The enhancement of fingerprints using digital image processing has been through three Frye hearings (*Commonwealth of Virginia v. Robert Douglas Knight*, 1991; *State of WA v. Eric Hayden*, 1995; *State of Florida v. Victor Reyes*, 2003). In each of these cases, the digital imaging technology met the court requirements and was determined to meet the threshold requirements of Frye. Additionally, the Hayden case was upheld on appeal in 1999. These three cases provide a strong foundation for the use of image processing techniques for image enhancement in court.

Additionally, thousands of cases using digital photographs are used in court every month throughout the United States. It is rare that a digital image is challenged at all, and there have been no cases to date that I am aware of in which a digital photograph has been excluded solely because it is digital.

The rules of evidence and the case law regarding digital images do not prevent legitimate challenges to the veracity of any image or to the legitimacy of any specific adjustment, correction, or enhancement made to an image. For this reason, it is important that anyone involved in presenting images for court use methods that will yield the same results when repeated and use valid imaging forensic techniques.

Four Aspects of Best Practices

The four basic aspects to best practices in imaging forensics are as follows:

- Archive the original image.
- Work only on copies of the original file.
- Use only valid forensic image processing procedures.
- Ensure that all processes are repeatable and verifiable.

Archive the Original Image

An unaltered copy of the original, or primary, image should be archived in its original format. This file should be stored for as long as your agency requires for photographic evidence. Whether this image is stored on a computer hard drive, server, CD, DVD, or other media is not important. What is important is that the image be maintained in its unaltered state and that it is stored in a manner to protect it from damage.

If the original image is a Raw file, the file is by default unalterable. That is, opening a Camera Raw file automatically creates a duplicate of the original, and that opened file must be saved in a different format. It is important to note that some metadata (such as file modification dates) in a Raw file may be changed, but not the image data. Converting Raw files to the open DNG format for archiving could help assure that the files can be opened at any point in the future, even if the camera manufacturer no longer supports the specific original Raw format. The DNG conversion does not alter the Raw file but places it in a larger container, making it a more universal, and less proprietary, format.

If the file is a JPEG or TIFF file, then it is important that policies and/or procedures be in place that require anyone who has access to open only duplicates of these files. This can be easily done by copying the files to a new location—leaving the originals untouched.

The archive should not allow rewriting of files. This will ensure that these original files remain unaltered and will also prevent them from being overwritten by other files that have the same name.

Work Only on Copies

Access to the original images can be easily limited through permissions on a server, passwords on an individual computer, or restricted access to stored media.

If images are stored on a server, access can be restricted through permissions protocols. The ability to write to the server should be restricted only to personnel uploading files. It is highly recommended that this capability be restricted to as few individuals as possible. Permissions can be set to Read and Write to allow uploading and viewing of files. To prevent anyone from making changes to files, deny the Modify permission setting. This is excellent security because it prevents files from being overwritten or changed in any way.

When trained personnel access files (whether from a server, a CD, DVD, or a directory on a personal computer), they can duplicate them to a working directory, leaving the originals untouched. There is never a need to work on the original archived file.

By working only on copies of the archived originals, you can maintain the integrity of the original archived files and can refer to them for comparison with corrected or clarified images.

Valid Forensic Procedures

As a general rule, we can use valid procedures to adjust the quality of the image but not to change the content of the image. But, as with most general rules, there are exceptions. Some techniques are intended to make a qualitative change but result in a change of content. And there are instances when changing the content is necessary.

Overprocessing an image so that image artifacts distort or alter the image content is an example of making changes that result in a change of content. Strong adjustments of contrast or brightness values can result in objects changing size or shape or blending into each other. Caution must be used in making any image adjustments so that qualitative changes are not overapplied.

As to necessary changes of content, examples include adding annotations to an image (as in a court chart) or changing the backgrounds of pictures in a photo lineup so that one individual does not stand out from the rest. In cases where the addition of text, lines, or other data is very obvious, the change stands for itself. In cases where an unusual background in a photo lineup is made to better match the individuals, documentation should be included in a report so that all interested parties are aware of the change.

Many image adjustments can be done in a nondestructive manner with adjustment layers. When you use this feature in Photoshop, the unchanged image resides as the base layer and the image adjustment layer is a separate layer that includes the parameters set by the technician. To make corrections and enhancements to images, one can turn off the adjustment layers and see the unchanged image and then turn on each adjustment layer to display what changes each has made to the image quality. The adjustment layer icon can be accessed to see the parameters used for each adjustment. Masks can be included for each adjustment layer to apply the adjustment to specific portions of the image.

Valid forensic methods are repeatable with similar results, are applied to groups of pixels, and provide explainable and predictable results. Image adjustments should be applied to a copy of the original, and an audit trail (either the procedure itself or notes) should be a part of any valid forensic workflow.

Repeatable Processes

It is frequently necessary to make adjustments to an image. Perhaps the image has a green cast from fluorescent lights or has very little contrast from being photographed on an overcast day. Or, perhaps a fingerprint image is obliterated by a stain and needs enhancement to see fine details. In all of these instances, changes need to be made to the image to improve its quality.

With any of these changes, the technician who made them must work on a copy of the original, use valid imaging forensic techniques, and be able to repeat them if required to do so. To enable the repeatability of the process, an audit trail may be used. An audit trail is the recording of the steps used to make any adjustments so that they can be repeated to obtain similar results. The audit trail may be a standard procedure that is routine and consistent, handwritten notes, a text document containing notes, or data that contains this information stored within the file itself, such as Photoshop's History Log.

Some adjustments are basic—such as a brightness or contrast adjustment—and may always be performed using the same techniques with similar settings. In these instances, retaining a copy of the modified image and an audit trail of the changes may not be necessary. The key here is that the procedure is a common one, is a standard routine, is a valid procedure, and can be easily repeated with similar results—even without notes. In such an instance, the standard operating procedure becomes the audit trail.

Audit Trail and History Log

When procedures are used that go beyond basic adjustments, a copy of the modified image should be retained. And there should be an audit trail of all steps used to make the adjustments. As mentioned in the preceding section, an audit trail may be handwritten notes, a text file, or data contained within the image file itself. With Photoshop CS and above, this can be done automatically using the History Log feature. It is important to note that Photoshop's History Log is not active by default, and must be turned on in the General Preferences window (Figure 1.1).

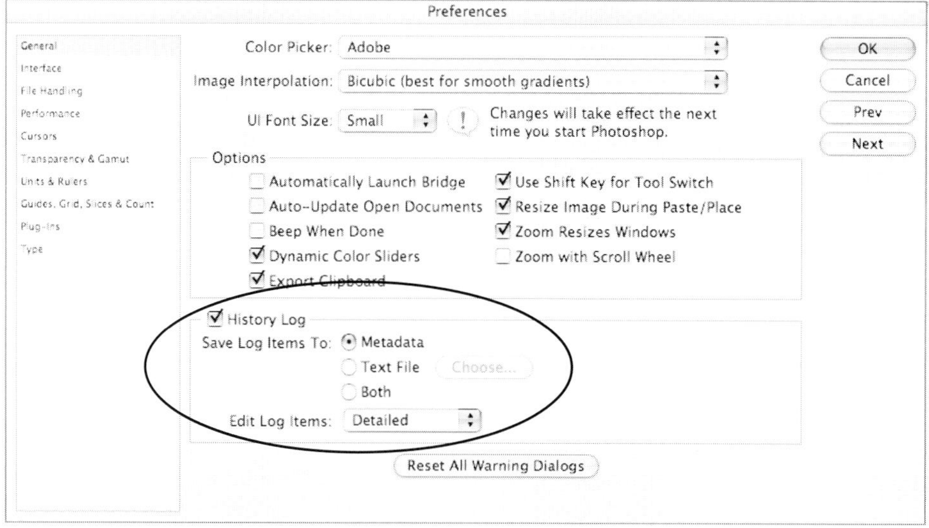

Figure 1.1 The History Log must be activated in the General Preferences window.

The History Log can be viewed in Adobe Bridge (see Chapters 4 and 6) or by choosing File > File Info in Photoshop and then clicking the History Log tab (Figure 1.2). See Chapters 3 and 6 for more information about the History Log.

Figure 1.2 The History Log is available as one of the tabs in the File Info window.

Summary

Utilizing best practices goes beyond the requirements of court, case law, and rules of evidence. Best practices provide us with standard operating procedures in your workflow to maintain the integrity of your images and procedures. By maintaining a digital negative, only working on copies of the original, using only valid forensic procedures, and maintaining an audit trail for any nonstandard enhancements or analysis, you can be assured that you have done the due diligence needed in forensics.

Reports and Testimony

All images taken in a law enforcement setting can potentially be used in court. Usually they will be used for illustrative purposes so a judge or jury can better understand the testimony of a witness. Some images will be used to illustrate an analysis, such as a latent fingerprint, a tool mark, blood spatter, a security video, a questioned document, or another comparative analysis process.

2

In either case, if your work involves image processing at anything beyond basic contrast, brightness, and color corrections, you may be required to testify in court.

Chapter Contents

Report Writing

Reports are an important aspect of the forensic imaging workflow, but not all aspects of imaging work require a report. For instance, if one is simply printing images for use in court, no report should be necessary—unless internal policies state otherwise.

Reports fall into two main categories: factual reports by personnel involved in the case and expert reports by those providing an opinion based on their expertise in a given field. The difference between the two reports is that the expert report will include an opinion and the methodology used to reach the opinion.

Most reports must include some basic information such as the name of the person writing the report, the date the report was written, the case name or case number, a list of the evidence reviewed or examined, and a listing of what was done. Police reports frequently use a form with check boxes for much of this information, with space for listing evidence and writing a narrative describing what was done.

It is important that all items of evidence are listed. If 15 images were examined but only 3 had information of value or required image clarification, list all 15 and state what information of value was on the 3 or what adjustments were needed.

When you're writing a report on image processing and steps beyond basic color, brightness, and contrast correction were performed, state what these steps were. The report should state what tools or filters were used or where this information resides (in the History Log, in case notes, or within Photoshop actions saved with the image files, for instance). The parameters used with the tools may be handwritten notes, other case notes, the History Log (see Chapters 3 and 6), or information from adjustment layers. For instance, if a color isolation technique was used to clarify detail in an image by increasing tonal contrast between specific colors, this should be stated in the report. The parameters can be in some form of the notes (including the History Log) as just stated. It is not necessary to fill your report with all the parameters used. The important thing is that by reviewing your report and notes, someone can repeat the steps with similar results.

The level of detail in a report may vary based on your workflow, the policies of your agency, or other factors. However, if you used image processing steps that exceed standard brightness, contrast, and color adjustments, a peer should be able to review your report and notes and understand the approach, perform the same steps, and achieve similar results. If this is not possible, either the report or the case notes (which may be the History Log or adjustment layers) should be more complete.

If the report includes an opinion, the opinion should be clear and to the point and should also contain the basis on which it was formed. For instance, if your report states that two prints were made by the same finger and this conclusion relied on image clarification, this should be stated in the report. The conclusion in this case is that two prints were made by the same finger. The basis includes the latent print analysis, but the conclusion is also based, in part, on the image processing. If these issues are not included in your report, the evidence may still be admitted, but cross-examination could be much more difficult and may call into question the validity of the process.

The bottom line in report writing is to include in the report and notes enough information that your work can be reviewed by another technician and can be explained in court. A technical review should validate the processes used and obtain similar results.

Court Testimony

Testimony in court may involve pretrial hearings, such as the Daubert and Frye hearings as described in Chapter 1.

There are two aspects to court testimony, whether as part of a preliminary hearing or part of the trial itself: the voir dire process and the testimony itself. The voir dire process is used to establish whether an individual meets the criteria to testify in court. Testimony on a case includes both direct examination and cross-examination.

The voir dire process is a part of trials in which there may be a question regarding the qualifications of the witness or the admissibility of the evidence. Sometimes voir dire is as simple as answering a few questions regarding your name, employment, title, number of years experience, and training in your field. Sometimes it can be quite a bit more extensive—especially when you're testifying as an expert in a specific field. Your education, work experience, and related training should all be listed on your curriculum vitae (CV) or resume. If you're testifying as an expert, the questions during voir dire may be more extensive and be very specific to show whether you have the education, training, and/or experience to provide the court with help in evaluating evidence in the case. Questions may also be asked about the technology used in the work performed in the case to determine that they are valid forensic processes and that you have the training and experience to use this technology.

When being qualified as an expert, it is important to avoid overstating your qualifications. Experts who attempt to qualify as an expert in a field that they do not qualify for are opening themselves up for potential problems. This is also doing a disservice to the case and potentially the entire field of forensic image analysis. First, they may not be allowed to testify by the court. Second, they may open themselves up to questions that they are unable to answer; they may even find themselves being led down a path of questioning that results in agreeing to conclusions that are contrary to their findings. And, if misinformation is presented in court, it can potentially result in changes to evidentiary rules.

It is best to work with the attorney in the case; let them know your qualifications and limitations, and stay within those boundaries. It is also important to note that an attorney may have misconceptions about your field of expertise, which should be clarified before testimony.

Under direct examination, testimony will generally involve the introduction into evidence of the images you processed and answering questions about how you received the evidence, what you did with it, and what conclusions you reached. In many cases this line of questioning is very basic and will provide an opportunity to explain to a judge and jury the procedures used, how these procedures are reliable, and how they provided information valuable to reaching your conclusion.

It is the job of opposing council to test the evidence in the case and possibly to present competing evidence. By using valid forensic procedures and having a thorough report, you should be able to ensure that your evidence remains solid. It's good practice to pause after each question is asked. This gives you time to be sure you fully understand the question, and provides time for opposing counsel to object to the question if they wish. If a question is ambiguous or vague, ask for clarification. If you do not understand a question, ask for clarification. If you are asked to answer a question with yes or no but that isn't appropriate or will lead to a misunderstanding of your testimony, explain that the question cannot be answered without an explanation. If you are unsure of the answer to a question, say that you don't know.

An important point to remember in testimony is that you are not an adversary for one side or the other. Your testimony should be neutral and should be basically the same regardless of whether you are testifying for the plaintiff or defense.

Sample Questions

In forensic imaging there are some general questions that may be asked in all cases and some that may be specific to the facts or procedures used in your case. Following is a list of potential general questions and some approaches to them. These can be used as a guideline for approaching testimony, but all answers to questions should be your own and should be based on the facts of your case.

Q: Did you examine all of the evidence in this case?

Unless you are the case detective, you may not know what all the evidence is, and much of the evidence probably did not make it to you. The best answer to this is to state that the evidence you examined is listed in your report. If you are asked to list what evidence you examined, ask the court if you can refer to your notes or report and list the items you examined. If you are asked if you examined items that you never received, state that you did not receive the items. If these questions are asked during cross-examination, you may be asked to clarify your answers under redirect examination.

Q: What did you do to the images in this case?

This question may be intended to be a general question, or it may be specific. If it is asked early in your testimony, it is probably general in nature. This question can be answered in general terms, by way of analogy, or with specifics regarding the tools and procedures used.

My preference is to answer the question using an analogy and then proceed to answer any follow-up questions with specifics if they are asked for. When asked this question, I have stated that I use software that enables me to clarify the details in an image, much like the controls on a television. These tools allow me to adjust color, brightness, contrast, and sharpness so that details are clearer in the image.

Grant Fredericks, an expert in forensic video analysis, teaches in the Law Enforcement and Emergency Services Video Association (LEVA) that he clarifies the information in an image without changing the image content. This makes details easier to see, much as turning on the light in a dark room provides better detail without changing the objects in the room. This is an excellent way to explain, in general terms, the basic concepts of image clarification.

Q: What specifically did you do to this image?

This question is obviously asking for very specific information. When asked for this level of detail, it is best to ask to refer to your report or notes and then state specifically what tools were used and what these tools did. For example, if an image was of very poor contrast and a Levels adjustment layer was used to expand the tonal range, state that this is what you did. Explain that this did not change the content of the image and that it provides better contrast in the image so that details are easier to distinguish.

Q: How did you make these adjustments?

If you anticipate needing to show a step-by-step of the process used in your work, you will need to have the images, a computer with the software you used, and appropriate monitors. Eventually, all courts may be set up for this, but at the time of this writing, most courts are not, and those that are frequently use LCD projectors, large-screen televisions, or monitors that are not calibrated to provide the best brightness, contrast, and color. It is important to either bring equipment, have the attorney rent equipment, or have the court equipment calibrated. If this is not done, you might show your work and it might not be visible on the uncalibrated monitors. It is unfortunate that many attorneys are unaware of the importance of this and that many forensic technicians have difficulty explaining the need for calibrated equipment.

Once the equipment has been set up, refer to your notes or other documentation (which may include a printout of the History Log) and display the original image and the clarified copy of the image. Then refer to your notes and repeat the process, step-by-step, explaining each step as you go through the process. This enables the judge and jury to see your process and understand what you did.

The opportunity to do this should support your testimony and show the judge and jury that you used valid forensic procedures, that you did not change the content of the image, and that the details revealed in the image processing are valid.

Q: Did you manipulate or alter this image?

This question is an obvious attempt to use a pejorative term to describe the image processing done in the image analysis process.

The question can be answered by asking for a clarification of the term *manipulate* and *alter*. Or, you can clarify the terms in your own answer, stating that if the term *manipulate* is meant to mean changing the content rather than clarifying detail in the image, you did not manipulate the image. You can then add to this answer the same information from the general question, What specifically did you do to this image?

Summary

The concepts we have covered in these first two chapters—using best practices, writing thorough reports, and answering difficult questions in court—may not have affected many forensic image analysts yet. If your work is limited to printing photos of graffiti and car burglaries, you may never go to court in your career. But this does not invalidate these concepts. Instead, these chapters should help you ease into a better workflow that will be less subject to potential challenges.

The day-to-day workflow of most police agencies doesn't require one to write reports for every print made in the digital darkroom, and these chapters are not suggesting that this should change. However, when performing more extensive tasks of image processing or analysis, using best practices, writing thorough reports, and preparing for testimony can make the difference between you and your images having integrity in court and the images being considered as manipulated with no validity by a jury.

Basic Imaging Settings

Before doing critical work with imaging on a computer, it is important that the computer monitor and Photoshop be set up to display information as accurately as possible and to create an efficient workflow.

If you don't make some initial settings for your display resolution, color bit depth, color profiles, and other preferences, the images displayed on your computer screen may be distorted or have limited color values.

The Preferences settings within Photoshop control the way some items appear (such as cursors), the way Photoshop uses memory and scratch disks, whether the History Log is invoked, where this information is saved, and so on.

3

Chapter Contents

Monitor Calibration

There are three aspects to setting up your monitor for the best possible output: setting the monitor's color and spatial resolution, setting the monitor's color temperature, and calibrating the colors displayed on the screen with a calibration device.

The first two settings are relatively simple and can be done without any additional equipment.

To set the color and spatial resolution on a Windows computer, right-click the Desktop and select Properties. Click the Settings tab. Monitor resolutions will be listed, such as 640×480, 800×600, 1280×1024, and so on. It is best to check the manual that came with your monitor and set this for the highest native resolution recommended by the manufacturer. An incorrect setting can result in image softness or in a distorted image display. To check this, I open an image of a circle in Photoshop and verify that it is round when I'm setting the monitor resolution to guarantee that my settings do not cause image distortion (see Figure 3.1).

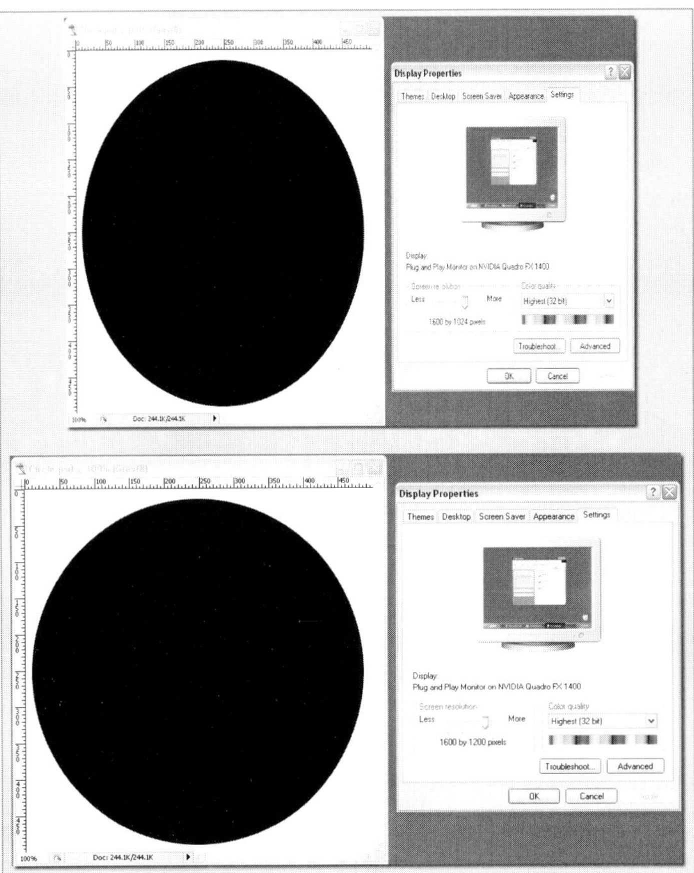

Figure 3.1 The image on the top shows the circle image distorted because of an incorrect monitor resolution setting. The image on the bottom shows the circle image with no distortion after the monitor resolution was corrected.

The color setting has different lists in different views in different versions of Windows, but the rule of thumb is to set the colors for the highest setting available, which may be called Millions, True Color, 24 bit Color, 32 bit Color, or something similar.

To set the color and spatial resolution on a Mac, open System Preferences, click the Display icon, choose the proper resolution based on the manufacturer's recommendation, and choose Millions for color.

The procedure for setting the color temperature may vary from monitor to monitor, so check your owner's manual. The setting that will provide a good color balance will be called D65, 6500K, or something similar. Many monitors are shipped with the monitor set to 9000K, which gives the image a blue cast—changing this setting will initially cause the display to look yellow by comparison, but will look much better once your eyes adjust.

Critical color calibration on a monitor requires the use of a calibration device. These devices use software to display a series of specific colors on the monitor, then read the colors through a piece of hardware (a spectrophotometer or colorimeter) placed on the front of the monitor. The software then builds a profile for your monitor that enables it to display more accurate colors. There are many calibration devices on the market—three that have received very good reviews and are reasonably priced are the Gretag MacBeth Eye-One Display, Pantone Huey, and the ColorVision Spyder.

Photoshop's Color Settings

The Color Settings in Photoshop are located under the Edit menu. This window, shown in Figure 3.2, is divided into five sections (including a Description section at the bottom that provides information about these settings when your mouse is over them) when the More Options button is clicked.

The top section, Working Spaces, controls the working space profile in which images will be managed within Photoshop. Photoshop ships with a limited color space profile (sRGB) set as the default. Changing the sRGB setting to Adobe RGB (1998) will display images with a much larger color gamut. The other settings in the Working Spaces section can remain in their default mode.

The second section allows you to turn your color management off, preserve a document's embedded profile, or convert to the working space you have set within Photoshop. You then can control what happens when you open an image that doesn't match your chosen color space. If you work in an environment where images come from many sources (including seized computers), I recommend setting all three options to Preserve Embedded Profiles and check the boxes so that you will get message boxes when there is a profile mismatch or a missing profile. If your environment is not likely to receive images from other sources, set your color policies to convert to the working color space, but check the boxes to provide messages letting you know when there are profile mismatches or missing profiles.

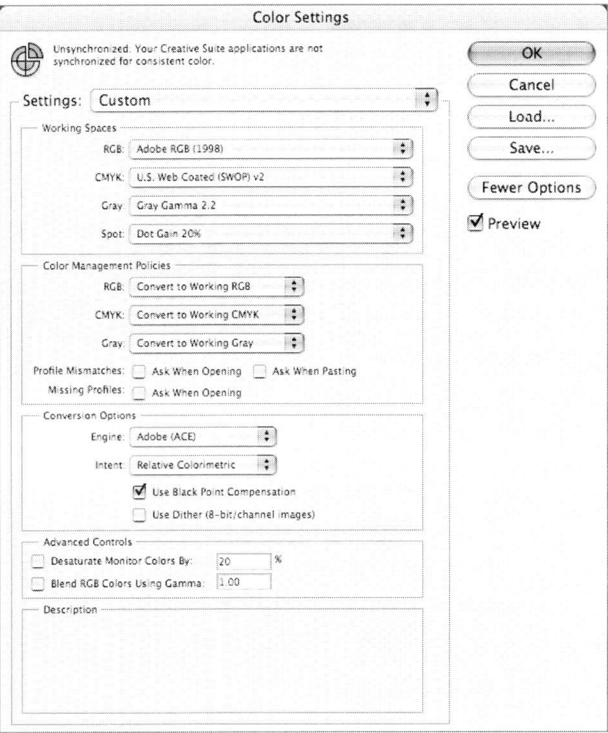

Figure 3.2 The Color Settings dialog provides options for assigning color profiles for your images.

In the Conversion Options section, it is my preference to uncheck the Use Dither box and leave the other settings at their defaults of Adobe (ACE) for Engine and Relative Colorimetric for Intent and leave the Use Black Point Compensation box checked. With Use Dither checked, Photoshop will change some pixel values randomly when converting files to 8-bit, which gives smoother, but less consistent results.

Clicking Save and providing a name for your new settings will make it easy to reset these should you ever lose them by deleting your preferences.

Note: For more information on color management, take a look at *Real World Color Management, Second Edition,* by Bruce Fraser, Chris Murphy, and Fred Bunting (Peachpit Press, 2004) or *Color Management for Photographers* by Andrew Rodney (Focal Press, 2005).

Photoshop Preferences

The Preferences settings in Photoshop are located under the Edit menu in Windows and under the Photoshop menu in Macintosh systems. There are 10 separate Preference panels in Photoshop CS3 (9 panels in Photoshop CS2) that can be accessed from within the General Preferences panel. This section shows the interface and recommendations for Photoshop CS3, and most can be applied easily for CS2 and earlier versions as well.

In the General Preferences (Figure 3.3), you can leave the top two sections at the default Photoshop settings, although I personally like to set Photoshop to automatically launch Bridge and I check the Zoom Resizes Windows box. I use Bridge almost every time I use Photoshop, so the autolaunching is a nice convenience. The zoom setting enables the window to increase in size when you're magnifying images, saving me the step of resizing the window manually.

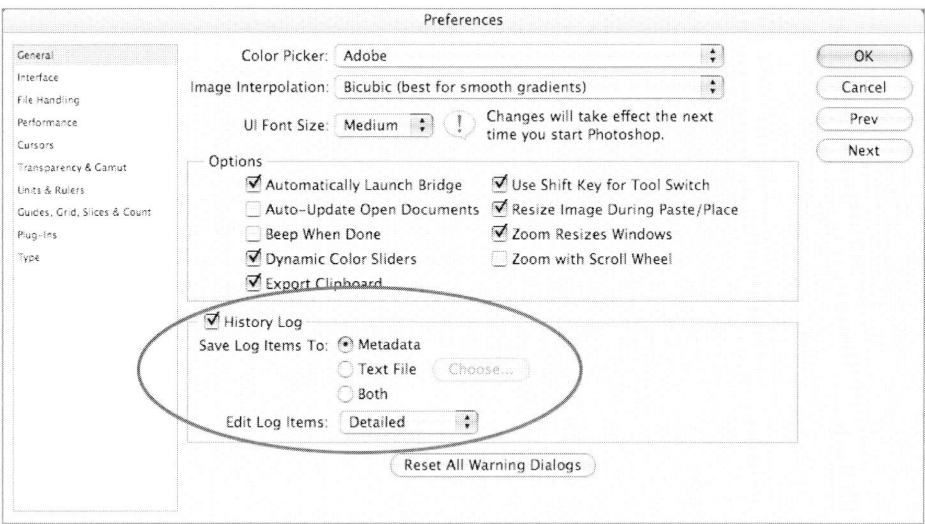

Figure 3.3 The General Preferences panel with the History Log enabled

The bottom section is for the History Log, which enables Photoshop to record a log of most of the adjustments you make to an image. To enable this feature, you must check the History Log box. There are three choices for where to keep the log: in the image metadata (making it part of the file itself), as a separate text file, or both. If kept as a separate file, the logs from all files are written to the same text file, which can become quite large over time, so I recommend saving to metadata only. The last option is to save sessions only, concise logs, or detailed information. Only the Detailed choice will record parameters for specific tools, such as the Amount, Radius, and Threshold settings in the Unsharp Mask dialog box. Therefore, Detailed should be selected.

It should be noted that some items do *not* get recorded in the History Log, such as freeform selections with the Lasso tool or brush strokes with painting, dodging, and burning tools. Specific steps and parameters in an action are also not recorded, although the action name is recorded when an action is run on a single image. However, when actions are run in Batch mode, even the action name is not recorded.

The Interface Preferences panel (Figure 3.4) allows you to control how some things appear in Photoshop, such as whether you want to view tooltips when you hover your cursor over a tool or palette or whether to autocollapse palettes to their icon state when you begin working on an image.

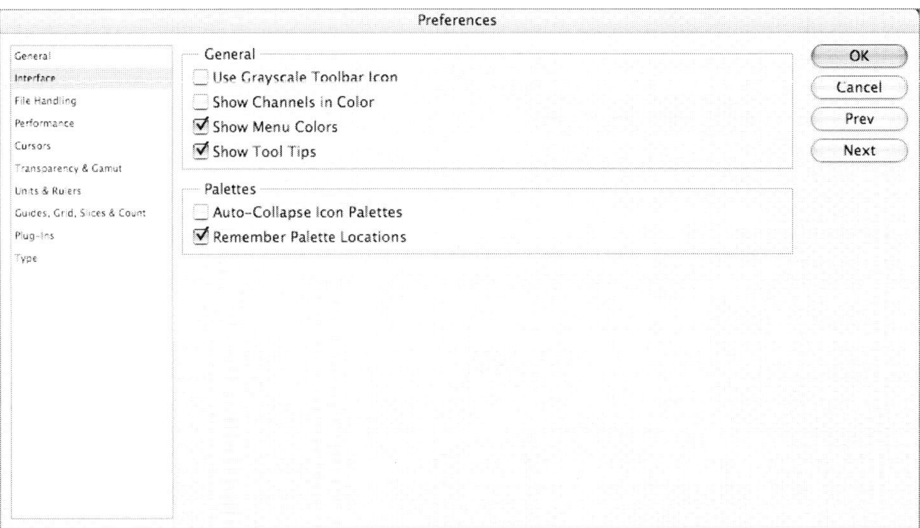

Figure 3.4 The Interface preferences

The File Handling Preferences panel (Figure 3.5) offers a choice called Ignore EXIF Profile Tag. If the digital camera you use incorrectly sets itself for the sRGB color space, you should check this box. Version Cue is a project management feature that can be turned off; it is intended for workgroups who work on the same project as a team. Selecting the Prefer Adobe Camera Raw For JPEG Files option enables JPEG images to be opened and adjusted within Adobe Photoshop Camera Raw—this is a new functionality in CS3. I leave this off; if I need to open TIFF and JPEG images into Camera Raw, I do so through Bridge instead by choosing the Prefer Adobe Camera Raw For JPEG And TIFF Files in Bridge's preferences and opening the images with the Ctrl+R/Cmd+R command.

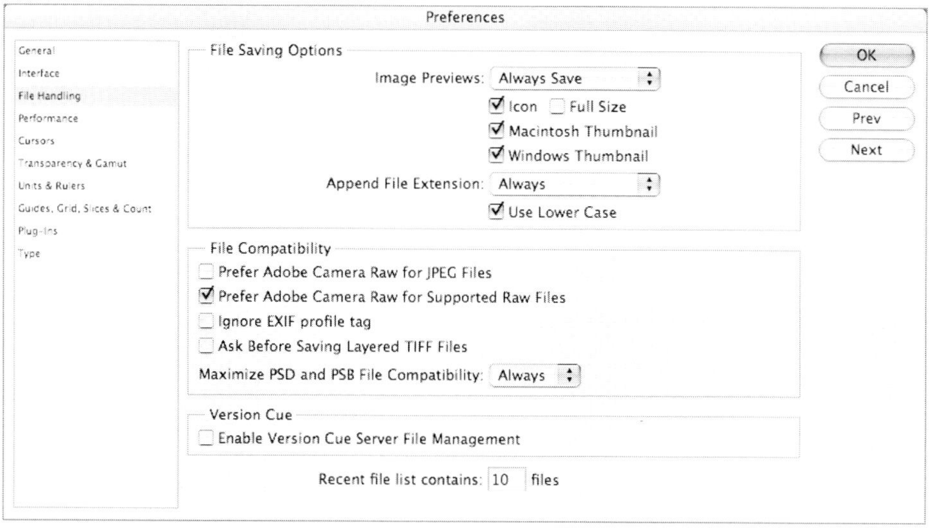

Figure 3.5 The File Handling preferences

The Performance Preferences panel (Figure 3.6) is new in Photoshop CS3. Some of the features of this panel were in other Preference panels in earlier versions, and some features are new to Photoshop CS3. As the name implies, the settings in this panel will directly affect performance within Photoshop.

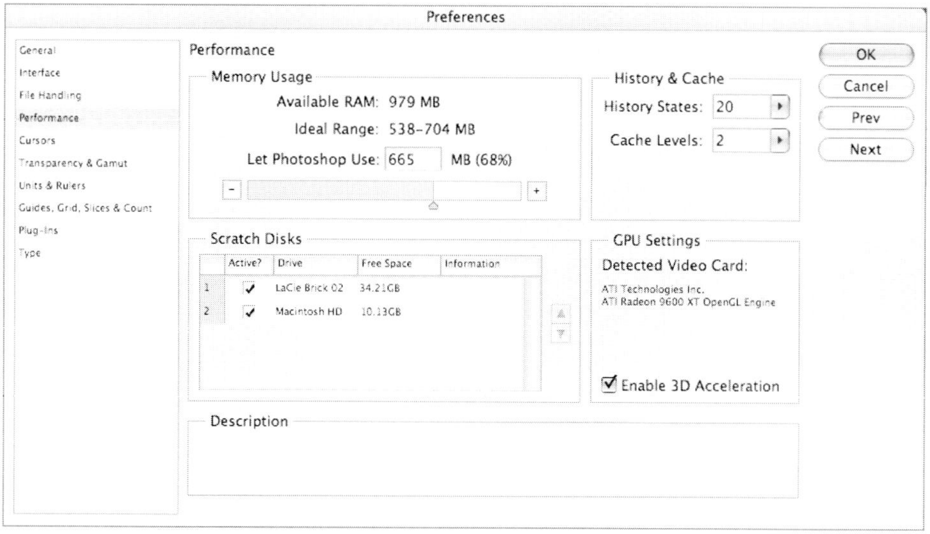

Figure 3.6 The Performance preferences

The recommendations for RAM are valid, and applying too much RAM to Photoshop can result in having too little available for the operating system, plug-in filters, or other open applications. Setting a defragmented, secondary hard drive as the primary scratch disk can help performance, especially if your system has limited RAM (this is true even if you set this as an inexpensive, external FireWire drive). Reducing the number of history states will help prevent RAM from being consumed, but it also reduces the number of undos available. Reducing the number of cache levels also prevents RAM from being consumed, but it can slow the screen redraw—a fair trade if your system has limited RAM.

In the Cursors Preferences panel (Figure 3.7), setting brushes to Full Size Brush Tip with Show Crosshair In Brush Tip checked allows for precise use of these tools when they are used. Having the Other Cursors option set to Precise provides for more accurate positioning, but the cursor is sometimes difficult to see.

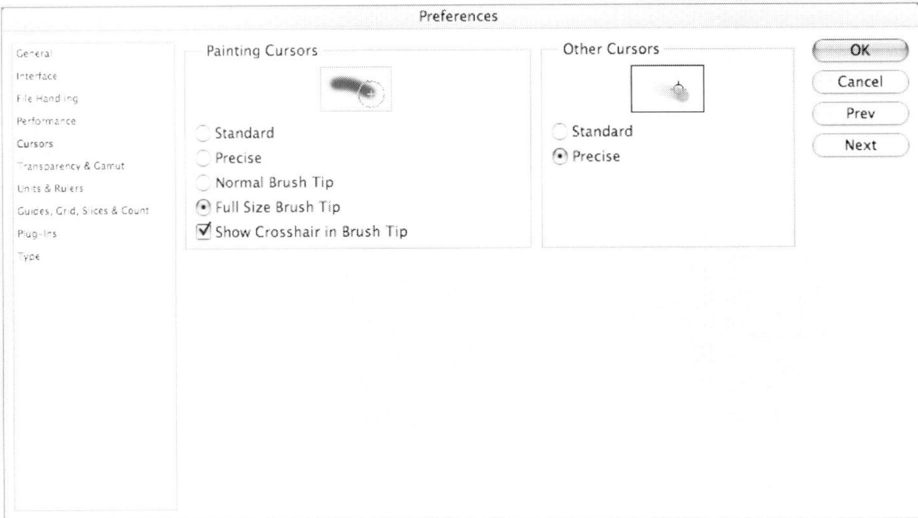

Figure 3.7 The Cursors preferences

The Plug-Ins Preferences panel (Figure 3.8) allows you to set a separate folder for Photoshop plug-ins. This is a good idea if you load many plug-ins and ever need to reinstall Photoshop. This is also the location to input the serial number for your previous version of Photoshop if this version is an upgrade.

Note: As far as imaging forensics is concerned, the Preferences panels named Units & Rulers; Guides, Grid, Slices & Count; and Type can all be left in their default state.

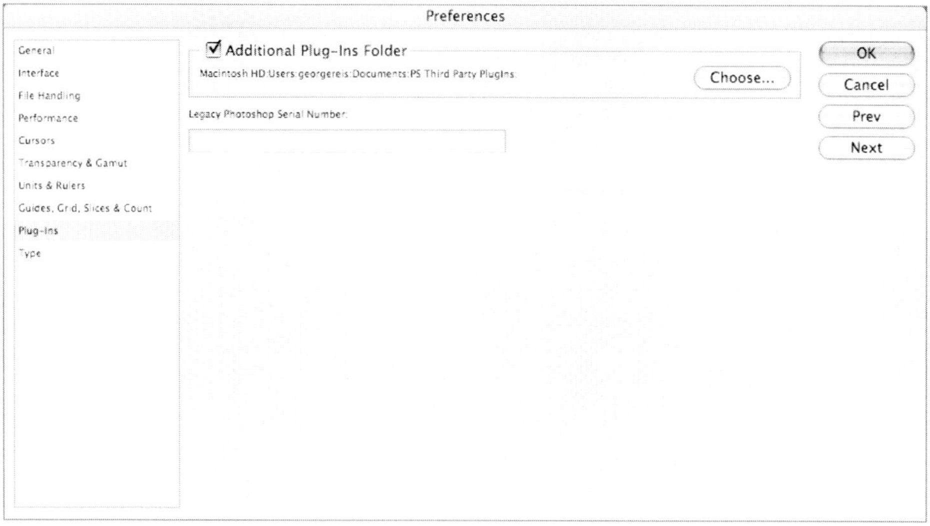

Figure 3.8 The Plug-Ins preferences

Personalizing Workspaces

Photoshop's palettes can be closed, moved around, resized, and recombined. In addition, with CS3, they can be collapsed to an icon state or hidden in a fully collapsed state. Photoshop's toolbar can be moved to any place on the window and viewed in a single column or in the traditional two-column view. Custom keyboard shortcuts can be designated. With Photoshop CS2 and CS3, one can even hide menu items that aren't used (or are rarely used).

Once you have spent some time with Photoshop, you may have different workspace configurations for different types of work—for example, different palettes open when you're just printing crime scene photos, when you're working on still images from a video, or when you're recording Photoshop actions. In fact, if you are sharing a computer with other users, it can be helpful to save workspaces in Photoshop to customize the preferences for each user.

Photoshop can save each workspace preference to easily allow you to switch from one workspace to another. To enable this feature, when a given workspace is set up, choose Window > Workspace > Save Workspace, and give the workspace an appropriate name. To return to any saved workspace, or to revert back to Photoshop's default workspace, choose Window > Workspace > (Workspace Name). Several workspaces are available from the Window > Workspace submenu.

Note: Other settings in Photoshop allow you to customize the workspace, create custom keyboard shortcuts, arrange palettes, create custom tool presets, and so on. This book is not intended to be an overview of all the features in Photoshop, so this chapter only touched on some of the key settings to set up in a forensic environment. For more detailed information about many of these settings, use Photoshop's Help menu or look at *Photoshop CS3 for Photographers* by Martin Evening (Focal Press, 2007); *Real World Color Management, Second Edition,* by Bruce Fraser, Chris Murphy, and Fred Bunting (Peachpit Press, 2004); and *Real World Camera Raw* by Bruce Fraser (Peachpit Press, 2005).

Summary

Setting up the monitor, color settings, and preferences is a task that will enable the Photoshop features we want to use (such as auto-launching Bridge and enabling the History Log), help our images to be displayed properly, and have good color. This task should only have to be performed once, however the settings should be double-checked periodically to ensure that they haven't inadvertently been reset.

Navigating with Bridge

With Photoshop CS2, Adobe introduced a new application called Bridge, which replaces the File Browser from earlier versions. This is a stand-alone application that can be opened and used without launching Photoshop, or it can be used in conjunction with Photoshop. In CS3, several enhancements have been made to Bridge, yet the main functionality remains basically the same as with CS2.

This chapter outlines the basic features of Bridge CS3, most of which will also apply to using Bridge CS2 and the File Browser in earlier versions of Photoshop.

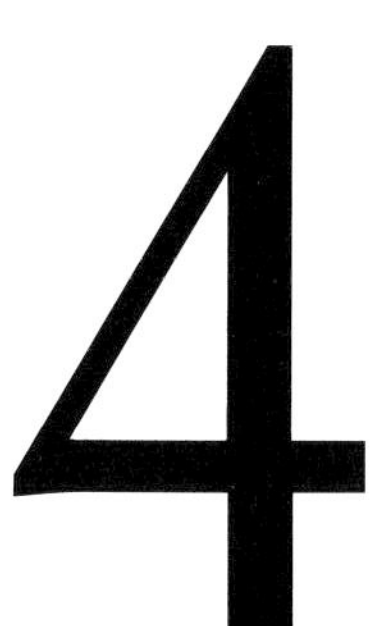

Chapter Contents

What Is Bridge?

Bridge is an excellent tool for locating, previewing, and organizing files. It is also the best place to review image metadata (information about images, including creation date and time, camera make and model, exposure information, date of modification, History Log information, and so on). Bridge hosts a version of Adobe Photoshop Camera Raw, so it can be the place where Raw files are previewed and Raw settings are applied. It provides thumbnails of images, a navigation window, a preview window, metadata information, and keyword searching. You can also access and apply Photoshop actions and automations from within Bridge.

Bridge is the first place for viewing images. In many cases you can do much of your work within it, without launching Photoshop at all. Once you have downloaded your digital images, Bridge is the first step in your digital imaging workflow. Before looking at this application's features, let's look at methods for downloading and archiving your images.

Bridge is a separate application from Photoshop, although it is tightly connected to it. There are several ways to launch Bridge. You can launch it in the same manner as any other application, or you can set your Photoshop preferences to automatically launch Bridge when Photoshop is launched (see Chapter 3, "Basic Imaging Settings"). If Photoshop is currently open, you can jump to Bridge by clicking the Go To Bridge icon on Photoshop's options bar (Figure 4.1), by choosing File > Browse, or by using the keyboard shortcut Shift+Ctrl+O/Shift+Cmd+O.

Figure 4.1 The Go To Bridge icon in Photoshop's options bar

When opening Bridge, navigate to the folder of images you want to view. This can be done by navigating in the Explorer-like Folders panel (Figure 4.2). If you click on a folder, its contents are displayed in the thumbnail portion of the window. If this is the first time you're navigating to this folder, it may take a few seconds for Bridge to build its cache, thumbnails, and preview. Text shows in the bottom-left corner of the window indicating the progress. Once the caches are built, you can preview and sort images; build keyword associations; perform searches for files; and rank, open, and rotate images. In addition, Photoshop actions can be invoked.

If there is a folder that you navigate to frequently, you can drag and drop it to the Favorites panel. In a forensics environment, having Favorites of the current year's and previous year's folders would be efficient. If your agency also does non-casework photography, another Favorite may be the Public Relations or Departmental History folder. Using Favorites merely provides a shortcut to the location, saving the need to navigate through the Folders panel to get to your commonly used folders.

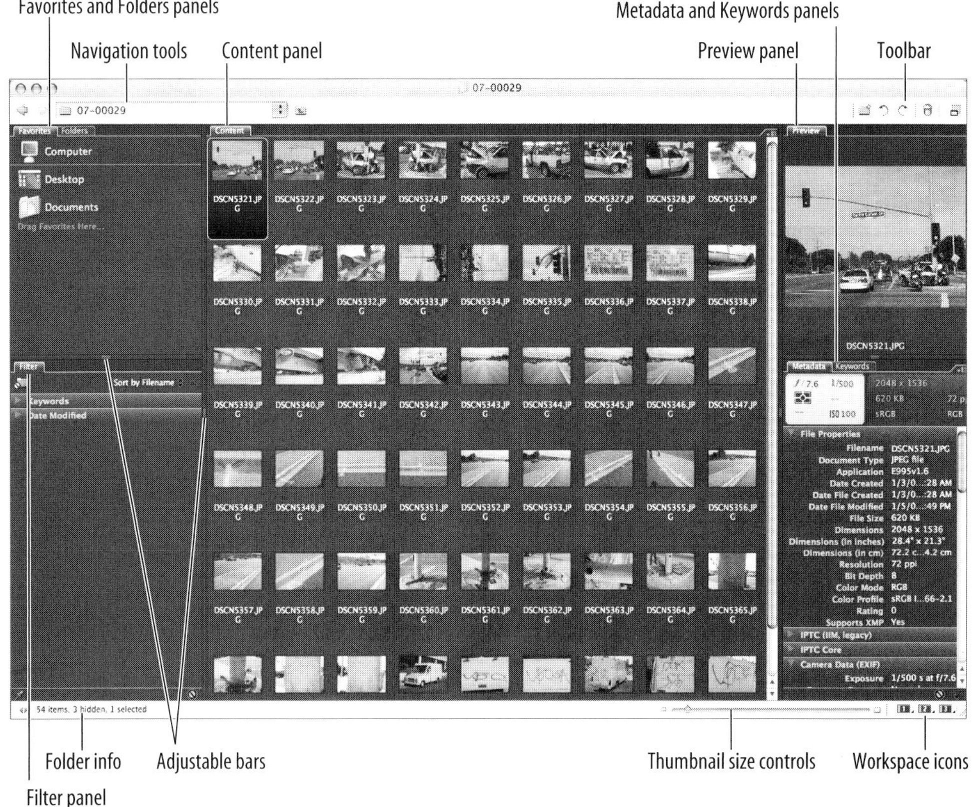

Figure 4.2 The default interface for Adobe Bridge

Downloading and Archiving Digital Images

Before viewing images, printing images, putting images onto a CD, and so on, you must download them from the camera media to a computer, server, or other media for long-term storage as discussed in Chapter 1.

There are many methods you can use to download your images, from using complex, proprietary systems to simply renaming folders to case numbers and copying them through Windows Explorer or the Macintosh Finder.

A simple method of downloading the images through Windows Explorer or the Macintosh Finder is to rename the innermost folder with the name of the photographer who took the photos. Rename the next folder up in the directory with the name of the case. Copy this folder to the location where your images are archived (Figure 4.3). Verify that all images are in the new location before formatting the memory card. You can then easily navigate to any file by case number.

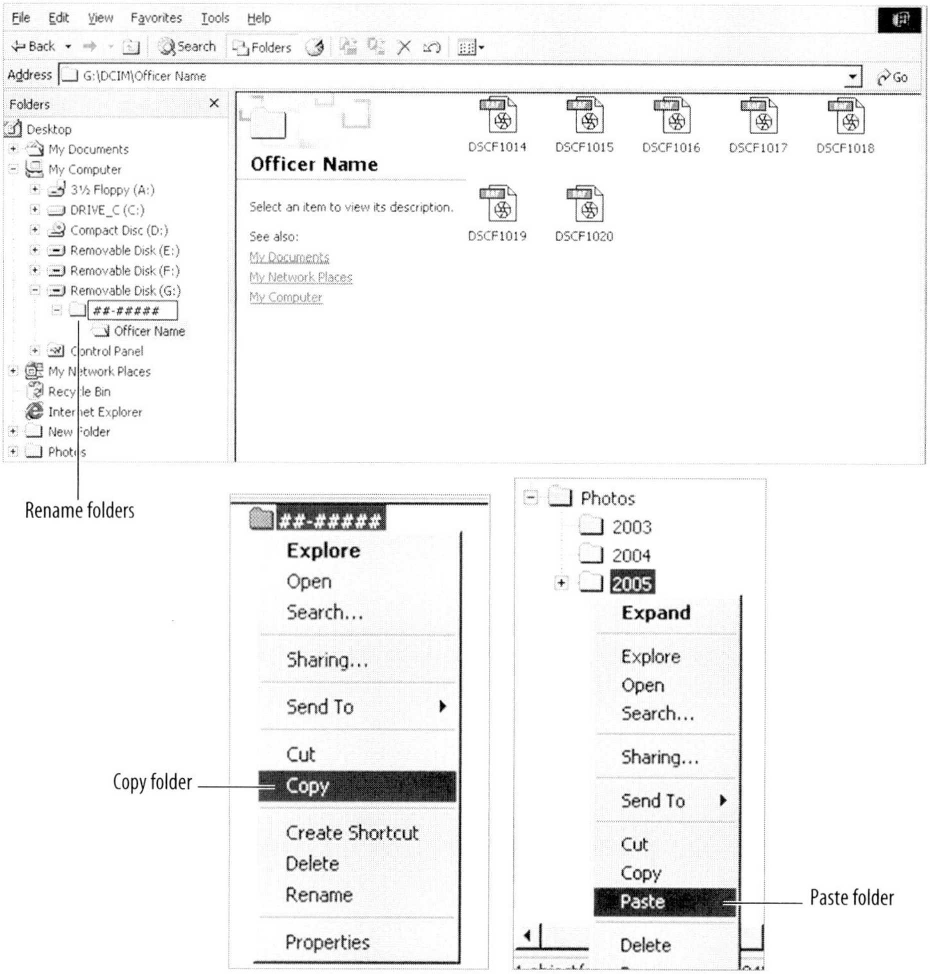

Figure 4.3 Renaming and copying folders from memory cards to an archive location is the simplest method for archiving digital photos.

Note: Your archive should provide a duplicate of all files regardless of the archiving method. This can be done by downloading the files, as described, to two separate locations or through the use of a mirrored RAID solution. RAID stands for Redundant Array of Independent Disks, which is a group of two or more hard drives that can provide autoduplication of records (through mirroring), faster file transfer (by writing to multiple disks simultaneously), and built-in recovery methods if a hard drive goes bad. In addition, a backup should be made daily of the archive files.

Bridge CS3 includes a photo download utility (Figure 4.4) that can be accessed by choosing File > Get Photos From Camera. There is an option in Bridge's Preferences to automatically launch this utility when a camera or memory card is connected to the computer. The standard view for this utility allows you to point to the memory card, select the location to download the images, select a second location for backup (if desired), rename the files if desired, preserve the original filename but with the metadata, open the download folder in Bridge upon completion of the download, and convert Raw files to Adobe's DNG format if desired. This simple utility provides a simple yet powerful interface for downloading memory cards to an archive location.

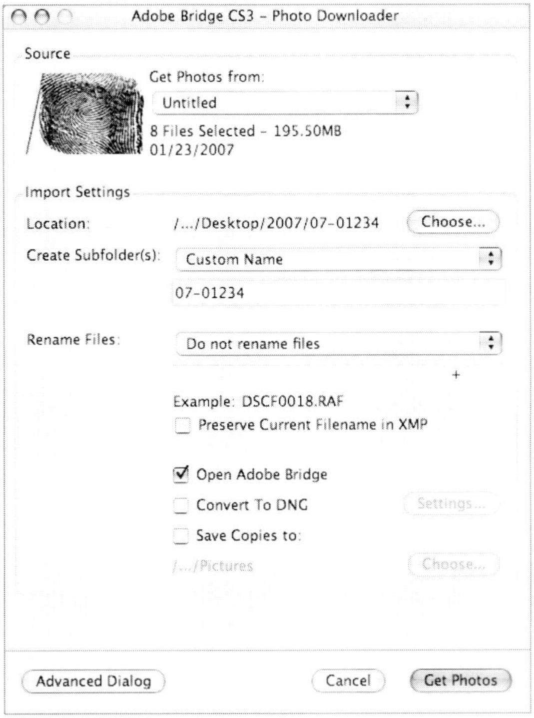

Figure 4.4 The Photo Downloader utility in Bridge CS3

Click the Advanced Dialog button at the bottom of this window to display all of the image files on the memory card. You can then choose which to download to a specific location, and this will also enable you to apply a metadata template to the images during download. A metadata template can place data in the IPTC fields of the file's metadata.

Adobe offers a free download utility at its website (www.adobe.com) called Import Camera, which offers similar functionality for Bridge CS2. It is a JavaScript file that can be accessed directly from Bridge. Once you've loaded the script into Bridge, it is available by choosing Tools > Import From Camera. The interface is simple—point to your memory card, choose any renaming options, and point to your archive locations.

Customizing Bridge

Every panel in Bridge can be resized and repositioned. Panels can also be hidden. For instance, you can hide all panels except the Content and Preview panels to make it easy to sort and compare images. Or you can hide all panels except the Content and Metadata panels to efficiently review file metadata.

The size of the thumbnails can be adjusted using the Thumbnail Size slider at the bottom right of the Bridge window. And you can control the size of the Preview panel (as well as all of the panels) by moving the adjustable bars.

The Window menu (Figure 4.5) provides several options for configuring the way Bridge looks and what is displayed within the Bridge window. You can choose which panels are visible and which are hidden. This can also be done by right-clicking on panels or panel tabs to bring up a contextual menu. Bridge also has several default workspaces that can be accessed either through the workspace buttons at the bottom right of the Bridge window or by selecting Window > Workspace and the workspace you wish to use. You can also save your customization by choosing Window > Workspace > Save Workspace. Once you have used Bridge for some time, you may find that there are workspaces that you prefer for viewing metadata, for entering keyword data, for reviewing fingerprint images, and so on. Saving each of these as a custom workspace and giving them appropriate names will make your workflow more efficient.

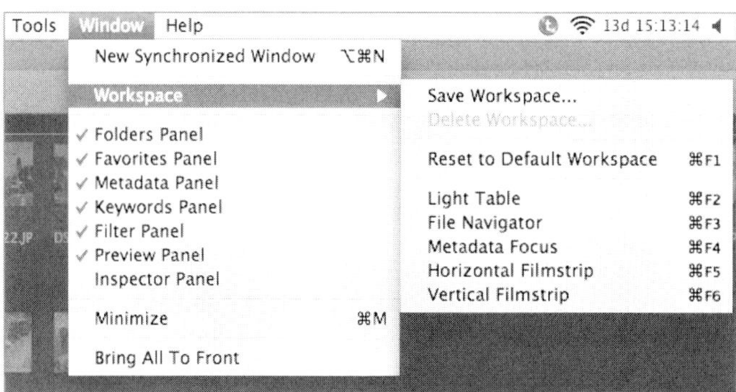

Figure 4.5 The Window menu provides several options for Bridge's layout and methods for saving and loading workspaces.

The toolbar, shown in Figure 4.6, provides several useful features that affect the way images may be viewed within Bridge. The New Folder icon will create a new folder within the selected folder, the Rotate icons will rotate selected images 90 degrees (counterclockwise or clockwise), the Delete icon will delete selected images (sending them to the Recycle Bin or Trash Can), and the Compact Mode button will convert the Bridge window to a small floating window. Bridge CS2 also had a Filter pop-up menu in this location; this has now become the more powerful Filter panel in CS3.

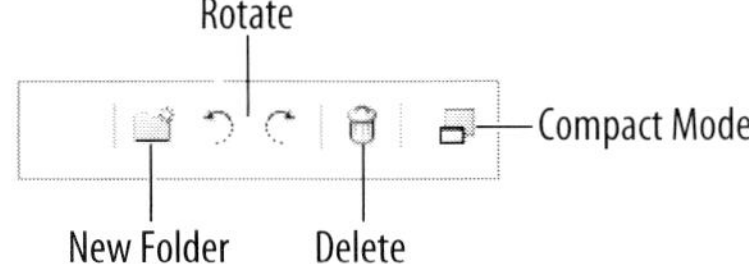

Figure 4.6 The Bridge toolbar provides an efficient method for creating a new folder, rotating images, deleting files, and putting Bridge into Compact mode.

Bridge Preferences

To access the Preferences settings for Bridge choose Edit > Preferences or press Ctrl+K/Cmd+K. Bridge's General Preferences panel opens.

In the General Preferences panel (Figure 4.7), settings can be made for the background color of the thumbnails and Preview panels (Image Backdrop slider) and the background brightness of the rest of the panels (User Interface Brightness slider). This window is also where you can set the Photo Downloader to automatically launch when a camera or memory card is connected. Reducing the number of items in the Favorites panel will make it faster and easier to navigate the items in that panel.

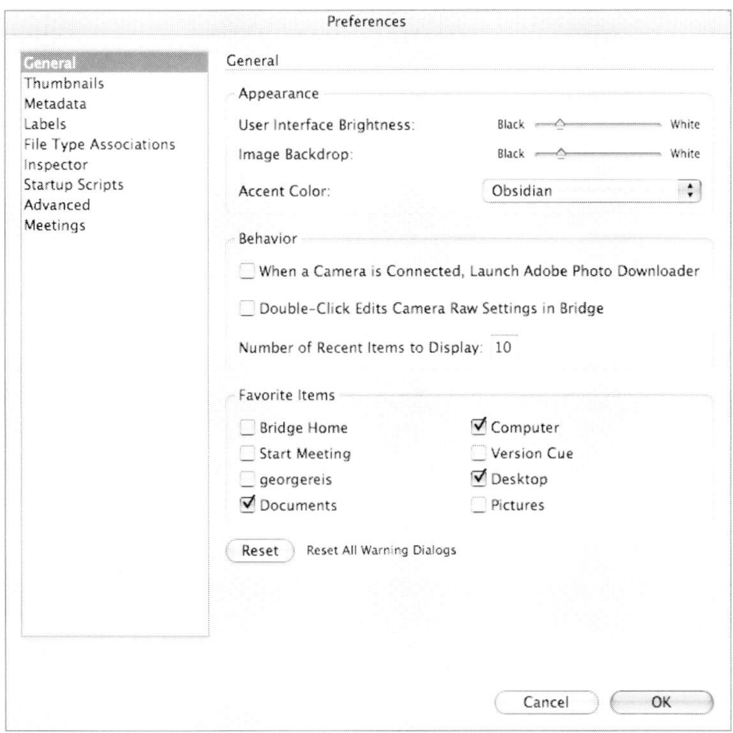

Figure 4.7 Bridge's General preferences

The Thumbnails Preference panel (Figure 4.8) enables you to select a new feature in Bridge and Adobe Photoshop Camera Raw 4—the ability to use Adobe Photoshop Camera Raw to adjust TIFF and JPEG images.

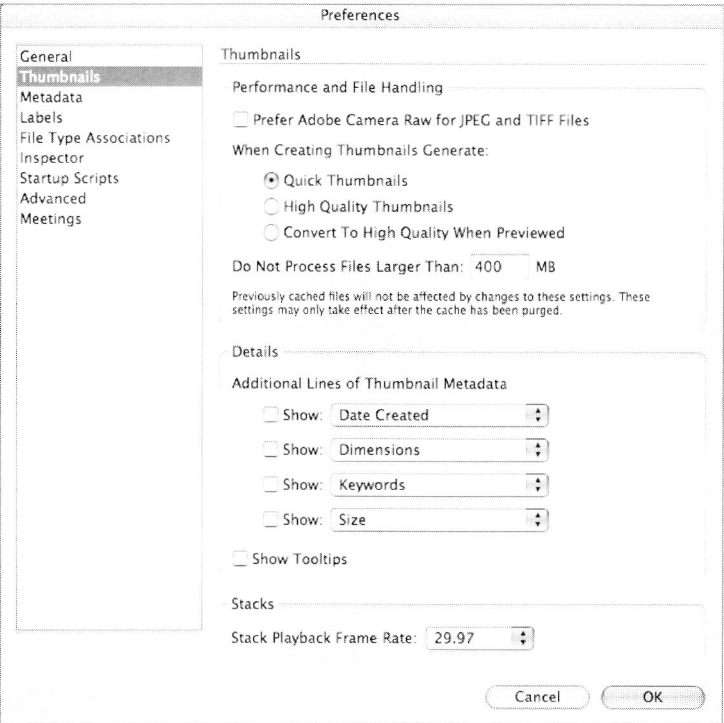

Figure 4.8 The Thumbnails Preferences panel in Bridge

Note: Although Adobe Photoshop Camera Raw (ACR) now supports opening TIFF and JPEG files, this does not change the quality or properties of those files. ACR is a powerful tool that can be used to quickly batch-process these files and is described in more detail in Chapter 5.

This panel has three choices for setting the thumbnail quality—it is important to note that the Quick Thumbnails setting will display the embedded thumbnail image in digital files, which may be important when performing image analysis. The High Quality Thumbnails setting will enable Bridge to build a thumbnail from the image file itself, which provides preview images of greater resolution and more accurate color.

This panel is also where you set what information is displayed under the thumbnails, whether to show tooltips in Bridge, and the frame rate for viewing image stacks that can be previewed in Bridge. Image stacks are files that are grouped together in Bridge by selecting multiple files and choosing Stacks > Group As Stack or pressing Ctrl+G/Cmd+G.

The Advanced Preferences panel (Figure 4.9) has an option called Enable Color Management In Bridge. For Bridge to display thumbnail and preview images using color management, this box must be checked and high-quality thumbnails must be enabled through the Thumbnails Preferences panel.

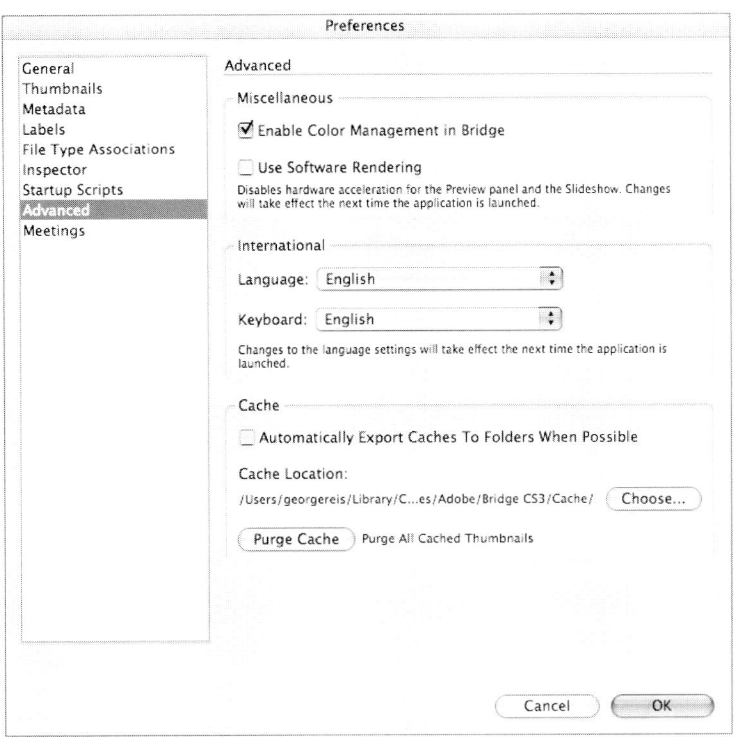

Figure 4.9 The Advanced Preferences panel with the Enable Color Management In Bridge option checked

We will cover the metadata preferences in Chapter 6, "Viewing Metadata," so we won't look at it here. Here's a summary of each of the other preferences categories:

The **Labels** preferences enable you to assign specific terms with the color labels that can be applied to images in Bridge.

The **File Type Associations** preferences enable you to choose which applications open which file types from within Bridge (this does not change the Operating System preferences when you double-click a file outside of Bridge).

The **Inspector** preferences are for use with Version Cue.

The **Startup Scripts** preferences control which startup scripts are launched when Bridge launches.

The **Meetings** preferences enable features for sharing your screen with other users over the Internet.

Keywords

The Keywords panel provides the capability to associate keywords with specific files. For instance, all images associated with a specific type of crime (homicide, rape, robbery, etc.), a specific reporting district, or a specific photographer can be assigned the appropriate keywords. Then, should you wish to locate all homicides in RD 34 through RD 42, you can simply do a search and the appropriate images will be displayed in the thumbnail view.

To set up this feature, click the Keyword tab and delete the default sets of keywords by highlighting each set and clicking the small Trash Can icon at the bottom of the panel.

New sets can be created by clicking the Keywords panel flyout menu and selecting New Keyword Set (Figure 4.10), by right-clicking in the Keywords panel, or by clicking the File Folder icon at the bottom of the Keywords panel (Figure 4.11). Give the set an appropriate name, like Crime, RD, or Photographer, and press Enter/Return. Next, highlight this set, and from the flyout menu, choose New Keyword, or click the New Keyword icon at the bottom of the panel. Give the keyword an appropriate name like Homicide, Rape, Burglary, etc., and press Enter/Return. Continue this process for additional keywords and keyword sets.

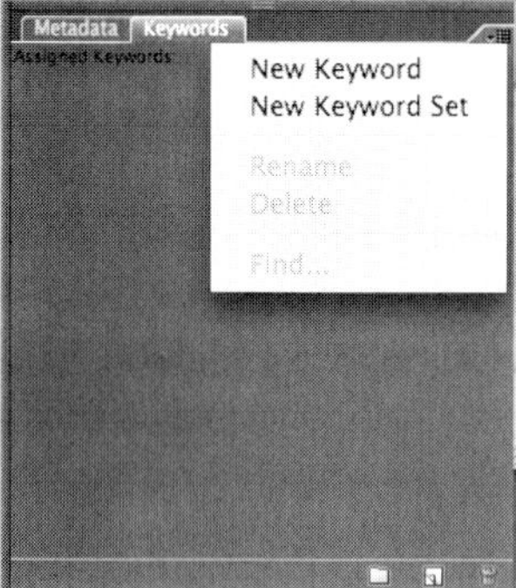

Figure 4.10 The default keywords can be dragged to the Trash Can icon to prepare for creating a new set; then new keywords and keyword sets can be created from the flyout menu or the contextual menu.

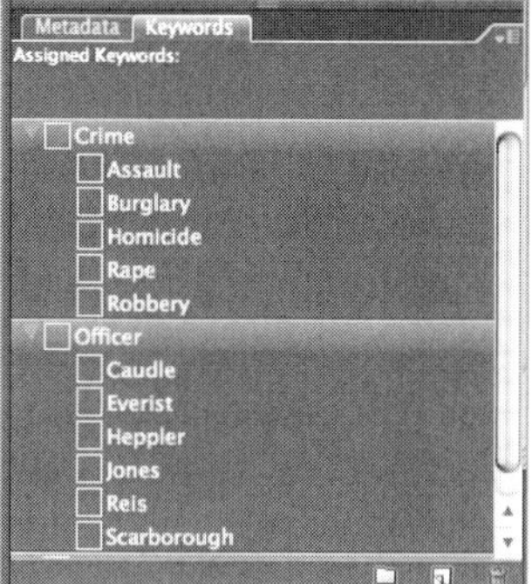

Figure 4.11 Custom sets of keywords can be created in the Keywords panel.

To assign keywords, simply highlight individual images or groups of images in Bridge and check the boxes to the left of the keywords you wish to assign to these images. To select multiple files, Ctrl+click/Cmd+click to select files individually, or select a group by clicking one file and then Shift+clicking another, selecting all consecutive files. As files are downloaded, keywords can be assigned for all images in each case as it is archived.

To then search the database, choose Edit > Find and enter the appropriate search criteria. In the Search window, choose the location you want to search (include subfolders if appropriate), and then choose the appropriate criteria, as demonstrated in Figure 4.12. You can search by keyword, filename, creation date, file type, and more. Multiple criteria can be used for a search by clicking the + key in the Criteria section of the Search window.

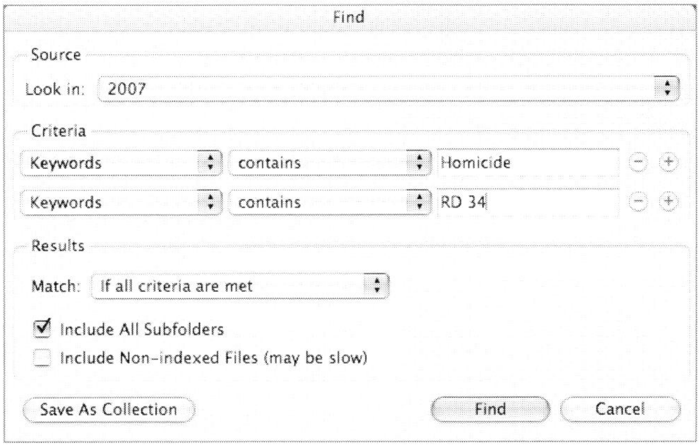

Find
Source
Look in: 2007
Criteria
Keywords contains Homicide
Keywords contains RD 34
Results
Match: If all criteria are met
Include All Subfolders
Include Non-indexed Files (may be slow)
Save As Collection Find Cancel

Figure 4.12 In this sample, I am searching for homicides in RD 34 in the 2007 directory.

Opening Files in Bridge

Individual files and sets of files can be opened from within Bridge. Double-clicking an individual file or selecting a file and pressing Ctrl+O/Cmd+O will open it in Photoshop.

To open a group of files, select them individually by Ctrl+clicking/Cmd+clicking individual files or by selecting one and then Shift-clicking another, selecting all consecutive files. With a group of files selected, double-clicking or using the keyboard shortcuts works the same way as with individual files.

Summary

Bridge can become a key part of the forensic digital imaging workflow. It can be the interface for downloading files from a memory card, navigating through directories, providing thumbnails and preview images, viewing metadata, opening and applying Camera Raw settings, applying and searching for keywords, and interfacing with Photoshop actions and other Adobe applications.

Because Bridge is a stand-alone application, it can run in the background, processing images and building thumbnails while you do other work within Photoshop or other applications

Bridge adds key functionality and efficiency to the forensic workflow.

Camera Raw

Adobe Photoshop Camera Raw (ACR) is an application that is included with Photoshop and is used to process and open files taken in a camera manufacturer's proprietary Raw file format. It can also process the open-standard DNG file format, and with Adobe Photoshop Camera Raw 4.0 and above, you can use it to process JPEG and TIFF files.

Raw file formats may be used when photographing fingerprints, footwear impressions, blood spatter, and other subject matter for which you want the best quality image.

5

Chapter Contents

What Is a Raw File?

Raw files are files from digital cameras that contain the "unprocessed" data, the data as it was captured. *Raw* isn't an abbreviation or even a single format; it's really a category of image file because each camera's version of Raw is a little different, as you'll see shortly. But all Raw files have much more in common with each other than with more accessible formats such as TIFF or JPEG.

Note: A minimal amount of processing is done to all image files, such as converting analog data to digital data. With Raw files, there is less processing done in-camera than with TIFF or JPEG camera-produced files.

Raw formats offer several advantages over TIFF and JPEG formats. When a digital camera converts the raw data into a TIFF or JPEG format, it reduces the bit depth to eight bits, applies a white balance that may not be ideal, and processes the image internally (image sharpening, JPEG compression, etc.), which may reduce the overall quality of the image.

Most digital cameras now offer a Raw file format at the professional and prosumer level. Each camera manufacturer uses its own proprietary Raw file format and provides free software that can open the files. Both Photoshop and Bridge include the Adobe Photoshop Camera Raw plug-in, which can open most Raw file formats.

Raw files are essentially digital negatives because the pixel data cannot be altered from within a photo editing program and saved back to the Raw file format. To open a Raw file, you must convert it with a Raw processing/converting application such as ACR to another format. The resulting file cannot be saved back to the original Raw file format; it must be saved in a non-Raw file format such as TIFF, JPEG, or the Photoshop format.

Raw formats offer greater bit depth than camera processed formats—usually 10 or 12 bits per channel (depending on the camera)—providing a much greater tonal range. An 8-bit image has up to 256 tones per channel; a 10-bit image has 1,024. The higher bit depth enables you to capture very subtle tonal differences and enables substantial image processing with better results.

I recommend that Raw file formats be used for any work in which comparative analysis will be done, including fingerprint, footwear, tire impression, and blood spatter photography. When choosing the best format to use in any forensics application, it is important to consider the use of the final image and all aspects of the system (camera, resolution, format, image processing steps, and output). For more information on this, see Chapter 1, "Best Practices." I have come up with my recommendations through my own testing. Each technician, examiner, or photographer should test their own equipment and evaluate their results when determining which formats to use in a forensics workflow.

Adobe Photoshop Camera Raw

Adobe Photoshop Camera Raw is a plug-in to Adobe Photoshop and Adobe Bridge. Version 4.0 provides a way to open Raw files from over 137 camera models from 16 camera manufacturers. This plug-in provides control over Raw files for correcting exposure errors, color balance, lens chromatic aberrations, and so on. When you make these adjustments in ACR, you are applying them to the linear file data, which can have significant benefits (as described later in this chapter).

Beginning with ACR 4.0, this plug-in can also be used to process JPEG and TIFF files. It will not convert the JPEG or TIFF file back into a Raw file, it doesn't remove JPEG artifacts, nor does it recover any loss of file quality that occurred when the JPEG or TIFF files were created in the camera. But it does enable you to open multiple files into ACR and apply the same adjustment to all of these files very efficiently. This concept is also discussed later.

ACR also provides a way to convert files from a proprietary file format to the open-source DNG file format. Each camera manufacturer uses a proprietary Raw file format—for example, Nikon uses NEF, Fuji uses RAF, and Canon uses CRW. These camera manufacturers may decide to stop supporting a given file format in the future, and it may be difficult to then open the images. Because DNG is an open-source format, it is likely that DNG files will be supported by multiple software companies for a longer period than proprietary file formats are supported.

Adobe Photoshop Camera Raw Preferences

Before using Adobe's Camera Raw functions, it is important to set up a few preferences that are specific to Adobe's Camera Raw converter. To access ACR's preferences, launch Bridge and choose Edit > Camera Raw Preferences / Bridge > Camera Raw Preferences (Figure 5.1). ACR preferences cannot be accessed directly from Photoshop, but they can be accessed from within the ACR window when a Raw file is open.

Because adjustments made in ACR do not change the pixel values of the Raw file, adjustments made in ACR are written to a separate file. The image settings can be saved in a central database or as individual sidecar files. The sidecar files are separate files for each image that include information about the settings made within ACR for things like color balance, brightness, and contrast. My recommendation is to choose the sidecar option because this makes it easiest to keep this information with the images when moving them to a storage location, a CD or DVD, and so on.

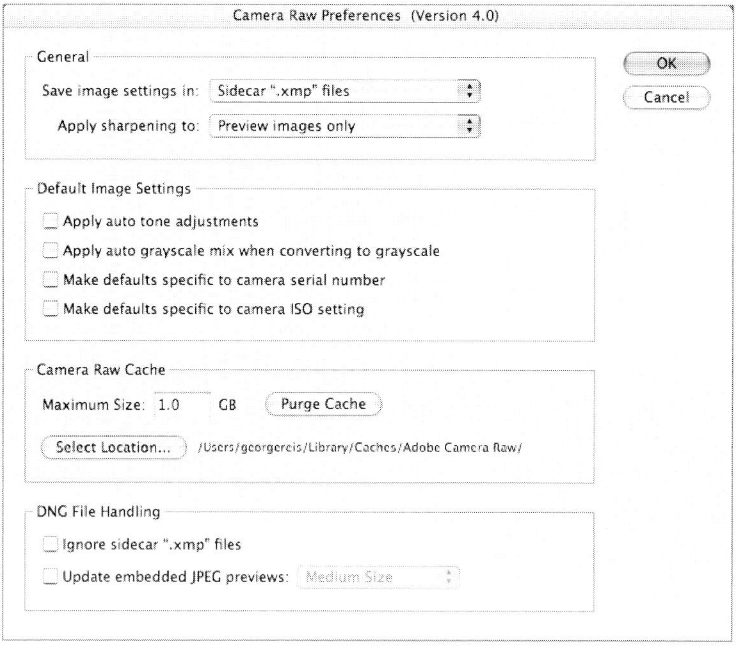

Figure 5.1 The Camera Raw Preferences dialog box

The second setting in the ACR Preferences dialog box determines if any sharpening applied within ACR will be applied only to the preview image onscreen or if it will be also applied to the file when it is opened. I recommend applying sharpening only to the previews so that you can apply it with better precision directly in Photoshop.

The next set of preferences controls how Adobe's Camera Raw defaults are applied to images opened in Camera Raw. If we were studio photographers, always shooting under the same lighting, I would recommend using some of these settings. But because our lighting changes with every crime scene, and from shot to shot within a single crime scene, I suggest keeping these boxes unchecked.

Even if you choose to save image settings in XMP sidecar files, image thumbnails and some other data are still stored in a separate cache file. The cache files can grow substantially over time. The next set of preferences gives you the ability to set the location for the cache files, purge the cache, and set a size limit on it. I leave the location and size limitation set to the defaults. If your agency creates a large number of Raw files, accesses them frequently, and has plenty of storage space, increasing the size limitation would make accessing older Raw files more efficient.

The last items in the ACR Preferences dialog box affect how ACR works with DNG files. If you convert Raw files to the DNG format for archiving, it makes sense to check both of these boxes for a more efficient workflow.

Using Adobe Photoshop Camera Raw

Now that the preferences have been set, point Bridge to a folder of Raw files. In versions of Photoshop prior to CS, it was best to wait for the File Browser to complete building thumbnails, previews, and cache files prior to working on images. With Bridge, this wait is no longer necessary. That is, you can select, rank, rename, sort, and open images while Bridge is still building thumbnails and previews, getting metadata information, and so on.

For a given scene, you generally need to apply the same color, brightness, and contrast adjustments to all the images in that lighting situation. Camera Raw with Bridge allows you to do this in a fairly automated manner. The method is to make all settings to one image and then apply them to all selected images in Bridge. Then, the correct adjustments will be applied when you open any of the images. We will cover this in more detail after first looking at how to make adjustments to individual images.

Select a raw image file (by clicking its thumbnail) that is representative of the correction you will want to make, and open it in Camera Raw by pressing Ctrl+R/Cmd+R. This opens the image in the ACR window within Bridge. Another approach is to select multiple files and open them as a group into ACR.

If your Raw files initially look darker or have a different color balance than your JPEGs do, it is only because no initial processing has been done. By making the adjustments described later in this chapter, you will find that your Raw files are superior to any JPEG or TIFF files produced by your camera.

Once one or more images are open in ACR and adjustments have been made, click Done to close the ACR window and create sidecar files for each adjusted image. The files can then be reopened in ACR or Photoshop with these adjustments applied. Clicking Cancel closes the ACR window without any adjustments being made. Choosing Open Object will open the files in Photoshop as Smart Objects with the adjustments applied. The Open Object button will be an Open button if Open Files As Smart Objects is unchecked in the Workflow Options dialog box (which we'll look at a little later). Clicking the Save Image button will provide options for saving the file(s) as a DNG, JPG, TIF, or PSD format. The Raw file will not be overwritten when saving a copy in any of these formats.

The ACR Interface

The Camera Raw window is divided into six main sections: thumbnails, toolbar, preview image, workflow settings, image adjustment settings, and control buttons. ACR 4.0 is the version that ships with Photoshop CS3. Older versions of ACR have many of the same features, although the 4.0 upgrade is substantial in both the interface and functions of this tool.

If more than one image is open in ACR, the thumbnails appear on the left (Figure 5.2). Multiple images can be selected to apply the same settings to all of the images. You can select multiple images—by Shift+clicking, Ctrl/Cmd+clicking, or clicking the Select All button—and then make the desired adjustments. Alternatively, you can apply adjustments to multiple images by first making the adjustments to one image and then selecting multiple images and clicking the Synchronize button.

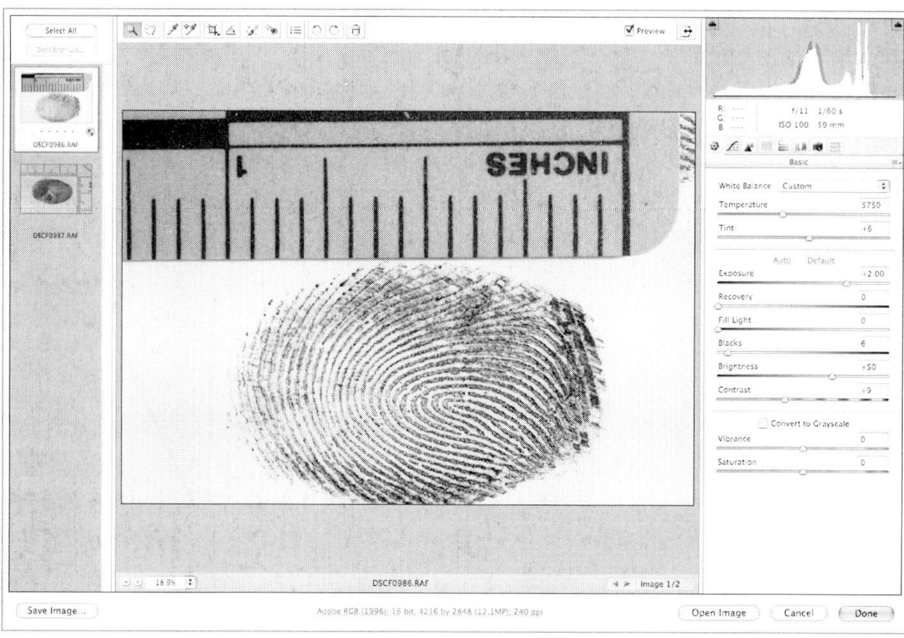

Figure 5.2 The Adobe Photoshop Camera Raw 4.0 window with two images open

The Preview Image section takes up most of the screen and the zoom level can be adjusted using the Zoom tool, the Zoom pop-up window, or keyboard commands (Shift+Ctrl+- / Shift+Cmd+- to zoom in; Ctrl+- / Cmd+- to zoom out).

The tools in ACR 4.0 (Figure 5.3) provide quite a bit of functionality. I recommend using these tools as a starting place in the ACR workflow.

The **Zoom** tool will magnify the image if you clicking in the Preview window, or zoom out if you Alt/Option+clicking.

The **Hand** tool can move the image when you click and drag in the Preview window to show different areas of a magnified view.

The **White Balance** tool allows you to make a quick color correction by clicking a value that should be neutral in tone (light, medium, or dark gray)—this is a great first step in color balance correction.

The **Color Sampler** tool allows you to click up to nine points in the image area to view readouts of their color values.

The **Crop** tool is for cropping the image. (I recommend not cropping images in a forensic workflow.)

The **Straighten** tool will correct an image that is askew—just choose this tool and drag a line along a feature that should be perfectly horizontal or vertical.

The **Retouch** tool has two options when invoked (clone and healing), and these options and the corresponding tools in Photoshop work similarly for dust spot removal. (I don't recommend using this tool in a forensics workflow.)

The **Red Eye Removal** tool is for fixing red eye.

The **Preferences** button will open the ACR Preferences dialog box.

The **Rotate** tools rotate the image by 90 degrees clockwise or 90 degrees counterclockwise.

The **Delete** tool will move selected files to your computer's trash upon exiting ACR.

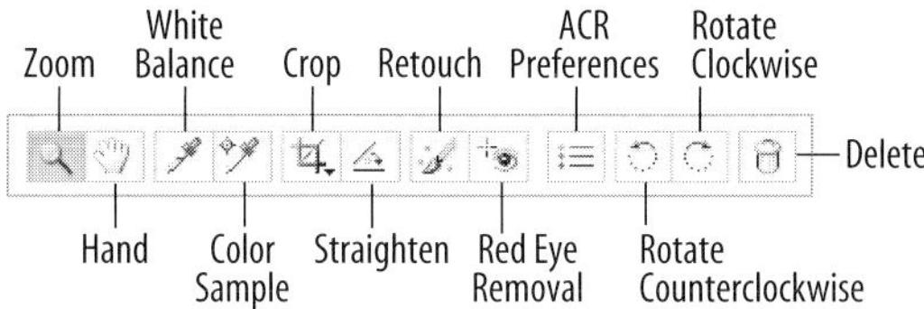

Figure 5.3 The toolbar from ACR 4.0

I use these tools in my workflow. First I open images into ACR and rotate them if needed. I then use the Zoom and Hand tools to see the level of detail needed for any adjustments that I plan to make (generally color, brightness, or contrast adjustments). I will then use the White Balance tool for an initial color correction, which I may further adjust with the Image Adjustment settings later in the workflow.

The controls in the Workflow Options window (see Figure 5.4) let you choose the color space, bit depth, pixel resolution and ppi of the image after conversion. Clicking the text opens a window to change these settings. I recommend setting the color space to Adobe RGB (1998) or to ProPhoto RGB—both of these spaces have a very large color gamut.

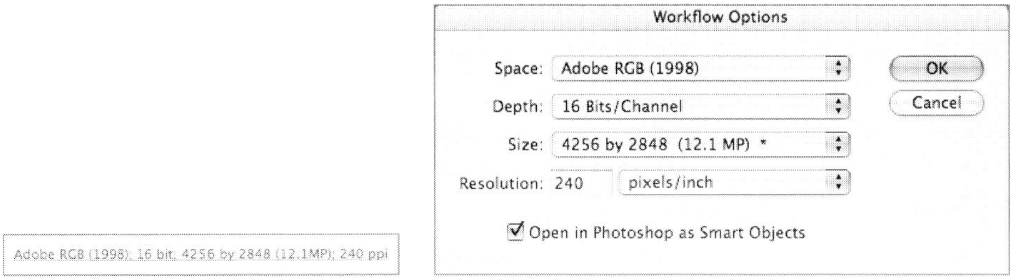

Adobe RGB (1998); 16 bit; 4256 by 2848 (12.1MP); 240 ppi

Workflow Options

Space: Adobe RGB (1998)
Depth: 16 Bits/Channel
Size: 4256 by 2848 (12.1 MP) *
Resolution: 240 pixels/inch
Open in Photoshop as Smart Objects
OK
Cancel

Figure 5.4 Click the hyperlink text at the bottom of the ACR window to open the Workflow Options window.

If any additional image adjustments are going to be made to the image, and/or if the image is going to be used for precise measurements or comparative analysis, then 16-bit images will allow for better results when you're applying image adjustments in Photoshop. Even if no additional adjustment is anticipated, the image can always be converted to 8 bit later.

The Size setting allows you to open the image at the pixel resolution in which it was photographed, to upsample to create more pixels, or to downsample to provide fewer. I recommend using your camera's native resolution. (A possible exception to this is the Fuji cameras that use hexagonal pixels, which may provide slightly sharper images by upsampling one level.) In this window, downsampled settings have a minus sign and upsampled settings have a plus sign. The asterisk in Figure 5.4 indicates that this is the one-step upsampled setting for a Fuji camera. The Resolution setting can be set to whatever printing resolution is used in your workflow. This setting does not affect the quality of the image itself, only the description of pixels per inch for printing.

As a general rule, these workflow options can remain set and will need to be changed only if you are preparing images for different purposes—printing 8×10s of crime scene images as opposed to preparing fingerprints for analysis, for example.

Making Image Adjustments in ACR

The entire right side of the ACR window (Figure 5.5) contains the image adjustment settings: adjustments for brightness, contrast, and color with several parameters for each type of adjustment. There are eight icons that represent tabs for the tools available in ACR to adjust brightness, contrast, curves, saturation, and chromatic aberration and to access presets. We'll take a look at the adjustments in the Basic tab in detail because that's where you'll make most of your adjustments in a typical workflow. We'll also briefly review the other tabs that may be used on occasion although they may not typically be used in a forensics workflow.

The Image histogram shows the graphical representation of the values in the image. It is updated as adjustments are made to the image within ACR. The icons in the top left and top right are black if no tones in the image are clipped, but they will display in a color if one or two channels have clipping and white if all three are clipped. Clicking on the icons will display the clipped pixels in the Preview window.

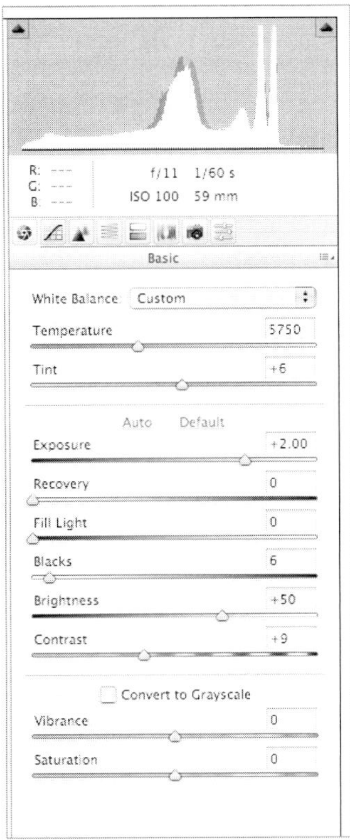

Figure 5.5 The right side of the ACR window has a histogram at the top, icons to open several different tabs, and an area to make image adjustments. Here are the settings available with the Basic tab selected.

Just below the histogram are the icons to display several tabs. The leftmost icon displays the Basic settings, which is the default view for ACR. There is an icon in the top-right corner of every tab view to open a flyout menu to save, load, and apply ACR settings (see Figure 5.6).

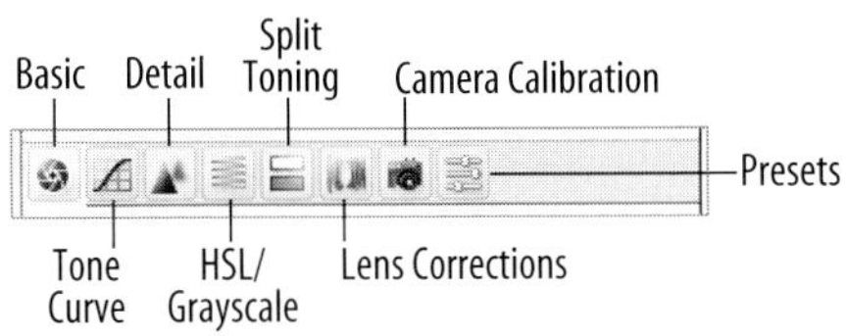

Figure 5.6 These icons access the adjustment tabs.

The Basic Tab

The Basic settings tab is where most of the basic image adjustment functionality in Camera Raw resides. This tab has a pop-up menu for setting preset color balance settings and sliders that are divided into three general categories—Color Temperature settings, Brightness/Contrast settings, and Saturation settings.

The color temperature settings are to adjust color temperature and tint. If the color sampler tool is used to correct the color balance in the image, no further adjustments may be necessary. If they are, the Temperature slider will adjust the blue/yellow range and the Tint slider will adjust the green/magenta range.

The brightness/contrast settings are used to adjust the brightness and contrast in some unique ways with considerable precision. I generally adjust the exposure to provide an overall correction first. It works in a similar way to changing the exposure in the camera. Moving this slider to the right increases the exposure (lightens the image), and sliding it to the left decreases the exposure (darkens it). Next I adjust the Blacks slider to adjust the shadow portion of the image. Very slight changes to this setting will make substantial changes to the image, so it is best used conservatively. I then adjust the Brightness and Contrast sliders if needed, and the Fill Light slider will lighten the darkest tones if needed.

The saturation settings adjust the intensity of the colors. Checking the Convert To Grayscale box will convert the image to grayscale.

As a general rule for crime scene, evidence, and traffic accident photography, the default settings should be very close, if not perfectly acceptable. To open images directly into Photoshop, applying the default ACR settings, just press the Shift key while double-clicking them in Bridge. If, however, corrections to Raw files do need to be made, it is preferable to make these adjustments within ACR rather than in Photoshop because more detail will be preserved.

The key to making the best corrections within the Basic settings tab is to make the largest corrections first and minor corrections last. That is, if the color is way off but the exposure and contrast are close, make color adjustments first. If the exposure is way off but the color is close, make adjustments to the exposure settings first.

Other Tabs

The second icon opens the Tone Curve tab, which provides an advanced curves interface. There are two separate curves interfaces available in the Tone Curve tab.

The Detail tab provides control over sharpness and noise reduction. Because we already set the Camera Raw preference to apply sharpness to the preview image only, the amount of sharpening set here will only affect the preview image. The 25 percent default setting tends to generate good previews. If graininess is a problem—especially with long exposures or high ISO settings—the noise reduction adjustments can be quite helpful. My experience is to avoid overcorrecting, so I recommend conservative settings.

The next two icons are the HSL/Grayscale and Split Toning tabs. These both offer capabilities for photographic artwork but are less significant in a forensics workflow.

The Lens Corrections tab is next. It provides adjustments for correcting chromatic aberrations (red/cyan or blue/yellow fringes along edges of objects) and vignetting (dark or light edges in the image).

The Camera Calibration tab allows you to calibrate your specific camera in a specific lighting environment. In a lab environment, with the same lighting used regularly, this may be useful to correct for any modest color shifts that exist in your captured images. Photograph a color chart with known color values and use the sliders in this tab to reproduce the colors and tones as precisely as possible. This can be done for any number of different configurations—and each can be saved via the flyout menu button just above the tab.

Last is the Presets tab, which lists all saved presets. Clicking one of the presets will apply it to the selected images.

Working with Multiple Images

ACR and Bridge allow you to work with multiple images in a couple of ways: by opening multiple images within ACR or by applying ACR settings to multiple images directly in Bridge. There are advantages to each method of working with multiple files. If you are working with a set of raw images that have similar lighting conditions, and therefore similar adjustments, using Bridge to apply the same adjustments to multiple images is a huge timesaver. If you are working with multiple Raw files that all need different adjustments, you can save time by opening multiple files in ACR rather than opening them individually in ACR, making corrections, applying them, relaunching ACR, making new adjustments, and so on.

To open multiple files in ACR, simply choose the files you want to open in Bridge by clicking the first image and Shift+clicking the last image to choose a sequence of images, or Ctrl/Cmd+click individual files that are not listed consecutively. Then double-click any of these images to open them in ACR (don't hold down the Shift key while double+clicking or the images will be opened directly into Photoshop and the default ACR settings will be applied.

To work on each image, select the thumbnail by clicking it. Multiple files can be selected by Shift+clicking or Ctrl/Cmd+clicking. For each image selected (or group of images), make the appropriate adjustments in ACR and click the appropriate control button.

A typical workflow using ACR with multiple images would be to open multiple files into ACR, work on each image, and click Done after all images are complete or open them into Photoshop by choosing the Open or Open Object button.

If all of the raw images in a set need the same basic adjustments, this can be done by correcting one image, then applying this adjustment to multiple images directly in Bridge (see Figure 5.7). You can basically copy the ACR settings and then paste them to other images. To do this, first open one Raw file into ACR, apply the appropriate settings, and click Done. Then return to Bridge.

Figure 5.7 Synchronizing the same adjustment settings to multiple images. Adjustments were made to the first image, then I clicked the Select All button at the top left followed by the Synchronize button.

An icon shows above the image thumbnail to indicate that ACR settings have been applied to an image (this icon shows below the thumbnail in Bridge 1.0). Right-clicking/Control-clicking the thumbnail will open a contextual menu that allows these settings to be copied. You can then select the rest of the images that you wish to apply these settings to by Shift+clicking or Ctrl/Cmd+clicking them. Right-clicking/Control-clicking any of the selected thumbnails will then show a contextual menu that allows you to paste the ACR settings to the selected images. Choose Paste Camera Raw Settings to open a window that allows you to choose all of the ACR settings or a subset of ACR settings. Choose which settings to apply and click the OK button to apply these settings to all selected images. Now these files can be opened without having to bring them through ACR.

JPEG and TIFF Images in ACR

ACR 4.0 introduced the ability to process JPEG and TIFF images within this interface. This offers two key advantages. First, it provides a very efficient workflow for making the same adjustments to multiple JPEG or TIFF files. Second, it doesn't apply those adjustments to the pixel values directly, making this a relatively nondestructive workflow.

There are several ways to set up a workflow to use ACR to process JPEG and TIFF files. Select the Bridge preference Prefer Adobe Camera Raw For JPEG And TIFF Files to enable JPEG and TIFF files to be opened in the Bridge hosted version of ACR by selecting them and pressing Ctrl+R/Cmd+R. If you don't select that option in Photoshop, JPEG and TIFF files will still open directly into Photoshop when you double-click them. Regardless of these settings, if a JPEG or TIFF file has been processed with ACR, it will open through ACR only when you reopen it.

A typical workflow for using ACR to process JPEG or TIFF files is to select multiple images in Bridge. Press Ctrl+R/Cmd+R to open them in ACR. Select all thumbnails in ACR, apply the desired settings, then click Done to apply the adjustments and close ACR or click Open or Open Object to open the adjusted images into Photoshop.

Summary

Raw file formats offer some key advantages to forensics users. Raw files function as digital negatives because changes cannot be saved back to the Raw format. Raw files have a higher bit depth than camera-created JPEG or TIFF files, which can provide substantially greater tonal information. Raw files do not have camera-applied processing such as image sharpening, color balance, and lossy compression. For these reasons, Raw file formats are a preferred format for photographs of images that will be used for image enhancement or comparative analysis.

Adobe Photoshop Camera Raw provides the ability to process individual images and groups of images. Adjustments can be made to color balance, brightness, and contrast as well as noise reduction, chromatic aberration correction, and calibrations to individual cameras. ACR is a powerful image processing tool and can be used to process JPEG and TIFF files in addition to most Raw file formats.

Viewing Metadata

In this chapter, you'll see how you can view a file's metadata and how that information can be valuable in a forensic workflow.

Chapter Contents

What Metadata Is

In an image file, metadata is the data that isn't describing the pixel-by-pixel content of the image. This includes information generated by digital cameras, such as camera make and model, shutter speed, aperture setting, ISO, the date and time when the image was digitized, the color space, and pixel resolution. It also includes information that might be generated by the operating system or software that is used to open or save the image, such as the name and version of the software used to process the image, the date and time the file was downloaded and modified, and information about any processing that was applied to the image. All of this metadata is automatically generated by digital cameras, operating systems, and imaging software (although in the case of Photoshop's History Log, this feature must be activated in Photoshop's General Preferences panel).

Metadata also may include information entered by an individual, such as case number, the name of the officer who took the photos, the crime type, reporting district, and whether the photos are of a crime scene, traffic accident, autopsy, and so on.

Our primary interest is in the metadata associated with the image capture and any subsequent processing that may have been done to the image. This is valuable for technical case review, to verify when photos were taken and downloaded (assuming the date and time are correctly set on your camera and computer), what image processing was performed (with Photoshop's History Log; see Chapter 3), and also as a part of image analysis to determine if the image is what it purports to be.

Entering Metadata

You can enter metadata as keywords and as IPTC data in your images.

Keywords are valuable in helping you locate specific images (such as homicide photos taken by Officer Jones in 2004). Keyword categories can be set for criteria such as crime type, officer name, or reporting district; then a future search can locate images that match specific keywords within these categories (see more on using keywords in Chapter 4).

IPTC stands for International Press Telecommunications Council, and in the case of IPTC metadata, it refers to a set of fields an individual can use to enter text data within a file's metadata. Because the IPTC is an organization associated with journalism, the field names that can be entered are oriented toward that discipline. But forensics users can repurpose these fields for their own use.

To enter IPTC metadata, select one or more files in Bridge, or the active image in Photoshop, and choose File > File Info; then click IPTC Contact or any of the IPTC options in the menu on the left (see Figure 6.1). When you're choosing multiple images in Bridge, the entered data is applied to the metadata of all selected images.

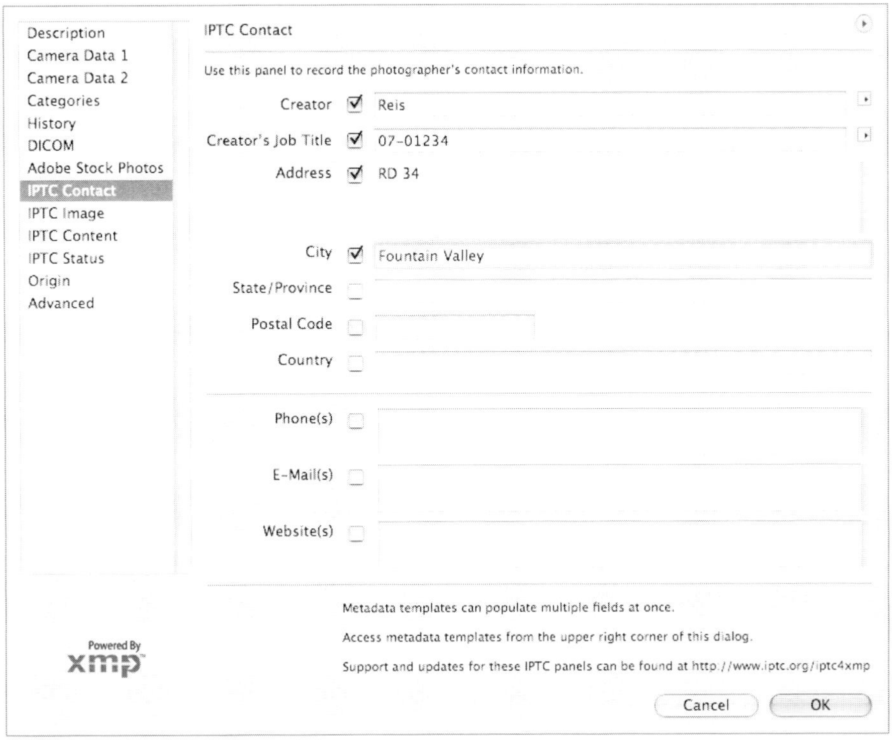

Figure 6.1 The IPTC Contact panel with several fields entered to represent the officer's name and the case number, reporting district, and city

This IPTC data can then be viewed by returning to the File Info panel or in Bridge's Metadata panel.

Metadata in Bridge

Metadata can be viewed in Photoshop or in Bridge.

To view the metadata in Photoshop, choose File > File Info. The Description, Origin, and Categories panels contain information that can be entered only to individual files, and some of the fields are duplicated in other panels. The Camera Data panels contain some of the Camera EXIF data (more complete Camera EXIF data can be viewed in Bridge, which we'll get to in a moment). The History panel displays the information recorded by Photoshop's History Log. The DICOM panel is for data from DICOM images that are used in the medical field. The Adobe Stock Photos panel contains data about images purchased from Adobe Stock Photos. The IPTC panels are for IPTC data as described earlier—fields with check boxes can be applied to multiple images at once.

Some fields are duplicated in more than one panel. The Advanced panel contains other metadata file information, including some file creation and modification date and time information.

Viewing metadata in Bridge offers two key advantages—the data is easier to read, and it is more efficient to move from one image to the next from within Bridge.

The Bridge window can be modified to almost any configuration by moving the adjustable bars, choosing which panels are visible, adjusting the size of the thumbnail images, and so on. I configure the Bridge window as shown in Figure 6.2 for viewing file metadata—it provides a large Metadata panel, a small Content panel, and a large Preview panel. This makes it easy to navigate from one image to another, see a large preview image, and see the largest number of metadata fields as possible.

Figure 6.2 A customized metadata workspace in Bridge

Showing or hiding specific panels is done by going to the View menu and selecting or deselecting the specific panels you want to show or hide or by right-clicking in a panel or on a tab and choosing to show or hide a panel from the contextual menu.

The size of the panels can be changed by clicking and sliding the adjustable bars to the position you prefer. The size of the thumbnails can be adjusted by moving the slider at the bottom-right corner of the Bridge window. Once the window is set up, a couple of preferences can be set for the metadata panel.

To access the metadata preferences, click the flyout menu button from the metadata panel and choose Preferences, or choose Edit > Preferences and click Metadata on the left of the window that opens. This will open the Preferences window to the Metadata panel (see Figure 6.3).

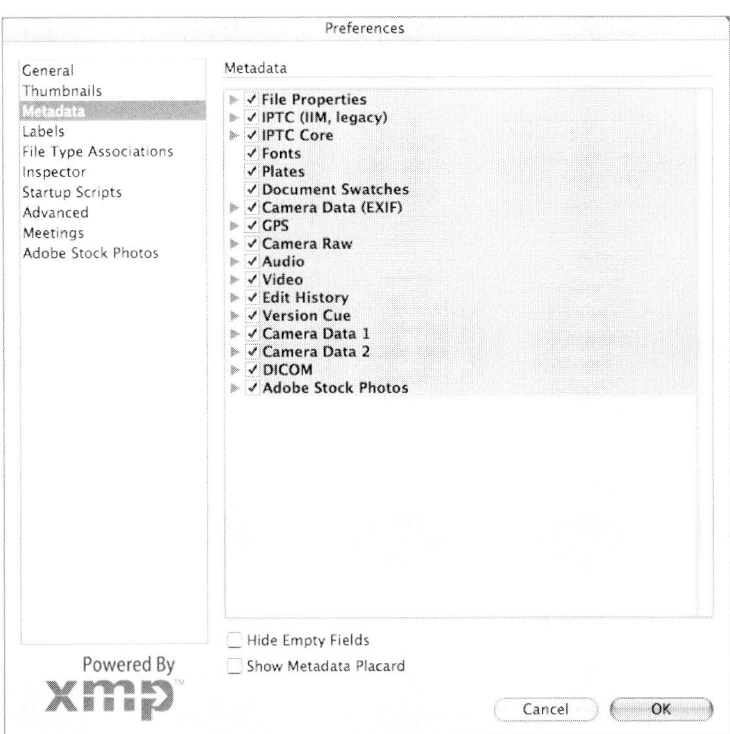

Figure 6.3 The Metadata Preferences panel is accessed from the General Preferences window by clicking Metadata on the left.

In the Metadata Preferences panel, check the boxes that represent the metadata you will want to see; I check all boxes so that I can see all metadata associated with the image. Unchecking the Hide Empty Fields box will make all fields visible, even if they contain no data.

Showing all fields, including empty fields, requires more scrolling, but it allows you to verify that everything is working properly and that you aren't missing any information.

Bridge's Metadata panel now displays the camera information (including camera make and model, lens focal length, shutter speed, aperture setting, date and time information from the camera, whether the flash fired, and so on), the IPTC data, GPS information (if a GPS device was connected to and data was recorded by a camera), and Photoshop's History Log.

Unchecking Show Metadata Placard will hide the icon in Bridge's Metadata panel that contains a graphic showing some exposure information that is also listed in text format. The metadata placard is duplicate information, so I choose not to display it. Figure 6.4 shows Bridge's Metadata panel.

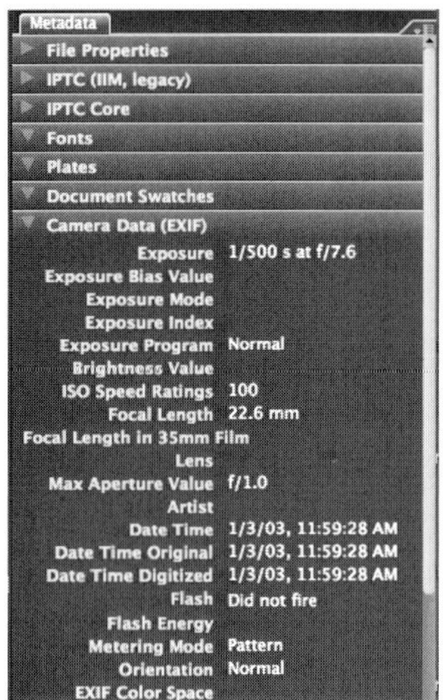

Figure 6.4 The Metadata panel in Bridge

Each metadata category in Bridge's Metadata panel can be expanded or contracted by clicking the triangle toggles. I begin my review of metadata by expanding each category and browsing the fields.

Using Metadata

The five categories that are likely to have the most relevant data for image analysis are File Properties, Camera Data, Camera Raw, IPTC, and Edit History data.

In image analysis, including image authentication, a review of the date and time stamps can help verify the date and time a photo was taken. It is important to note, however, that the date and time recorded is only as accurate as the date and time set in the camera. If the date and time are different than claimed by the photographer, this data, combined with information about when and how the date is reset in a specific camera, can be used to determine if the date and time difference is easily explainable (a one-hour difference due to daylight savings, a one-day or one-month difference due to user error in setting the date, for example). A difference of three months, two weeks, and six hours is probably not easily explained by simple user error, daylight savings, changing time zones, or a power reset.

Other camera information, such as the recorded shutter speed, focal length, and aperture settings, can be reviewed to determine if they correspond with the image sharpness, angle of view, and depth of field. If not, this may indicate that the image data has been replaced with a different image, that it is a composite image, or that it has been manipulated in some other way.

The History Log is valuable for technical review. If a technician has made image adjustments and has the work reviewed by another technician, this data can verify what adjustments have been made to the image, and the reviewer can apply these same adjustments to a copy of the original to determine if they obtain similar results. If a suspect used Photoshop and had the History Log enabled, reviewing it can also show what processes they applied to the image.

The IPTC data can be viewed to see what user-entered information has been set. This can help show the origin of an image if the data was recorded by the original creator and not deleted later. It may also help show a correlation between multiple images based on the types of information recorded.

Summary

Image metadata can be valuable in a forensics workflow for several reasons. Keywords and IPTC data can be used for identifying information about your images and make it easy to find specific images based on information such as crime type, case number, reporting district, and so on. Camera data can be used in image authentication. The History Log is valuable in a forensic workflow for performing technical reviews. However, even with this valuable information, it must be remembered that some data, like the data in the IPTC fields, is entered by a user (and could be deleted); date and time information is only as accurate as the settings in the camera and computer; and the History Log is recorded only if it has been enabled in Photoshop's preferences.

The Digital Darkroom

II

This section deals with items related to general crime scene, traffic accident, and evidence photographs and preparing them for printing or for CD or DVD distribution. This includes methods for making basic enhancement, printing images, batch printing, and making contact sheets, multipage PDF documents, and court displays.

If images are stored on a server or within a specific directory on an individual workstation, you can guarantee that you're working on copies by copying the files to the host computer. If you're working from images on a CD or DVD, this is guaranteed by the nature of the media. Regardless of the method of archiving images, it should be understood that all image processing is performed on duplicates of the images.

7 Basic Image Adjustments

In a typical forensic workflow, viewing and printing most crime scene, traffic accident, and evidence photographs should not require making any corrections for color, brightness, or contrast. However, some images are either over- or underexposed or may have a color shift. There are several ways to correct color, contrast, and brightness in Photoshop—some methods will apply corrections to the entire image and others will apply them to local areas. Here we will review two types of adjustments: global adjustments and adjustments to localized areas of an image. But first we'll discuss how to prepare for these adjustments in a nondestructive workflow.

Chapter Contents

Global Adjustments with Levels

One of the easiest and most efficient methods for making corrections to color, brightness, and contrast is Levels adjustment. Levels adjustments can be made directly to the pixels in the image by choosing this tool from the Image > Adjustments menu. Levels adjustments can also be made by applying them as an adjustment layer. Adjustment layers hold the instructions for adjustment to an image so that the original pixel values are unchanged adjustment layers that can be modified without any changes being made to the original Pixel values. This provides a nondestructive workflow because the original pixel values remain unchanged.

Smart Objects, Smart Filters, and Bit Depth

Photoshop introduced Smart Objects with CS2 and expanded their capability in CS3 by adding Smart Filters.

A Smart Object is an image layer that enables you to work in a more nondestructive manner with your images. Smart Objects keep the original image content so that the available adjustments can be re-edited or undone without a loss of image quality. In CS2, the capabilities offered by Smart Objects used in a forensics workflow were primarily in image resizing.

With CS3 and the introduction of Smart Filters, almost all filters and adjustments can be applied in a nondestructive and re-editable method with Smart Objects. All processes and examples done in the following chapters will be on images that have been converted to Smart Objects. Although it isn't required to work with Smart Objects, it is good practice. To convert an image to a Smart Object, choose Layer > Smart Object > Convert To Smart Object, or simply open it as a Smart Object by choosing File > Open As Smart Object.

A Smart Object icon is placed in the lower-right corner of the image thumbnail of the Layers palette after an image has been converted to a Smart Object. There are a few functions that cannot be directly applied to Smart Objects, including Perspective Transforms, cloning, and painting. If these are needed, the Smart Object must be converted back to a raster layer by choosing Layer > Smart Objects > Rasterize.

Finally, all images in this workflow are also in the 16 Bits Per Channel mode. It isn't necessary for images to be in 16-bit mode, but as with Smart Objects, it is good practice. You can convert to 16 bits by choosing Image > Mode > 16 Bits / Channel.

The 16-bit mode provides a larger tonal range when working with images. It doesn't add any tonal values to the image when it is converted from 8 bits, but it provides a larger container. The advantage of this larger container is that with some adjustments, a better result can be achieved.

The original image in Figure 7.1 is very underexposed and has a color shift. By applying a Levels adjustment to the entire image through an adjustment layer, you can correct the exposure error and the color shift.

Before starting, I like to convert the image to 16 bits per channel and to a Smart Object as described in the sidebar ("Smart Objects, Smart Filters, and Bit Depth"). I also zoom the image to a size that will avoid screen-based artifacts (100 percent or an even factor or multiple of 100, such as 25, 50, or 200 percent).

Figure 7.1 Left, the original image; right, after a Levels adjustment.

To make a color correction using Levels adjustment, you will first need to set the Eyedropper tool to sample a 5×5 pixel sample (or larger). To do this, select the Eyedropper tool in the toolbar or press the I key. With the Eyedropper tool selected, set the pop-up menu in the option bar to 5 By 5 Average, as shown in Figure 7.2.

Figure 7.2 Choose the Eyedropper tool and set it to 5 By 5 Average.

Create a Levels adjustment layer by clicking the adjustment layer icon and choosing Levels from the contextual menu (see Figure 7.2) or by choosing Layer > New Adjustment Layer > Levels (Figure 7.3). This will open the Levels dialog box (Figure 7.4).

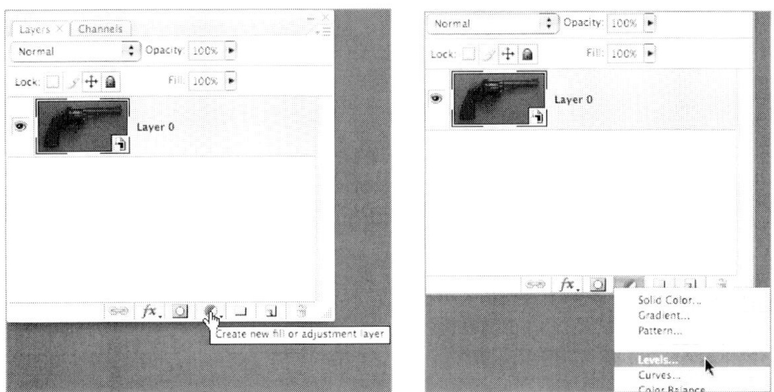

Figure 7.3 Click the adjustment layer icon and choose Levels.

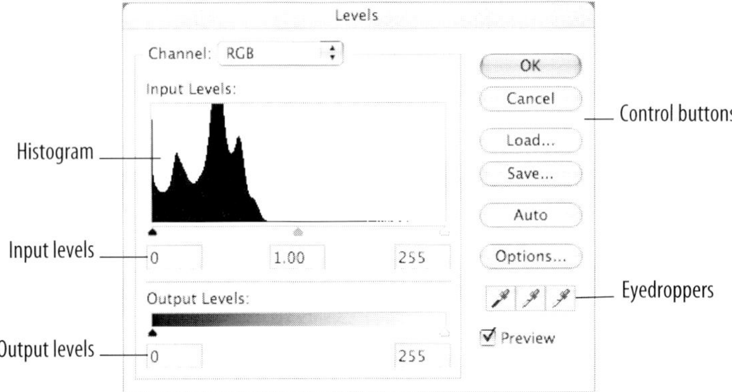

Figure 7.4 The Levels dialog box

The large graph is a histogram, which displays the tonal range of the image. The darkest pixels are represented on the left, the brightest on the right, with the midtone in the center. Understanding the histogram is key to evaluating photographs and correcting poor exposures. In this image, the histogram tells us that most of the pixels are dark because most of them are to the left of the midpoint—that is, most are darker than middle gray.

Moving the input sliders, or changing the values in the Input Levels text boxes, can adjust the contrast and/or overall brightness of an image. The left slider is the black point slider; any pixels to the left of it will become black. The slider on the right is the white point slider; any pixels to the right of it will be pure white.

When these sliders are moved within the outside parameters of the graph, some pixel values will become pure white or pure black, which is called clipping because the values are all clipped to the minimum or maximum brightness. Clipping can cause a loss of tonal variations in these areas, so it is important to not overcorrect when making these adjustments. Sliding the outside sliders toward the center will increase the contrast and potentially clip the darkest and brightest values. Sliding the center slider to the left lightens the overall image by moving more pixels to the right of the midpoint, and sliding it to the right darkens the overall image by moving more pixels to the left of the midpoint.

A general rule of thumb is that one should move the black and white point sliders to the edges of the histogram graph to get the fullest tonal range possible. Sometimes there will be highlights or shadows of little value and the sliders may be moved beyond these pixels. Holding down the Alt/Option key while moving the white point and black point sliders will show which pixels will be clipped in the preview image.

For the image shown in Figure 7.5, I slid the white point slider to the left to expand the tonal range. I clipped some pixels and held the Alt/Option key down while clicking the white point slider, which provided me with feedback to see which pixels I was clipping. I tend to make an adjustment, then click and release my mouse while holding down the Alt/Option key, which toggles between the adjusted image and the clipped values. Areas that are white are being clipped in all three color channels, those showing red are clipping in the red channel only, those in blue are only being clipped in the blue channel, and so on. Notice that sliding the white point slider also changed the white point value in the levels value field. The value in any of the input value fields can be adjusted very precisely by using the up and down arrows on the keyboard, or a value could be typed in.

The image is now a little light and has a color shift, so you're not yet done with it. You'll adjust the overall brightness next.

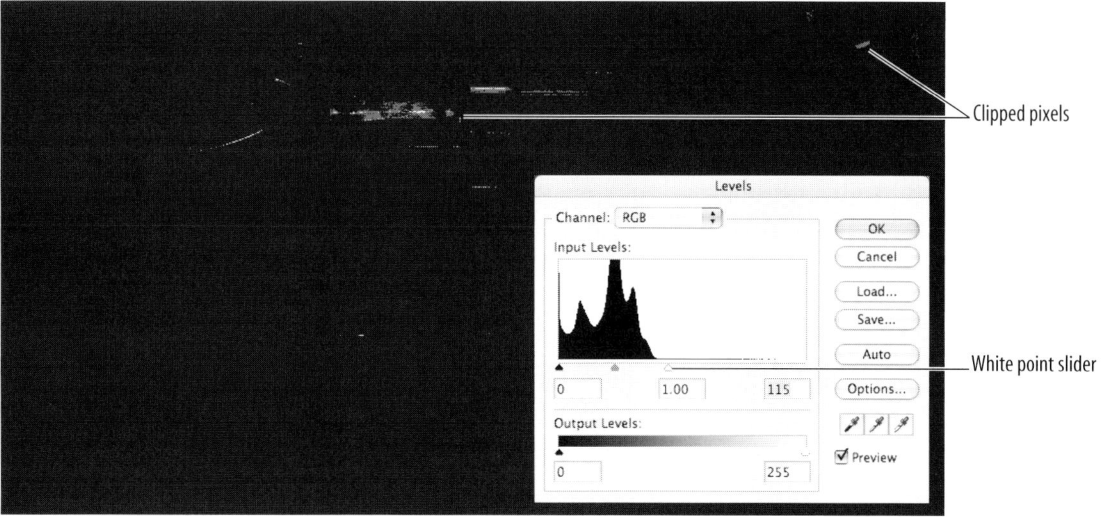

Figure 7.5 The image displays the pixels that will be clipped with the setting made on the right.

Sliding the midpoint slider to the left, as shown in Figure 7.6, lightens the image overall—it moves more pixels to the right side of the midpoint slider, which means that more pixels will be lighter than middle gray. Sliding it to the right places more pixels on the left of the midpoint, making the image darker. For this image, the extreme adjustment of the white point made the image a bit light, so a slight adjustment brings back the midtones in this image.

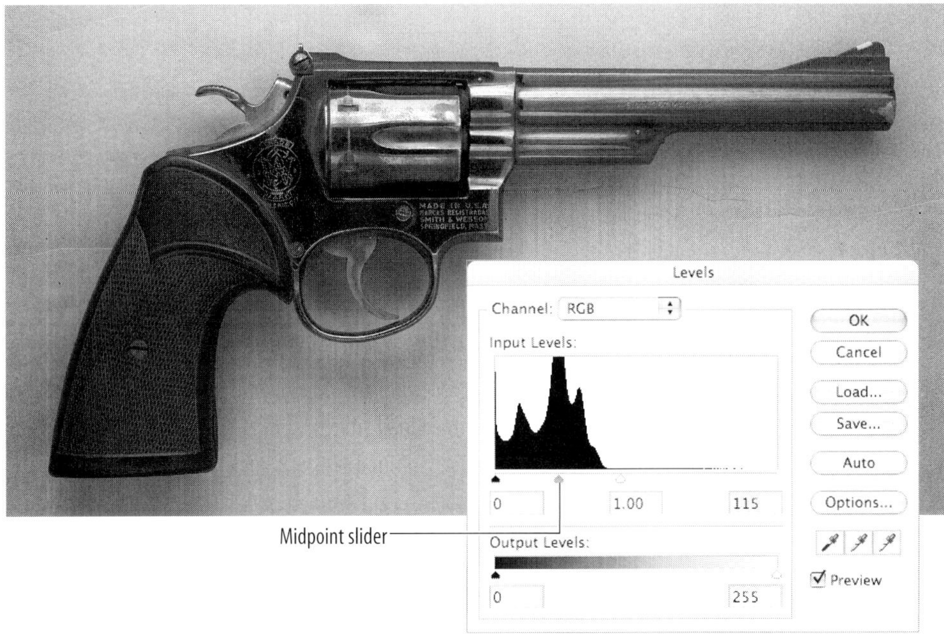

Figure 7.6 Adjusting the midpoint slider will lighten the image by using the settings shown on the right.

The only remaining problem with this image is the red color shift. If the color shift were more extreme than the exposure problem, we would have adjusted it prior to adjusting the midpoint. It is best to correct the biggest defect first, and it will sometimes be necessary to then go back to fine-tune it after other adjustments have also been made. In the case of this image, either adjustment could be done first.

Now we'll correct the color shift. To color-correct an image within Levels, select the gray point eyedropper and click something in the image that is supposed to be neutral in color. In the image in Figure 7.7, I chose a shadow area on the gray background. I purposely did not choose the gun metal because blue steel should have a slight blue cast. Neutral, in this instance, means light gray, medium gray, or dark gray—something that has no hue. Gray items may include a gray card, tires, asphalt, some walls, furniture, clothing, and hair. If the color is off in the image, this area may appear to have a color cast, and clicking it will apply the proper filtration to make it neutral. The same correction is applied to the entire image, correcting the overall color shift. The gray point eyedropper samples an area of the size set in the Eyedropper tool options. If the sampled area is a single pixel, the correction will be more difficult because individual pixels may have slight color shifts that are not representative of the area—that is why you set the Eyedropper tool for a 5×5 pixel sample area (or larger) earlier.

Note: In Photoshop CS3, Adobe has given us the capability to go up to a sample area of 101×101 pixels. But that large a sample will rarely be useful. The key is to set the sample size large enough to offset undue influences of bad pixels but not so large that areas of color are included in the sample.

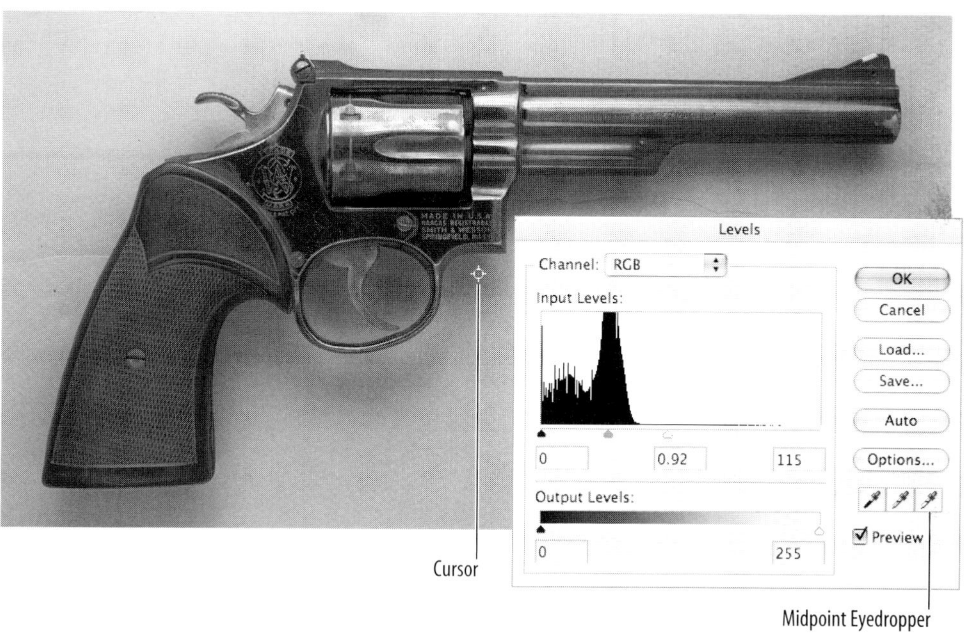

Figure 7.7 The image shows the color-corrected image from using the gray point eyedropper as shown.

After you have completed your adjustments, click the OK button to apply them to the adjustment layer and dismiss the Levels dialog box. The adjustments are all contained within the adjustment layer that can be seen in the Layers palette. A thumbnail is visible showing the original image, and another thumbnail represents the adjustment layer. Clicking the visibility icon for the adjustment layer will toggle the adjustment on and off, showing the original image with no changes and showing it with the adjustments applied. Double-clicking the levels icon will reopen the Levels dialog box and show the exact adjustments that were made to the image. No adjustments need to be made to the layer options—the mode should be Normal and the opacity and fill should both be 100 percent.

This image can now be saved and closed or sized for printing. If you're saving the image, you must save it in TIFF or PSD format to retain the separate adjustment layer.

If I'm saving the image, I like to name the layer with the parameters used for the adjustment layer. If the only adjustment made within Levels is a brightness/contrast adjustment, all the parameters can be seen in the primary Levels dialog box. However, color adjustments (as you made with the Eyedropper tool) cause changes to the separate red, green, and blue channels. To view the separate color channel adjustments in the Levels dialog box, choose each channel separately from the drop-down menu at the top of the window or press Ctrl+1/Cmd+1 for the red channel, Ctrl+2/Cmd+2 for green, and Ctrl+3/Cmd+3 for blue. Ctrl+~/Cmd+~ will return to the composite mode.

In the case of this image, I have renamed the layer, L RGB 0 0.92 115 0 255; R 0 0.86 255 0 255; G 0 1.04 255 0 255; to represent the changes made in the adjustment layer (Figure 7.8). These parameters are also recorded in the History Log, and the layer is renamed simply to provide a quick way to see this information within the Layers palette.

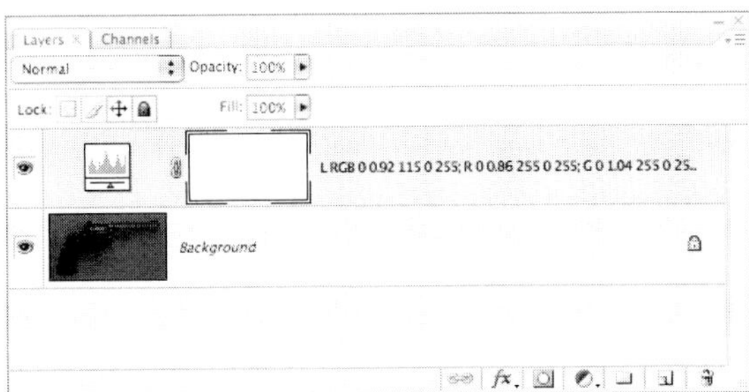

Figure 7.8 The Layers palette with the renamed layer

Automatically rename Adjustment Layers

Included on the CD with this book is a JavaScript script called AdjustmentLayers.jsx, which will automatically rename adjustment layers. This script was written for me by X Bytor (xbytor @gmail.com) to add this functionality to Photoshop, and we are making it available at no charge through the GNU licensing agreement. It will work with most of Photoshop's adjustment layers and eliminates the need to note the settings in any adjustment layer and then rename the layer manually.

To install this script, place it in the Scripts folder, which is located in Adobe Photoshop CS3/Presets/Scripts. After you restart Photoshop, it will appear on the menu as File > Scripts > Adjustment Layers.

Automatically rename Adjustment Layers *(Continued)*

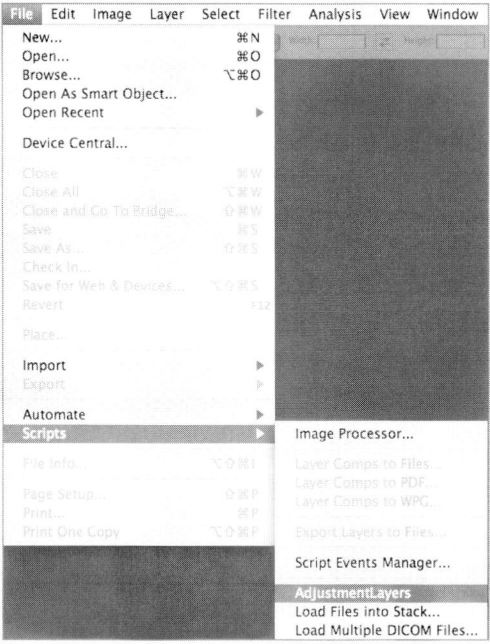

The dialog box provides a drop-down menu to select your adjustment layer of choice. Only the supported adjustment layers are available in this menu. It also provides an option to create an adjustment layer or modify an adjustment layer. If there are no current adjustment layers, the option to modify an adjustment layer is not available.

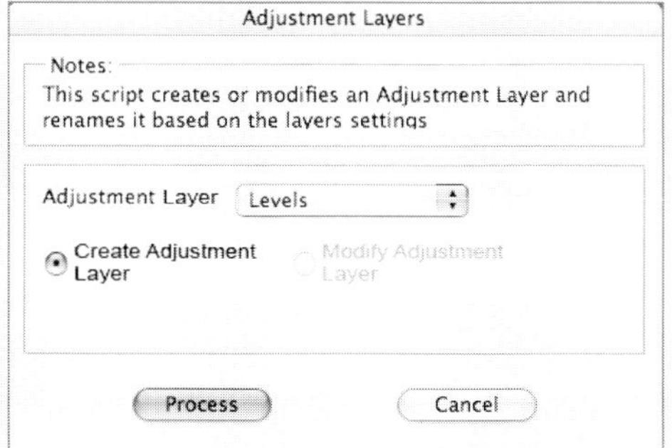

Selecting an adjustment layer type and the Create Adjustment Layer option will create a new adjustment layer of the type selected and, after making any adjustments, will then rename that layer with the settings used. Select Modify Adjustment Layer when an adjustment layer currently exists to make the modifications set and rename the layer to reflect these adjustments.

Using Layer Masks for Local Adjustments

By using adjustment layers to make brightness, contrast, and color corrections to an image, you can add a layer mask to apply the adjustments only to local areas of the image. The advantages of this method are that the Levels adjustment layer can be turned off to show the unchanged, original pixel values of the image; the layer mask can be viewed to show exactly where the adjustments were applied; and the Levels dialog box can be accessed to show exactly what changes were made.

In Figure 7.9, the foreground was properly exposed with the flash, but the background is very underexposed. Making an adjustment to the entire image to brighten the background would result in the foreground going too bright. A layer mask will enable the adjustment to be made only to specific areas of the image—in this example, to the background, bringing in detail in the background and showing separation between the tires and black sky without blowing out the foreground details.

Original

After layer mask adjustment

Figure 7.9 The original image on the left and the same image after applying an adjustment layer with mask to only lighten the background.

The simplest way to make an adjustment mask is to let Photoshop create one automatically. This is done by first selecting the area you want to adjust and creating an adjustment layer. Photoshop will then create a mask so that the adjustment is applied only to the area that was selected. Because this will be a mask, it can be adjusted later if needed, and the mask can be viewed to illustrate precisely where the adjustment was made.

There are several tools available to select one or more parts of an image. The selection tools are located at the top section of the toolbar and include the Marquee tools, Lasso tools, and Wand tool.

For this image the Wand tool will work well. Each selection tool has several options available on the options bar along the top of the screen (Figure 7.10). The icons in the first set determine if clicking will create a new selection, add to an existing selection, subtract from an existing selection, or intersect existing selections. The Tolerance setting determines how close in the average brightness value pixels must be to be selected. The Wand tool works by selecting the pixel you click, then selecting other pixels that are similar in value. Setting the tolerance to 32 will select pixels that are within 32 brightness values from the pixel that was clicked. Selecting the Contiguous box will restrict the selection to only pixels that are in contact with each other. Choosing New Selection, limiting the tolerance, and choosing a contiguous selection is an excellent way to select all the dark or all the light pixels in a portion of the image.

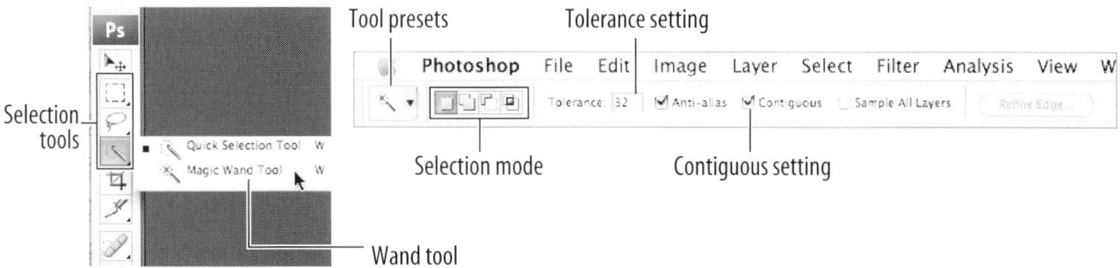

Figure 7.10 These options are available when you select the Wand tool on the toolbar.

For Figure 7.11, clicking virtually anywhere in the dark sky will select all of the sky, parts of the tires, and all connected dark parts of the image. The selected area shows as a dotted line. If an adjustment were made to the image now, the transition would be too harsh, so I need to soften the transition using the Feather feature.Choose Select > Modify > Feather to open the Feather Selection dialog box (Figure 7.12). The Feather Radius setting controls how gradual the transition along the edges of the selected area is. For this image, a radius of 35 provides a gradual transition.

Figure 7.11 The cursor position shows in the upper-left area of this image and the selected area can be seen surrounded by light dashed lines.

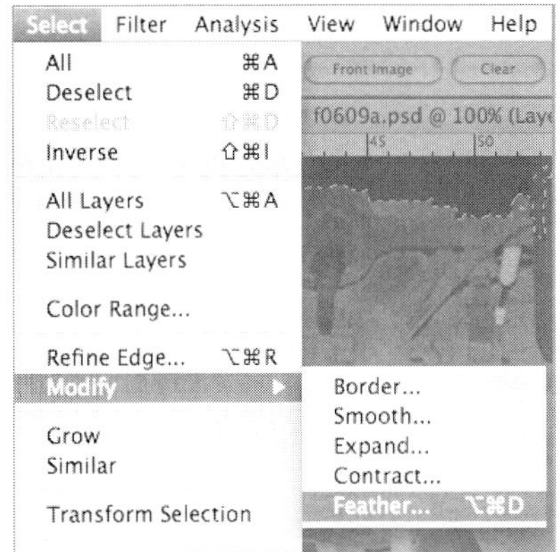

Figure 7.12 Choose Select > Modify > Feather to access the Feather feature. The only parameter is to set the radius for the blending.

If I now apply a Levels adjustment layer, the adjustments will show only in the areas that are fully selected. To create a Levels adjustment layer, choose the adjustment layer icon at the bottom of the Layers palette and select Levels from the contextual menu, or choose Layer > New Adjustment Layer > Levels. Areas that are not selected will not be adjusted at all, and transition areas will be partially adjusted. For the image in Figure 7.13, an adjustment that shows some detail in the background and provides separation between the tires and sky is adequate.

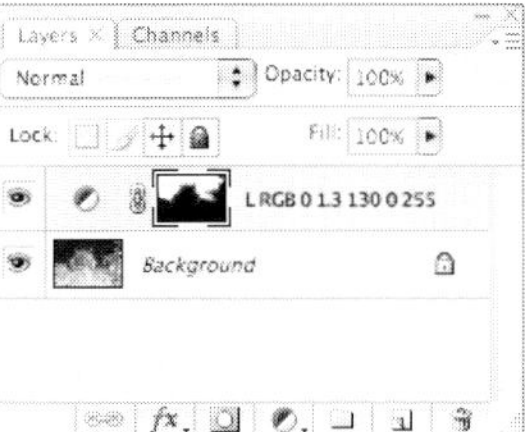

Figure 7.13 The image with the Levels adjustment on the left and the layer with the layer mask on the right

The Layers palette shows the original image as the bottom layer (it will be named Layer 0 if it has been made into a Smart Object). The next layer is the adjustment layer with the mask. I like to rename the adjustment layer with the setting used for the adjustment—in this case, this is L RGB 0 1.3 130 0 255 (see Figure 7.14).

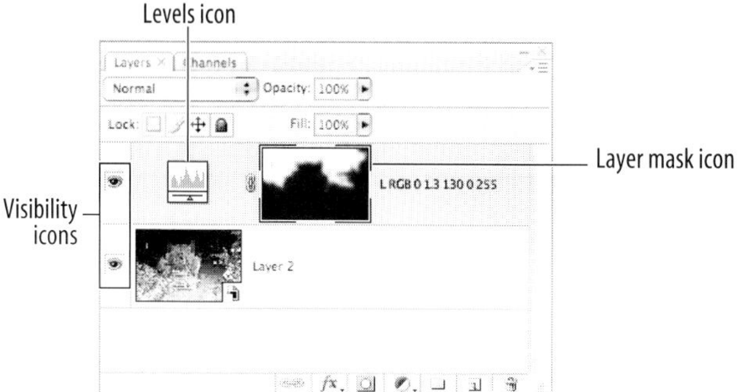

Figure 7.14 The Layers palette showing the visibility icons, renamed palette and layer mask.

To view the mask at any time, Alt/Option+click the layer mask icon. This shows the mask filling the image window. To toggle back to the image, Alt/Option+click the layer mask icon again. A layer mask shows the original pixel values where the mask is black, displays the full adjustments where the mask is white, and shows a percentage of the adjustment where the mask shows various shades of gray.

There are several advantages to using an adjustment layer mask in a forensics workflow. It is easy to show the original image with no changes made (only display the background layer); the exact adjustments that have been made to the image can be displayed by double-clicking the adjustment layer icon, the mask can be viewed in the image window by Alt/Option+clicking the mask icon, and the adjusted image can be viewed by clicking on the visibility icons for all layers.

This is a form of nondestructive image correction because the original pixels in the image are unchanged in the background layer. In addition, all adjustments can be re-edited if needed. And, all adjustments can be easily seen and shown in court if needed.

Adjustments with the Shadow/Highlight Feature

Another tool that can be used to make localized adjustments to an image is the Shadow/Highlight feature. This feature enables you to lighten the shadow areas and darken the highlights, with control over the amount and the transition between the corrected areas and those left alone.

In Photoshop CS3, this adjustment can be made to a Smart Object and applied as a Smart Filter. Smart Filters are very similar to adjustment layers—they are nondestructive (preserving the original pixel values within the Smart Object); they can be re-edited (just double-click the name of the adjustment or filter in the Layers palette); you can apply masks to localize the adjustment; and you can turn their effect on or off by toggling the visibility icon on and off.

In Figure 7.15, the interior of the garage, the driveway, and the bushes are underexposed, yet the sky is a bit overexposed. The adjustments needed are to lighten the areas in the garage, driveway, and bushes while either leaving the sky as it is or darkening it somewhat to better reflect the tonal range of the day it was photographed.

Figure 7.15 The original image on the left and the image after a Shadow/Highlight adjustment on the right.

As with all of the examples in this chapter, there are several ways that this image can be corrected, including using layer masks. However, a faster and simpler method for this image is to use the Shadow/Highlight feature.

If you are using Photoshop CS3, converting the image to a Smart Object by choosing Layer > Smart Objects > Convert To Smart Object will enable this adjustment to be applied as a Smart Filter in a nondestructive, re-editable manner.

Note: In Photoshop CS2, the Shadow/Highlight feature does change the pixel values as it is applied. Therefore, in CS2 I prefer to duplicate the background layer so that the original pixel values are retained there and all adjustments are done on the duplicate layer. To duplicate the background layer, simply drag it to the new layer icon in the Layers palette. This creates a new layer that has the default name of Background copy, which can be changed later.

To access the Shadow/Highlight feature, choose Image > Adjustments > Shadow/Highlight. The Show More Options box should be checked to expand the dialog box to show all of the adjustments available, as shown in Figure 7.16. For both the Shadows and Highlights sections, Amount controls the intensity of the brightness change; Tonal Width controls the number of tones that are adjusted (for instance, a small tonal width in shadows will affect only the very darkest tones), and Radius determines the size of the grouping of pixels used to determine if they fall into the Shadow or Highlight category (a larger radius may result in either halos around objects or an overall image adjustment instead of a localized adjustment). The Adjustments section provides the ability to make slight adjustments to the color balance and midtone contrast.

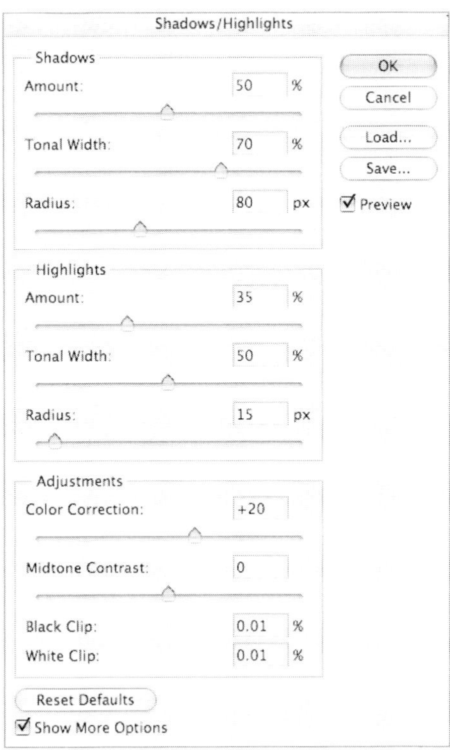

Figure 7.16 Checking the Show More Options box expands the Shadows/Highlights dialog box to show all of the available parameters.

I made a rather strong adjustment to the image in this example because the image was very underexposed and to illustrate what is possible with this feature; however, more reserved adjustments are more likely to be the norm with this feature.

If I'm using Photoshop CS2, the last step I do when using this tool is to rename the Background copy layer with the parameters used with this tool. In this example, I set the parameters in the Shadows section to 50, 70, and 80; the parameters in the Highlights section to 35, 50, and 15; the Color Correction value to +20; and the Midtone Contrast value to 0. I then changed the layer name to SH 50,70,80,35,50,15,20,0. These parameters are also recorded in the History Log, but I use them for the layer name as an easy reference. In Photoshop CS3, Smart Filters cannot be renamed.

The image can now be saved or prepared for printing.

Summary

Making basic adjustments to correct for a poor exposure, bad lighting, or a color shift should be simple and quick. For most crime scene, traffic accident, and evidence photos, adjustments shouldn't be needed. When they are, using the methods described in this chapter should enable you to make them quickly and efficiently to individual images.

If the same adjustment needs to be made to a group of images, this can be done easily using Photoshop actions (see Chapter 9 for an overview of actions) or by batch-processing with Adobe Photoshop Camera Raw 4.0 (see Chapter 5).

Printing Images

Two primary issues come up with printing images: properly sizing the image and choosing the right color settings. Sizing the image involves setting both the physical print dimensions and the image resolution to get the best sharpness, color, and efficiency. Incorrect color settings can result in prints that have color shifts or inconsistencies from one print to another. Having a workflow that addresses these issues will provide consistent, high-quality prints.

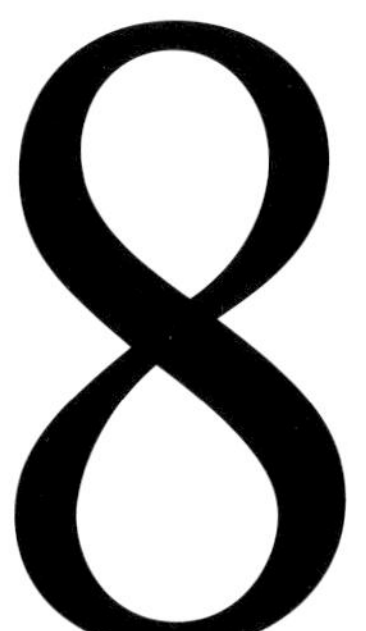

Chapter Contents

Print Overview

Preparing an image to print involves working within the proper color space and color profile and telling the printer what size to print the image. Chapter 3 deals with setting up color space, and this chapter will deal with many of the other issues for printing crime scene, evidence, and traffic accident images—and other images of a general photographic nature. Printing contact sheets will be covered separately in Chapter 10. The special issues surrounding printing video frames that need pixel aspect correction are covered in Chapter 23.

One of the difficulties with printing, and controlling the color, is that there are two interfaces for printing: one within Photoshop and the separate print driver. The print driver is a product of the printer manufacturer, and each manufacturer uses its own terminology for various features. Because of this, the step-by-step methods for printing to a Canon printer will be different than the step-by-step methods for printing to an Epson printer. However, the concepts will be the same. When reading this chapter, keep that in mind, and focus on the concepts rather than the specific steps—especially regarding the printer driver issues.

Another issue with printer drivers is that because they are not part of Photoshop, they can't be controlled by Photoshop. However, most print driver settings are sticky (at least until you quit Photoshop or restart the computer). This means that once you set up the first print, any remaining prints should not require rechoosing each parameter within the printer driver. Additionally, many print drivers allow for saving presets, making it simple to choose common settings simply and quickly.

Image Size

The first step in preparing an image to print is to determine what size the print will be and what resolution to set for the image.

In forensics, you will generally print all images full frame; that is, without any cropping of the image. Depending on the format of the original negative, slide, CCD, and so on, this may make prints that are square, panoramic, or most likely some rectangular shape between the two. This means that what you commonly call an 8×10 isn't necessarily 8×10 inches. It may be closer to 6.5×10 inches for prints from 35mm negatives and many digital cameras or 8×8 inches for prints from many medium-format cameras.

The resolution that you set will be in pixels per inch (ppi) and will determine the sharpness of your print and the speed at which your image is printed. The important concept here is that pixels and dots are frequently not the same thing, and therefore, ppi and dpi are frequently not the same thing. If you have a printer that can print 1440dpi (dots per inch), the best resolution for printing will not be 1440ppi for several reasons, but the most important reason is that in ink-jet printers and laser printers, it takes many dots to print a single pixel.

In my own tests, and in tests that I have read of, most ink-jet and laser printers will print very good quality prints at 200 to 300ppi and excellent quality prints at 300 to 400ppi. A good rule of thumb is to print at a resolution that is an even factor of the printer's dpi for efficiency and in the range listed here for quality. That is, if your printer will be set to 1440dpi, a ppi of 240 for very good quality prints and 360 for excellent quality prints should work well. For a printer capable of 600dpi, settings of 200 and 300 would be substituted.

Access the Image Size dialog box by choosing Image > Image Size. In Photoshop CS2 and CS3, the keyboard shortcut is Ctrl+Alt+I/Cmd+Option+I.

The Image Size dialog box (Figure 8.1) is divided into three sections: Pixel Dimensions, Document Size, and Interpolation Options.

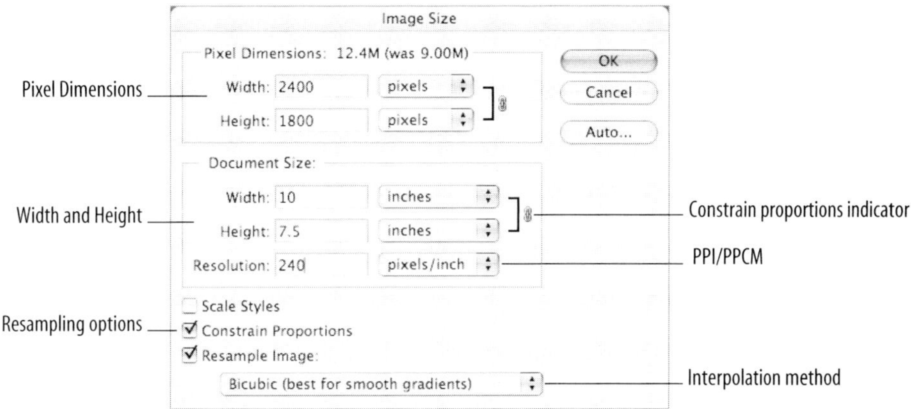

Figure 8.1 The Image Size dialog box

- The Pixel Dimensions area shows the number of pixels in your image. The pop-up menus can be changed from pixels to percent. The values for these can only be changed if the Resample Image box is checked.
- The Document Size area allows you to change the width, height, and/or pixel resolution of the image. The Height and Width settings can be made in percent, inches, centimeters, millimeters, point, picas, and columns. The Constrain Proportions indicator is locked on the width and height if the Constrain Proportions box is checked. Resolution is also constrained if Resample Image is unchecked.
- In the resampling options section, you can choose whether to resample the image (change the number of pixels in the image) and, if so, what method to use and whether to constrain proportions. Resampling an image will usually cause some degradation to the image, but it is generally not noticeable when sizing a photographic image of modest resolution for printing.

To print an image as an 8×10, I have made several choices. First, I decided to resample the image and checked the Resample Image check box. If I didn't resample the image, it may be too pixilated or I may not be able to print it at my preferred printing resolution. It is accepted practice in forensics to resample an image for printing. Not doing so could lead to images that don't match your monitor in image quality or apparent resolution. Constrain Proportions is also checked. This will generally be the case; if this box is not checked, the image will be stretched or squashed when it's resampled (the primary exception will be when printing images that are at an incorrect pixel aspect ratio, such as many video images; see Chapter 23). I set Width to 10 inches, which automatically set Height to 7.5 inches because Constrain Proportions is checked. I set the resolution to 240ppi because I will be printing to an Epson 1280 printer. I left the interpolation method set to Bicubic, which is a good general interpolation method. If I were making a substantial change in image size, I would choose Bicubic Sharper to make the image smaller or Bicubic Smoother to make the image larger.

The Print Dialog

Clicking OK prepares you for the next step of setting the print orientation and printer profiles. In Photoshop CS2, there are five menu items associated with printing: Page Setup, Print With Preview, Print, Print One Copy, and Print Online. Photoshop CS3 has brought this down to three menu items. In CS3, select Print from the File menu, and in CS2, select Print With Preview—in either case, this gives you a dialog box that includes a preview window and several options. You can access the page orientation from this window, and you can control color management issues. The key advantage of this dialog box is the ability to color manage your printing.

If a printer is giving you incorrect colors, such as a magenta or green shift, chances are that one of three things is happening: the color is not being managed in Photoshop or the print driver, the color is being managed in both Photoshop and the print driver, or the wrong paper/ink combination is being used. By first managing color in Photoshop, then making some choices in the printer driver, you can avoid color shifts and have consistently good quality prints—assuming that everything is in good working order.

The Print dialog box in CS3 (Figure 8.2) is slightly different than the Print With Preview dialog box of CS2, but most features are similar, although their placement in the window may be different. The left side displays a large preview window with icons for changing print orientation below it. Clicking the Landscape or Portrait icon will change the size and shape of the preview window.

Choose the printer you will be printing to in the top center of the window. If your printer of choice isn't listed, download the most recent drivers from the printer manufacturer's website and reinstall.

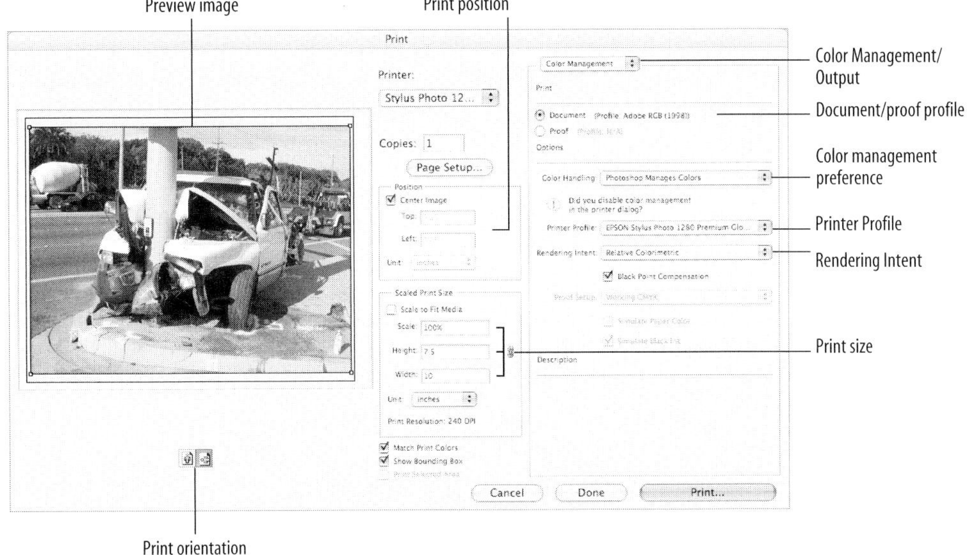

Figure 8.2 The CS3 Print dialog, now with preview by default, is used to set print orientation and color management policies for printing.

I already set the print size and resolution in the Image Size dialog box, so I generally leave the Center Image box checked in the Print Position section, and I make sure that Scale To Fit Media is not checked. Because I set the print size and resolution in the Image Size dialog box, I don't want that to be undone or redone here. If I were to check this box, the image resizing would be done by the print driver and I would have no control over the method of file interpolation.

The Color Management/Output menu allows you to select between these choices (color management or output settings). The right side of the window in CS3 (the bottom half in CS2) changes depending on which setting you make here. If you choose Output, you can set several options such as printing registration marks, caption information, and a border on the print. Most of the settings are self-explanatory, so I'll focus on the Color Management settings.

The first section in the Color Management section is for determining whether Photoshop handles the color management or if the printer handles it. Photoshop is an excellent color manager, so I recommend choosing Photoshop Manages Colors.

Below this you set the printer profile. The printer profile you set will be for the specific printer and paper combination that you are using. In this example, I am printing to an Epson Stylus Photo 1280 with premium glossy photo paper, so that is the setting I will choose. The rendering intent is usually best left at the default setting of Relative Colorimetric.

Once you have set these parameters, you can click the Print button to open your print driver, click Cancel to close the window without retaining any of the settings you made, or click Done to dismiss the window while retaining these settings for this image. I'll click Print, and in the next section, we'll take a look at the print driver options.

The Print Driver

The following sections describe the print driver for the Epson Stylus Photo 1280 for Windows XP Pro and for Macintosh OS X; other printers and operating systems may look different and may have different names for various functions.

The Print Driver in Windows

The first window to open allows you to choose your printer and to access additional functionality. Select the printer of choice here, and then click Preferences or Properties, depending on the driver and OS (see Figure 8.3).

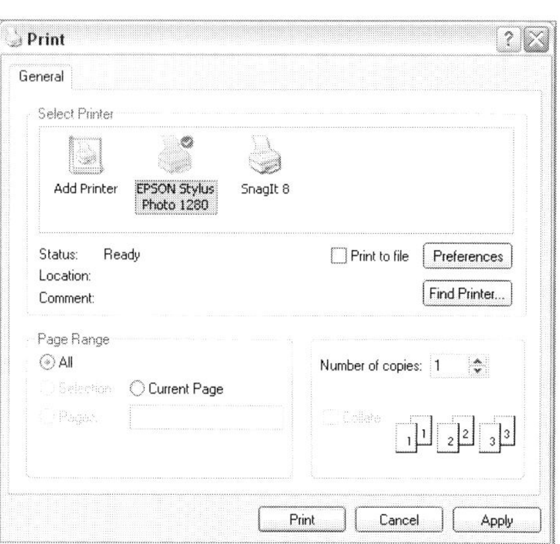

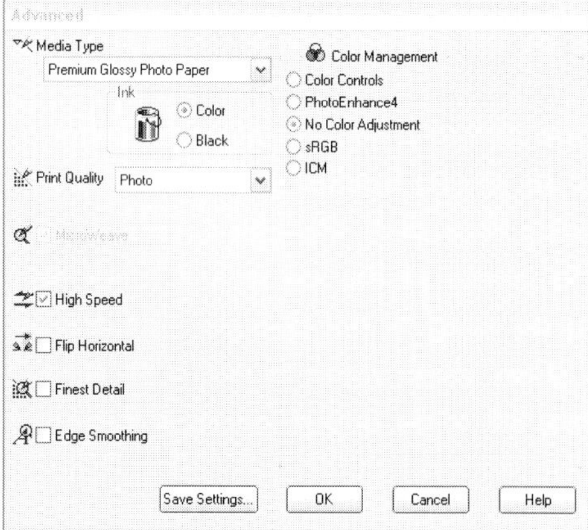

Figure 8.3 The Windows print driver windows for the settings described in the text, with the main print driver window on the top left, the Preferences window in the top right, and the Advanced window (for color management) on the bottom.

This opens the printer properties or preferences window, also shown in Figure 8.3. Select the paper type you will be using at the top of this window, and then select the Custom radio button and click the Advanced button, which will open the Advanced window.

It is now time to set the parameters in the Advanced window. The correct paper type should already be chosen in the top of the window—if not, change it. In the Color Management section, choose the No Color Management radio button. For Print Quality, select the appropriate setting; for the Epson 1280 in the XP-based driver, my preference is to select the Photo setting and check the High Speed box as in Figure 8.3.

These settings can now be saved for future use by clicking the Save Settings button and giving this an appropriate name. Then click OK to dismiss this window, click OK to dismiss the printer properties window, and click OK in the main print driver window to print the image. In the future, clicking the Custom radio button in the printer properties window will enable you to choose this saved setting from the pop-up menu.

The Print Driver in Mac OS

The Mac OS print drivers generally only have a single window with pop-up menus at the top to select the printer, presets, and various functions for the print driver. Choose the printer in the top section of this window, and then choose Print Settings (see Figure 8.4).

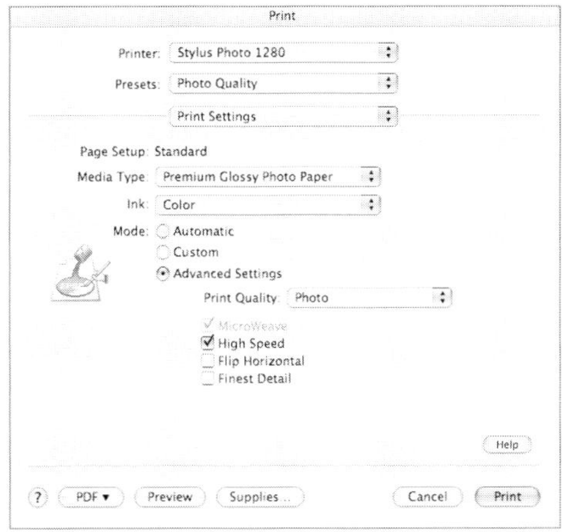

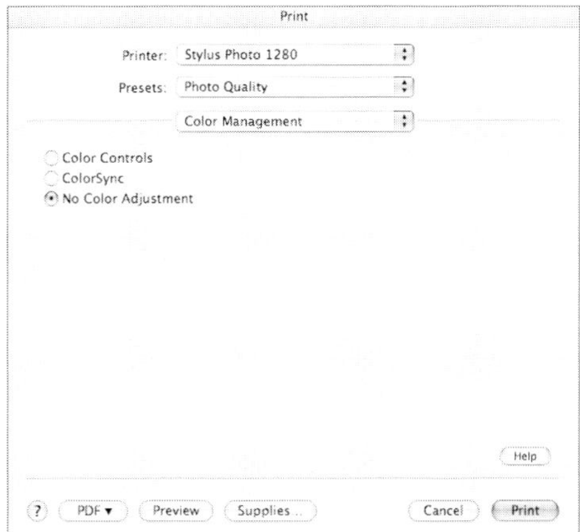

Figure 8.4 The Mac OS print driver windows for the settings described in the text, showing the Print Settings and Color Management options.

On a Mac, select Print Settings from the drop-down menu and choose the paper type you will be using. Also, select the Advanced Settings button and select the appropriate print quality. (I recommend choosing the Photo setting and checking the High

Speed box for good quality printing from the 1280.) In both cases, it is important that the paper type selected in this window is the same as that used in the Print window in Photoshop and also matches the paper type in the printer. If any of these do not match, color shifts can occur.

The last setting to make on the Mac is to choose Color Management from the drop-down menu and click the No Color Management radio button. Choosing Save As from the Presets drop-down menu will enable this group of settings to be saved with a unique name and accessed through the Presets drop-down settings in the future. Finally, clicking Print will print the image.

Summary

It may seem as though there is a lot to do to print an image in Photoshop. However, there are really only three steps—setting the image size, setting the parameters in the Print dialog box, and setting the parameters in the print driver—and by saving presets you can reduce that process even further. In the next chapter, you'll see how you can make printing even easier by batch printing—printing entire folders or all selected images from Bridge without having to input data for each image.

You saw how to set the print size and the resolution within the Image Size dialog box and the method for resampling—for example, 10 inches wide at 240 pixels per inch with Bicubic resampling.

In the Print window, you set the color handling option for Photoshop to color manage the document. The printer profile is set to match your printer and paper combination with Rendering Intent set to Relative Colorimetric. You also saw how to set the print orientation appropriately.

In the print driver, you again set your paper choice; turned off color management because Photoshop, not the print driver, will handle color management; and set your printer parameters to match the dpi settings for the printer.

Automating Photoshop through Actions

Photoshop actions are shortcuts that enable repetitive tasks to be done automatically. Actions can be applied to individual images or to groups of images. An action can be a single step, such as converting to 16-bit mode, or multiple steps, such as resizing an image and sending it to your printer.

In this chapter, I'll show you how to create a few different actions and run them on individual images and on groups of images.

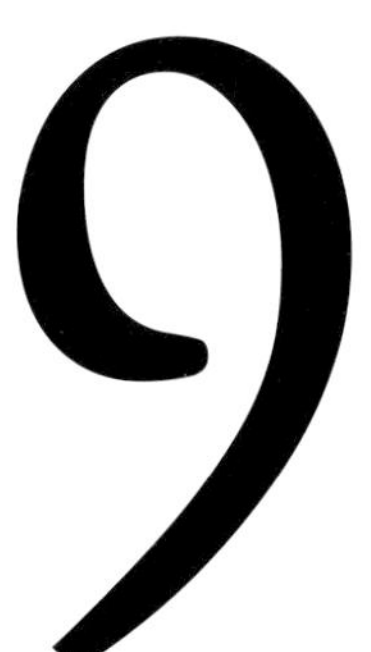

Chapter Contents

Introduction to Actions

In Photoshop, actions are shortcuts that enable repetitive tasks to be done automatically by the computer with very little user input. The process is simple—you "record" an action by accessing this feature in the Actions palette, performing the steps to do the task, then stopping the recording when the task is done. Later, when you want to do this same task to one or more images, it can be done in one or a few clicks and applied to a single image or to multiple images.

Any process that is done frequently is a good candidate for making into an Action. This may be a process that is done from case to case, such as converting to 16-bit mode or deinterlacing video; or it can be a process that is only done to multiple images on a single case, such as a specific Levels or Curves adjustment. In this chapter, actions will be created for converting images to 16-bit mode, deinterlacing video, and printing photos.

There are a few important things to note when creating an action:

- Not all features can be recorded in an action. If you create an action and it fails, it may be because it includes a feature that can't be recorded.
- It is important to name the action so that you will remember exactly what it does.
- Actions should include all parameters.
- Actions can be edited later if a mistake was made or if an alteration in the functionality is desired.

Many users are hesitant to use actions because they think actions are more complex than they really are. In this chapter, we'll create some straightforward actions that will show how easy it is to create and run actions. These actions will also be practical, so dig in and give it a try.

Action Setup

To begin, make the Actions palette active. If it isn't currently visible on your screen, choose Window > Actions. If it is in Icon mode, click the Actions palette icon to open it to the full palette (Figure 9.1). This palette needs to be in Text mode; if it is currently in Button mode, click the Flyout Menu icon and uncheck Button Mode in the flyout menu. Now clear the existing actions by either choosing Clear All Actions in the flyout menu or by dragging the Default Actions folder to the Actions palette Trash Can icon.

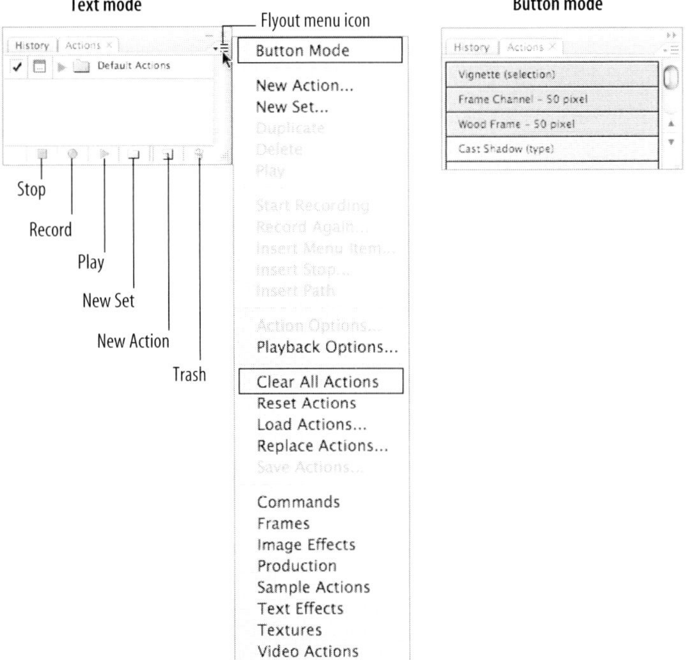

Figure 9.1 The Actions palette: left, in Text mode with the flyout menu, and right, in Button mode

The Actions palette is now ready to begin recording a new action. First, we will create a new set (which is like a folder that contains our Actions), and then we will open a file prior to recording the action. This is so that our action doesn't record the step of opening a specific file.

To create a new set, open the flyout menu and choose New Set, or click the New Set icon on the bottom of the Actions palette. This opens the New Set dialog box (Figure 9.2). Type a name for this set of Actions and click OK. The name may be a general name such as Forensic Actions, or it may be specific to the types of actions it contains, such as Video Actions or Latent Print Actions. If multiple users share the same computer, each user may want to personalize their own set of actions with the names they choose.

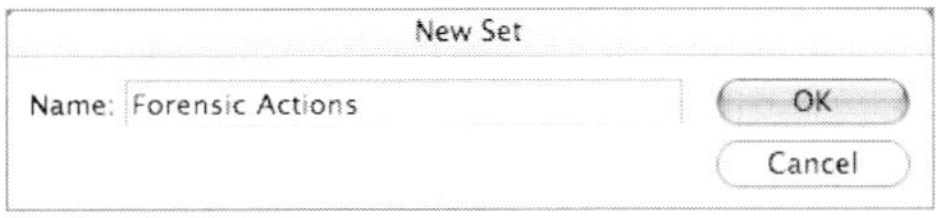

New Set
Name: Forensic Actions
OK
Cancel

Figure 9.2 The New Set dialog box

The next steps in creating actions are to begin recording a specific action, perform the individual steps of that action, and then stop the recording. Each action will have different steps, but the process will be the same. To illustrate this, we will create three actions, which should provide enough information to create actions for virtually any process in Photoshop that is performed on multiple images.

Creating and Running Actions

The first two actions that follow will be actions that perform a single step (converting to 16-bit mode and deinterlacing video); the actions following those will involve several steps (printing an image). In all cases, the steps to record and perform the actions will follow the same pattern and can be used as a basis for creating other actions.

Converting to 16-Bit Mode Action

The first action will be one that converts an image to 16 bits per channel. To begin, you should open an image that is not currently in the 16-bit mode. Then click the New Action button at the bottom of the Action palette. This opens the New Action dialog box (see Figure 9.3).

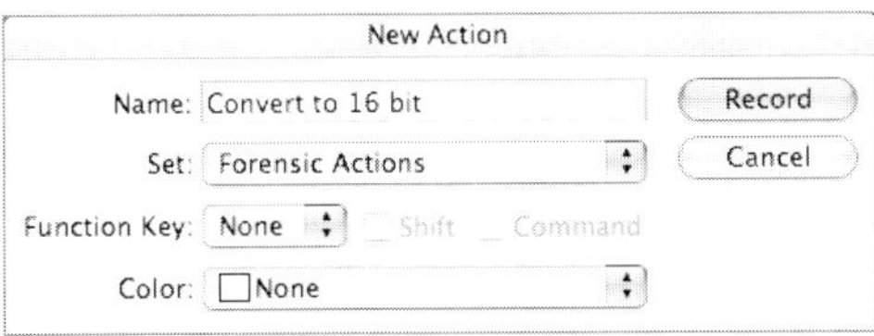

Figure 9.3 The New Action dialog box

Name the action specifically and thoroughly so that you will always know exactly what it does. In this case, I named the action Convert To 16 Bit, as shown in Figure 9.3. Choose the action set that this action belongs to—in this case, Forensic Actions. Choosing a function key in this dialog box would allow you to run this action by using a keyboard shortcut; this is a convenient for actions that may frequently run on open files. Choosing a color gives the action the selected color when in Button mode (see Figure 9.1).

Press the Record button to dismiss the dialog box and begin recording the action. The Record icon at the bottom of the Actions palette (second from left in Figure 9.4) displays as red to indicate that Photoshop is currently recording an action.

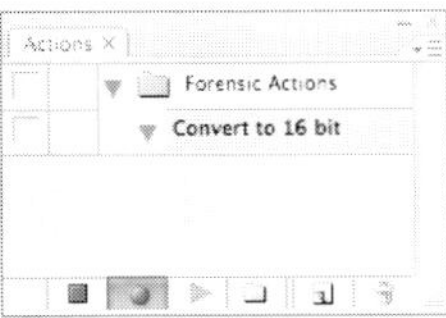

Figure 9.4 The Record icon is red when an action is being recorded.

The next step in recording an action is to perform the steps of the action. In this case, this is the single step of converting the image to 16 bits per channel. To convert this file, choose Image > Mode > 16 Bits/Channel (see Figure 9.5).

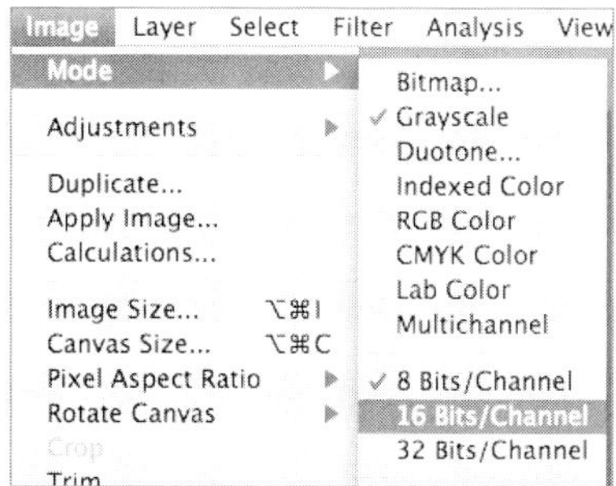

Figure 9.5 Selecting Image > Mode > 16 Bits /Channel converts the image to a 16-bit file.

The last step in recording an action is to click the Stop icon on the bottom left of the Actions palette (see Figure 9.1). This completes the recording of the action, and it is now ready to be run on other images. In the section "Running Actions" later in this chapter, you see several methods for running actions on individual and multiple images.

Deinterlace Action

Deinterlacing frames from video is a common task in forensic video analysis (see Chapter 23). Photoshop's De-Interlace filter has options for eliminating the even field or the odd field and for replacing the field using duplication or using interpolation. It is valuable to compare the results from each of these choices to get the best results, and using actions can make this much more efficient. I recommend creating four separate De-Interlace actions—one for each option for that filter.

As with any action, before beginning, first open an image to perform the steps of the action, then create the new action by choosing the New Action icon or New Action from the flyout menu, as described earlier. In the New Action dialog box, name the action specifically. The first of these four actions will eliminate the even field and create the new field by interpolation, so the action can be named DI Elim Even Inter, which is very descriptive in spite of the shorthand (see Figure 9.6). Assigning a function key can be useful for this action because it may frequently be performed on individual open files. Clicking the Record button will dismiss the dialog box and begin recording the steps performed.

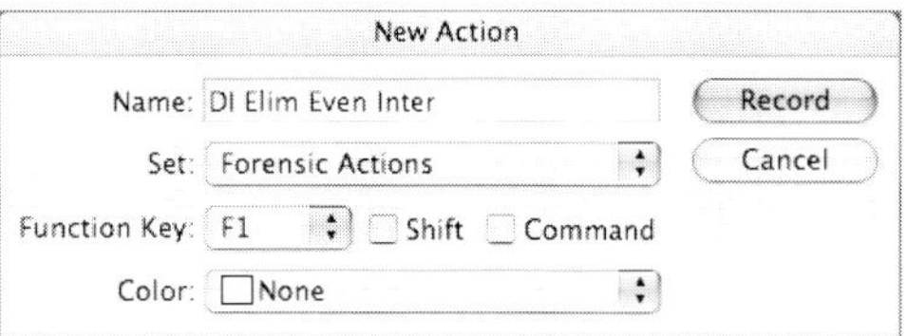

Figure 9.6 Naming the action with a good description and providing a function key

The next thing is to perform the action. In this case, it is a single step of deinterlacing the images with the parameters outlined when we named the action, as shown in Figure 9.7.

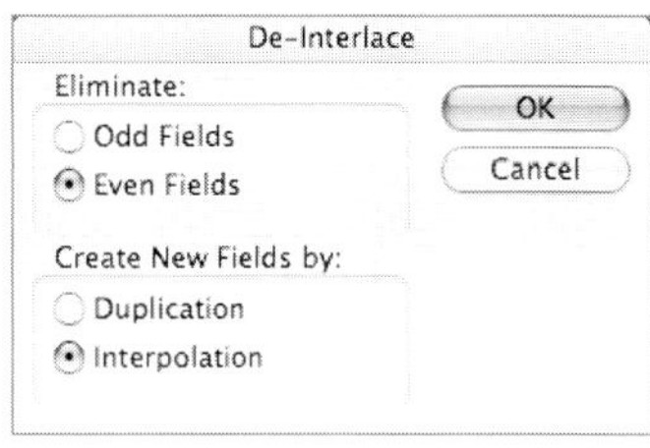

Figure 9.7 The De-Interlace filter with the parameters set to eliminate the even field and create the new field with interpolation

Once the deinterlace is complete, end the action by clicking the Stop icon as described in the previous section. This completes the first of the four deinterlace actions. Repeat these steps for eliminating the even field and replacing it by duplication and for both options in eliminating the odd field. Name each one specifically during the process, and provide function keys for each. Each of these actions can later be performed on individual files or groups of images, as described in the section "Running Actions" later in this chapter.

Printing Action

Open a typical file that would be printed to a standard size output such as 5 inches wide or 10 inches wide.

Create a new action by choosing New Action from the flyout menu or by clicking the New Action button. Name the action precisely and thoroughly so that it will always make sense. I named this action Print 10″ Wide, 240 PPI, Don't Save (Figure 9.8), which gives a good description of what it does—it prints a given image to 10 inches wide and doesn't save the image when complete. Since I only have one action set, my only choice of where to keep this is in Forensic Actions. I have given a function key shortcut so that I can run the action by choosing a function key, and I made the label red so that I can sort my actions when in Button mode by functionality—for example, red for printing, green for enhancement.

Clicking Record dismisses this dialog box and begins the recording process.

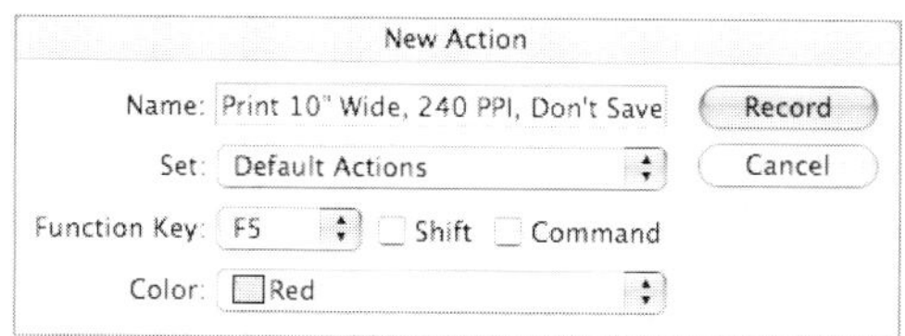

Figure 9.8 The New Action dialog box for the printing action

Next, you'll perform the steps to prepare and print the opened image, close the file without saving changes, and finally, stop recording the action. Because Chapter 8 covered sizing and printing an image, the steps will simply be summarized here.

For this example, set the parameters in the Image Size window to 10 inches wide at 240ppi with bicubic resampling. Then, open the Print with Preview window—set the Page Setup parameters and the Color Profile and Print Profile settings, and click the Print button. Set the print driver to the Preset made in Chapter 8, and click OK to print the image. Then click the Stop icon on the bottom of the Actions palette to stop recording this action.

Note: While the printing steps are recording, warning dialogs may pop up stating that some printing or page setup functions cannot be recorded. This is normal, and the windows can be dismissed by clicking OK.

As each step is recorded, it is written into the Actions palette. Details of each step can be viewed by clicking the Expand Content toggle, as shown in Figure 9.9.

Figure 9.9 The Actions palette showing the expanded view of the printing steps

Running Actions

As mentioned earlier, actions can be run on individual files or on groups of files. Performing an action on individual files is simply a matter of opening the file and running the action from the Actions palette. Performing actions on groups of files is done by running the action in Batch mode, which allows you to run the action on currently open files, on a folder of images, or on images selected in Bridge.

To run the action on a single file while in the Text mode, simply open an image, select the name of the action in the Actions palette, and click the Play icon at the bottom (Figure 9.10). Pressing the Play icon runs the action immediately. In Button mode (Figure 9.1), just click the icon and the action will run on the frontmost image. In essence, a series of files could be opened and this action played for each one in succession—but there is an easier way to run actions on a group of images: by using the Batch Action feature as described in the next section.

Note that running an action on individual files will record the action name in the History Log but will not record the individual steps of the action.

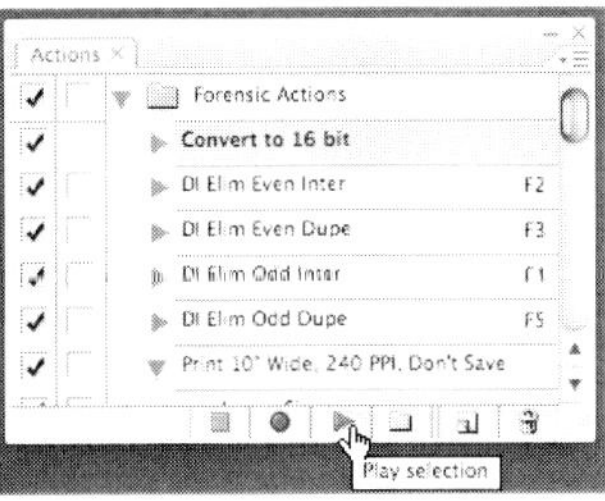

Figure 9.10 Selecting an action and clicking the Play icon will run the action on the active document

Batch: Running an Action on Multiple Files

Actions can be run on multiple files from Bridge or from Photoshop. Regardless of whether the Batch command is invoked from Bridge or Photoshop, the process itself takes place within Photoshop and the dialog for setting the parameters is the same.

To run an action on multiple images in Photoshop, choose File > Automation > Batch. To batch-process files from Bridge, select one or more files, then choose Tools > Photoshop > Batch. In either case, the Batch dialog box will open in Photoshop (Figure 9.11), providing many choices for selecting which action to run, the files on which to run it, and what to do with the processed files.

In the top section, select the set of actions that contains the action you want to run and the specific action to run.

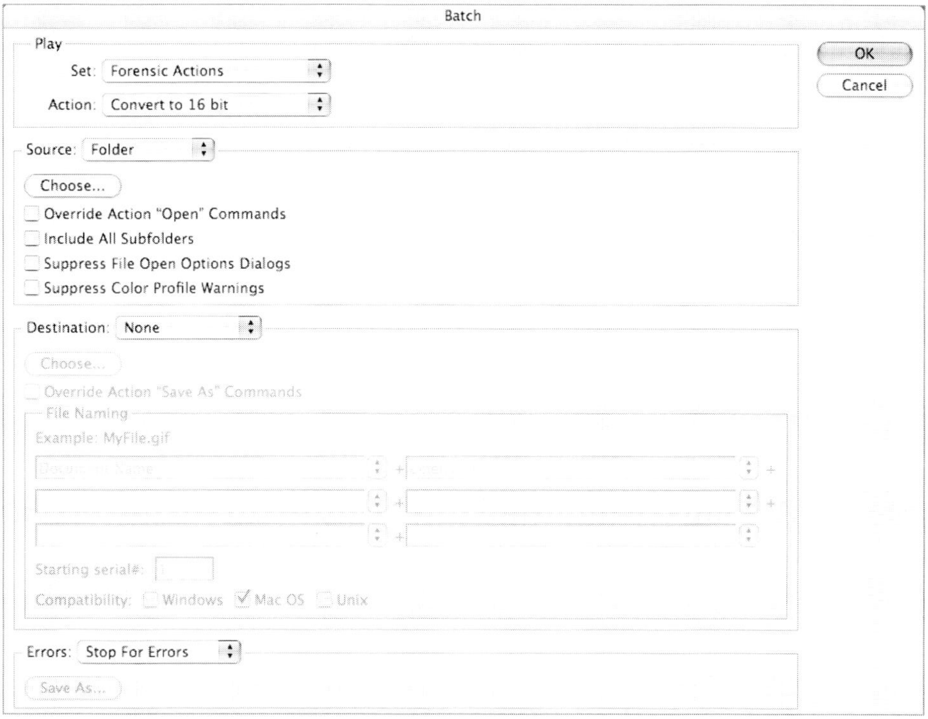

Figure 9.11 The Batch dialog box is divided into four sections.

In the second section, select which files to perform the action upon. If images were selected in Bridge and the batch process invoked from Bridge, then Bridge should already be listed as the source. Other options are Opened Files, Folder, and Import, which allow the action to be run on files that are already open, a folder of images, or images that are imported into Photoshop.

The third section determines what will be done with the files after the batch process is completed. Selecting None for the destination will leave the files open in Photoshop after the action has been completed. Selecting Save And Close will save the files in the same location, overwriting the original files. Choosing Folder will save the files in your folder of choice, using the file-naming parameters you set in this section. For example, you can run a batch process to deinterlace all files in a folder of images (eliminating even fields), save them in a folder, and append each filename with the letter *A*. Then a batch process can be run on the same group of images to deinterlace (eliminating odd fields), save them to that same folder, and add the letter *B* to the filenames. This would result in all the working image files remaining in their original location, with copies in the destination folder.

The bottom section determines how errors are handled when a batch process is run. Choosing Stop For Errors will stop the action when it encounters an error. Choosing Log Errors To File will enable the batch process to continue when it encounters an error and simply list all errors in a text file. The advantage of logging errors to a text file is that Photoshop may encounter an error with a file early in the batch process, preventing the remaining images from being processed if Stop For Errors was selected. The Log Errors choice will simply skip that image and continuing processing the remaining files.

Clicking the OK button closes the Batch dialog box and performs the selected action on the designated images. It is important to note that running a batch action will not record the name of the action in the History Log. However, copies of actions run on images can be saved with the image files (see the next section), providing full documentation of the processes performed with all actions used.

Printing Actions

Before running any printing action, it is wise to print one image manually, as outlined in Chapter 8. This will set some of the options for Print with Preview, page setup, page orientation, and the print driver that may not have been recorded in the action.

Saving Actions

There are two primary reasons to save actions: to keep an archive of them that can be reloaded into Photoshop if needed or shared with others and to save the actions used on images in a case as a form of notes.

Actions can be saved only as sets rather than as individual actions. If you have created a single set of actions, saving it to an archive location can save you from having to create new actions from scratch should Photoshop need to be reinstalled or removed from one computer when updating to another. A saved set of actions can also be shared with others.

To save a set of actions, select the set in the Actions palette that you want to save and select Save Actions from the flyout menu (Figure 9.12). In the Save dialog box, navigate to the location where you want to save the actions and click Save.

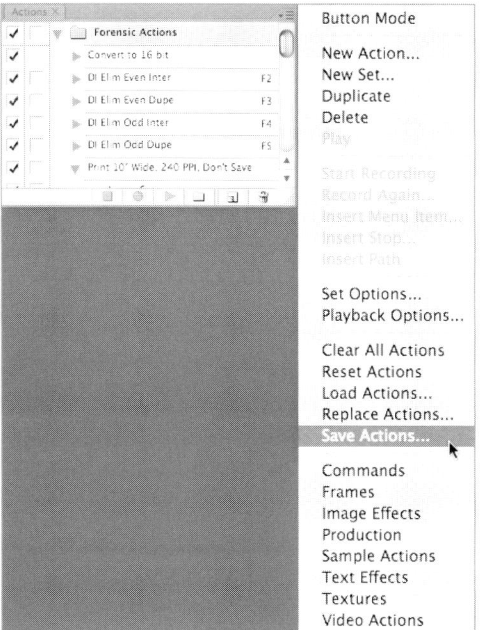

Figure 9.12 Selecting Save Actions

If you have used several actions on the images from a case and would like to save only those actions with the image archive, create a new set, name this set with the case number, and copy the actions used to that set. Figure 9.13 shows an action set named for a case number with actions copied to it. The steps are to first create the new set by clicking the New Set icon or choosing New Set from the flyout menu. Copy the actions by Alt/Option+dragging them from their present location to the new set, select this set, and choose Save Actions from the flyout menu.

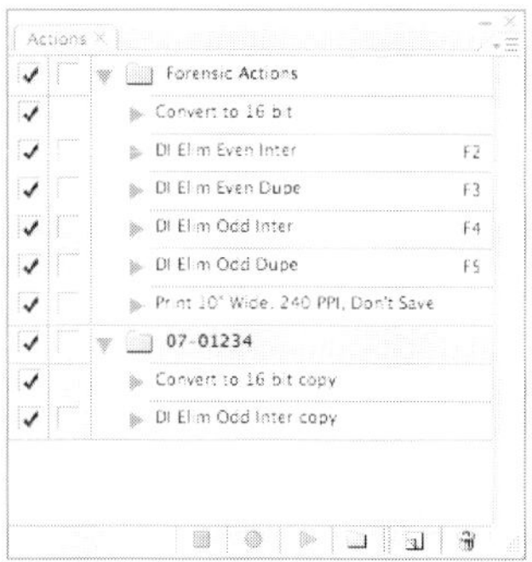

Figure 9.13 An action set containing the actions used for the images on a specific case

Summary

A primary advantage to using computers is their ability to perform repetitive tasks efficiently. Photoshop actions are shortcuts that enable Photoshop to perform tasks very quickly. Performing actions on individual images provides a reliable and repeatable processing method. Performing actions on multiple images adds substantial efficiency to your imaging workflow.

Creating actions is as simple as starting the recording, performing the steps, and stopping the recording. Playing the action is just a matter of clicking the Play icon or setting the parameters in the Batch dialog box.

10 Contact Sheets

Contact sheets show multiple images on a single page. These images are usually in the order in which they were taken. When you provide contact sheets to the investigating detective or a district attorney, they are able to see all of the images taken, know the order in which they were taken, and become better oriented to the entire scene. A contact sheet of the images from a security video can show the sequence of events, making it easier to see what took place.

Chapter Contents

Using Contact Sheets

Contact sheets traditionally are made by laying pieces or strips of film in contact with a sheet of photographic paper to see all of the photographs taken on a roll of film or on a group of sheet film negatives. The contact sheet would give you the ability to quickly and easily see all of the images taken at an event and make decisions as to which would make good enlargements.

An additional advantage is that contact sheets typically show the images in the order they were taken. In forensics, this is important because crime scenes and traffic accident scenes change over time. Viewing contact sheets enables an investigator, detective, or other interested party to see the images in their proper sequence to better understand how the scene looked over a period of time as well as gain a better understanding of how different parts of a scene relate to each other.

The disadvantages of traditional contact sheets is that the image size is limited to the film size and images can't be individually corrected for color, brightness, and/or contrast.

With the digital darkroom, you can still create contact sheets, and you can keep the images in order with a "frame number" under each one. In addition, the contact sheet can be made from files that have been individually corrected for color shifts or incorrect exposures. You can also control how many images are on each page, set the size of the images, and add additional information—such as the agency name, case number, and page numbers.

Using Photoshop's Contact Sheet Feature

In the example shown in Figure 10.1, I created the contact sheet with 12 images per page. I added the case number as a title and page numbering at the bottom-right corner of the image. When Photoshop creates the contact sheet, it automatically adds the name of each file as an option, but page numbering and titles must be added after the contact sheets are created; I'll show you how to do that a little later in this chapter.

To begin, select all the items in a folder within Bridge by clicking the first image and then holding the Shift key and clicking the last image (or press Ctrl+A/Cmd+A). Then choose Tools > Photoshop > Contact Sheet II (Figure 10.2), or select this command directly in Photoshop by choosing File > Automate > Contact Sheet II. This opens the Contact Sheet II dialog box (Figure 10.3).

Figure 10.1 A typical contact sheet with the case number and page numbering added

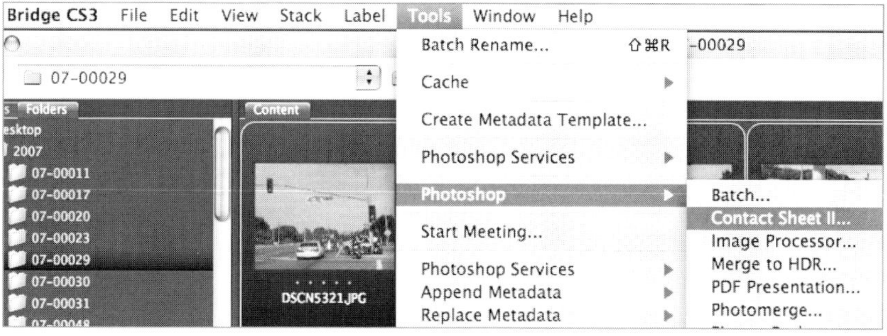

Figure 10.2 Selecting the Contact Sheet II feature from within Bridge

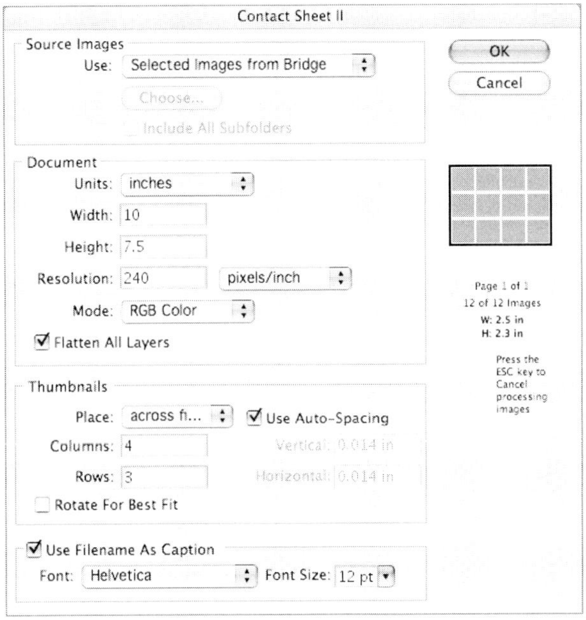

Figure 10.3 The Contact Sheet setup dialog

This window is divided into several sections that are pretty self-explanatory and follow a logical sequence.

Source Images options These allow you to choose the images you are using in your contact sheet. In this case, I first selected the images in Bridge, so I'll leave that as the source in this window. The advantage of selecting the images in Bridge is that you can choose to select only a subset of the folder and even rearrange the order of the images in Bridge. Or you could choose Folder from this pop-up menu and then click the Choose button to open a navigation window that will allow you to point to any file on your computer or network. It should be noted that even contact sheets should be made with duplicate images, not with your original files. Chapter 1 deals with this topic—but it is simplest to just copy the folder of images you are using onto your desktop, leaving your original images untouched.

Document options This section provides input for the page size, printing resolution, and color mode and an option to flatten the layers. As a general rule, I prepare contact sheets to have a landscape orientation and make them only 7.5 inches in height so that I can make room for a title and footer later. As discussed in Chapter 7, my standard printing resolution is 240ppi. The standard color space for color images is RGB. The process of creating a contact sheet creates new layers for each image and for the text under each image. Flattening layers reduces this to a manageable two layers—one for the background layer and one for the images and captions. To summarize, I choose to make my contact sheets 10×7.5 inches at 240ppi in RGB color and flatten the layers.

Thumbnails options This section is where you enter data about the way the contact sheet should look—how many rows and columns and how much spacing between images. In this example, I chose 4 columns and 3 rows—for 12 images to a page. When you're entering this data, the preview image is updated to show how the layout will look when finished. I leave the Use Auto-Spacing box checked. Photoshop will create multiple pages, if needed, based on the number of images selected and the layout chosen.

Caption options Checking Use File Name As Caption will place the name of each file under each image in the contact sheet. The specific font and font size can be chosen here for the caption data.

Click the OK button and Photoshop will create the contact sheet(s) based on the parameters you set. If there are too many images to fit on a single page, additional pages are created until all images have been pasted into pages.

Adding Headers and Footers

The next step is to add a title and the footer information. To do this, you need to make room on the top and bottom of the page. This is done by expanding the canvas size. But first, you need to make sure that the background color in the color picker is white.

To set the color picker (Figure 10.4) to the default black foreground color and white background color, press the D key on the keyboard.

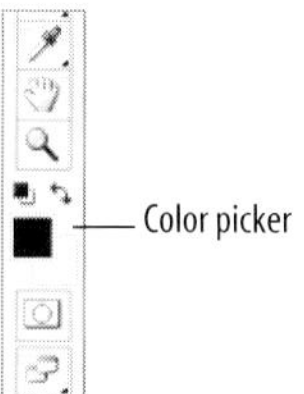

Figure 10.4 Set the color picker to black foreground, white background.

Choose Image > Canvas Size to open the Canvas Size dialog (Figure 10.5). This window will expand the size of the canvas based on the parameters entered. In this example, the image is 10 inches by 7.5 inches. If you keep the anchor in the center of the canvas and expand the height to 8 inches, the canvas is expanded by ¼ inch on the top and ¼ inch on the bottom. If you were going to add a title only and no page number, moving the anchor to the bottom would expand the canvas by ½ inch on the top only. Click OK and the canvas will have room for the title and page number information.

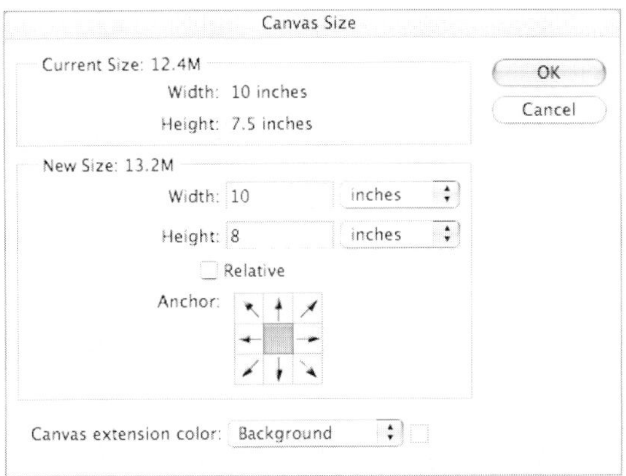

Figure 10.5 Increasing the canvas size

To add the title and page number information, choose the Text tool from the toolbar, either by pressing the T key or by clicking the Tool icon to select it.

In the Text tool options bar (Figure 10.6), several parameters can be set, including font, font size, and alignment. Choose the options you want for the title, click where you want the text to appear, and begin typing. Then commit the text by either pressing the Enter key on the numeric keypad or clicking the Commit button on the Text tool options bar. You can then similarly set the parameters for the page number, click, type, and dismiss the Text tool.

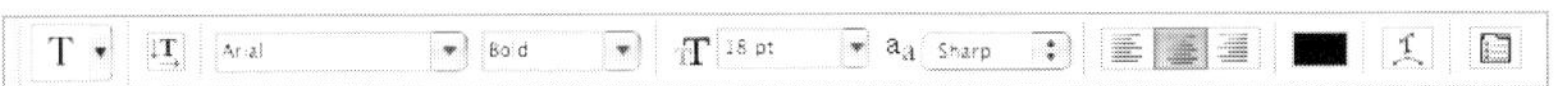

Figure 10.6 Text tool options

The contact sheet(s) can now be printed or saved. If saved as a PSD or TIFF file, the image can be saved with support for layers. In the example here, this would include the text layers, which could then later be edited. The Photoshop (PSD) format uses lossless compression and the TIFF format offers options to save the image with no compression, with lossless compression, or with the JPEG lossy compression.

The contact sheet could also be flattened and saved as a JPEG. To flatten the image, choose Layer > Flatten Image. You need to flatten an image to save it in the JPEG format because JPEG does not support images with multiple layers. Because contact sheets are for reference purposes, I usually flatten them and save them in the JPEG format.

Using the CSX Contact Sheet Script

Included on the accompanying CD is a JavaScript script called CSX (which stands for Contact Sheet X). It was written by X Bytor (xbytor@gmail.com) and is licensed under the GNU license for free distribution. It should be placed in the Adobe Photoshop CS3/Presets/Scripts folder for direct access to it from Photoshop's File > Automate menu.

This script offers several features not available directly in Photoshop's Contact Sheet II feature. First, a template can be used that controls the appearance and layout of the contact sheet—a department logo can be placed in all contact sheets, for example. Additionally, titles and page numbering can be generated as part of the process. Contact sheets can also be saved as part of the process, so saving files doesn't have to be done manually for each contact sheet created.

I have included two templates on the companion CD that provide for a portrait and a landscape layout to use to test this script and modify for your own templates. These templates are titled Police_Landscape.psd and Police_Portrait.psd. Figure 10.7 shows a contact sheet made with this script using the landscape template.

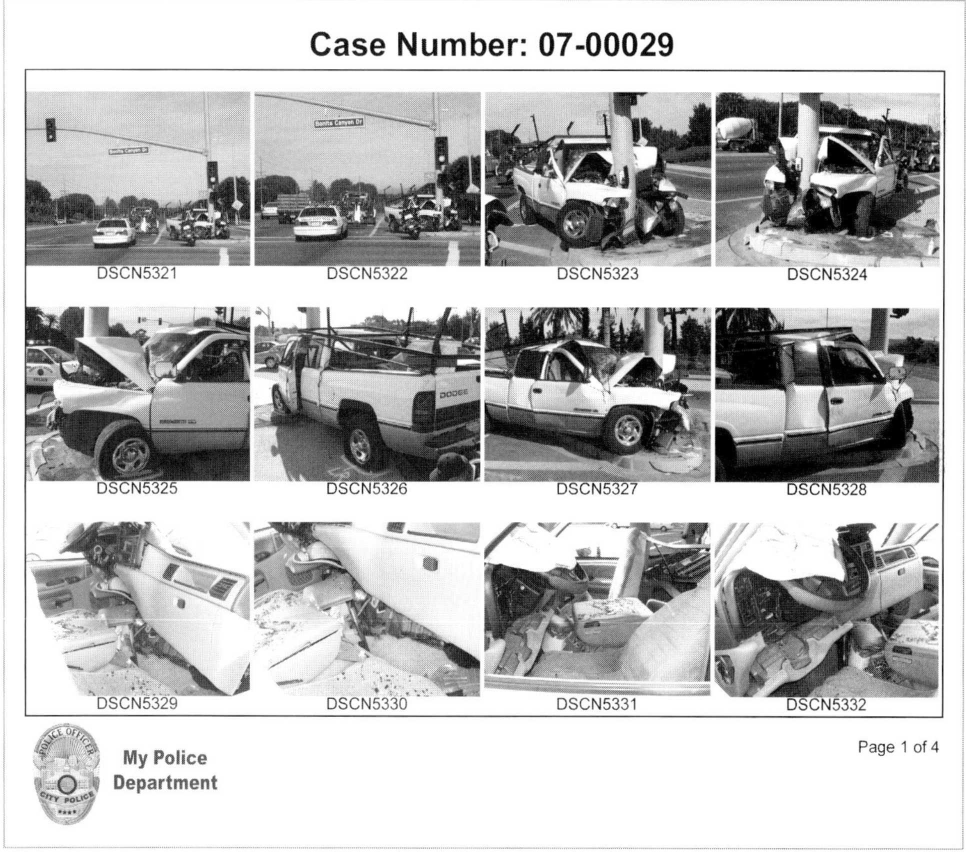

Figure 10.7 With the CSX script, contact sheets can include a title, page numbers, and logos as shown here.

To use CSX, choose File > Automate > Contact Sheet X. This opens the CSX dialog box, shown in Figure 10.8.

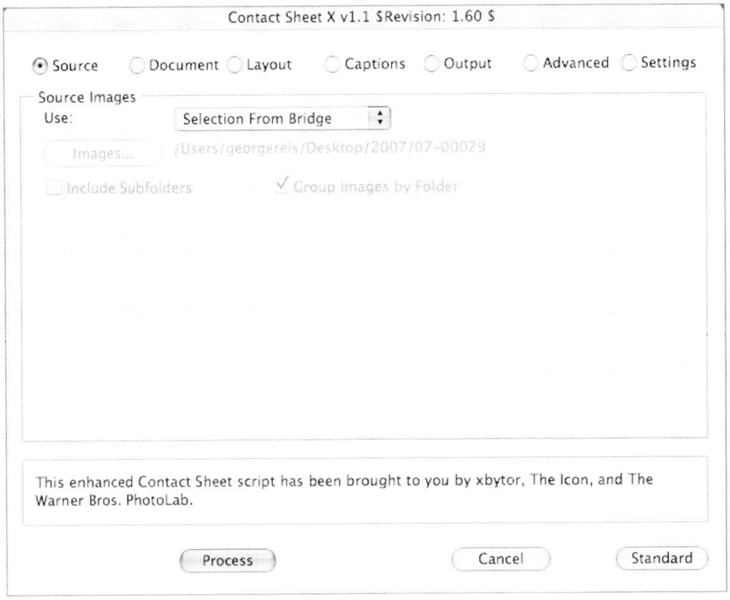

Figure 10.8 The Source tab of the CSX dialog box

In the Source tab, you can choose to create contact sheets from the current open files, the selected files in Bridge, or files accessed by choosing Folder and navigating to a folder of images.

The Document tab (Figure 10.9) provides options to select the paper size, resolution, margin settings, and color space or to select a template file that will control these settings. If you use a template, you'll type your title of choice in the Header field. Although you can't see the whole filename in Figure 10.9, I have selected the `PoliceLandscape.psd` template and typed a case number as the title. The script ignores the document dimensions if you use a template because they will be set in the template.

The Layout tab (Figure 10.10) controls the number of images per page, the order in which the images are placed (left to right or top to bottom), and whether images should be rotated. The settings in this tab are similar to the settings in Photoshop's Contact Sheet II feature and self-explanatory.

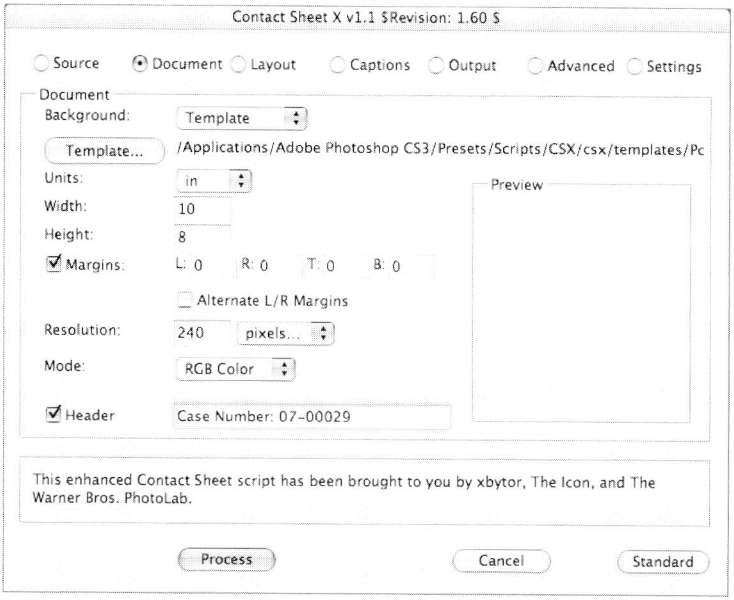

Contact Sheet X v1.1 $Revision: 1.60 $

Source · Document · Layout · Captions · Output · Advanced · Settings

Document

Background: Template

Template... /Applications/Adobe Photoshop CS3/Presets/Scripts/CSX/csx/templates/Pc

Units: in

Width: 10

Height: 8

Margins: L: 0 R: 0 T: 0 B: 0

Alternate L/R Margins

Resolution: 240 pixels...

Mode: RGB Color

Header: Case Number: 07-00029

Preview

This enhanced Contact Sheet script has been brought to you by xbytor, The Icon, and The Warner Bros. PhotoLab.

Process · Cancel · Standard

Figure 10.9 The Document tab with a template selected and a title typed in the Header field

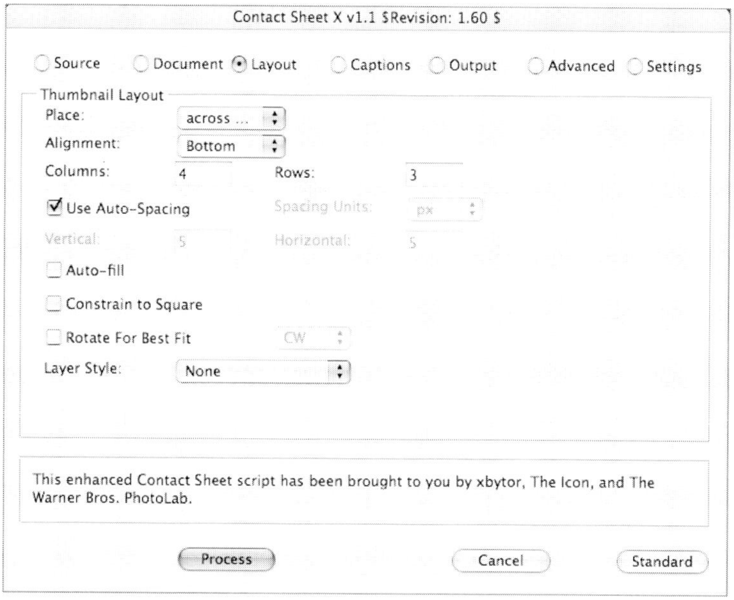

Contact Sheet X v1.1 $Revision: 1.60 $

Source · Document · Layout · Captions · Output · Advanced · Settings

Thumbnail Layout

Place: across ...

Alignment: Bottom

Columns: 4 Rows: 3

Use Auto-Spacing · Spacing Units: px

Vertical: 5 Horizontal: 5

Auto-fill

Constrain to Square

Rotate For Best Fit · CW

Layer Style: None

This enhanced Contact Sheet script has been brought to you by xbytor, The Icon, and The Warner Bros. PhotoLab.

Process · Cancel · Standard

Figure 10.10 The Layout tab of Contact Sheet X

The Captions tab (Figure 10.11) controls the individual captions under each image. Contact Sheet X provides options for including captions or not and for setting the font parameters for the captions. You can also choose to have the captions display the filename without the extension.

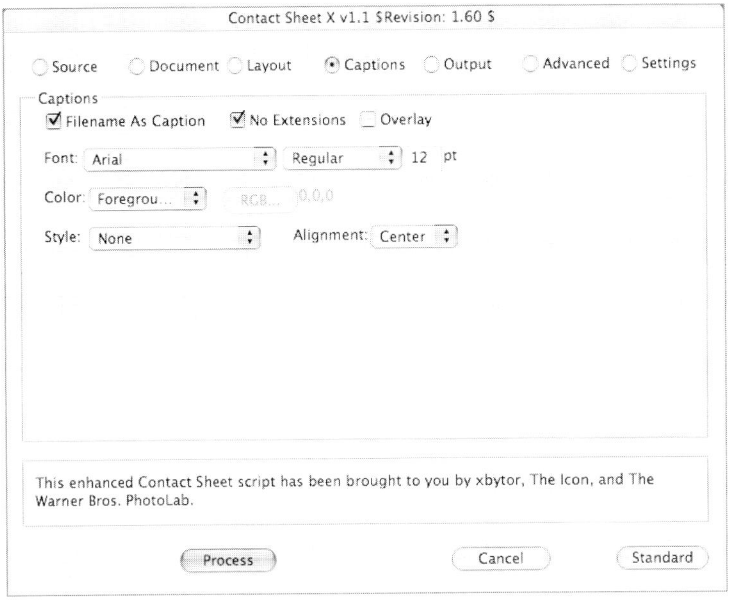

Contact Sheet X v1.1 $Revision: 1.60 $

Source | Document | Layout | Captions | Output | Advanced | Settings

Captions

Filename As Caption | No Extensions | Overlay

Font: Arial | Regular | 12 pt

Color: Foregrou... | RGB... | 0,0,0

Style: None | Alignment: Center

This enhanced Contact Sheet script has been brought to you by xbytor, The Icon, and The Warner Bros. PhotoLab.

Process | Cancel | Standard

Figure 10.11 Contact Sheet X's options for setting captions

A key feature of Contact Sheet X is the ability for this script to automatically save each page. This setting is in the Output tab, as shown in Figure 10.12. This is also where you set the naming preferences and file format for the contact sheets.

The Advanced tab provides options to add speed for this script; see the CSX documentation for information on these options. The Settings tab allows you to save and load presets.

Once all parameters are set, click the Process button and Contact Sheet X will create the contact sheets with the parameters set, including adding a title and page numbers and automatically saving the files if these options were selected (or are part of the template used).

Note: Other scripts and scripting information by X Bytor and others can be found at www.ps-scripts.com and www.ps-scripts.sourceforge.net.

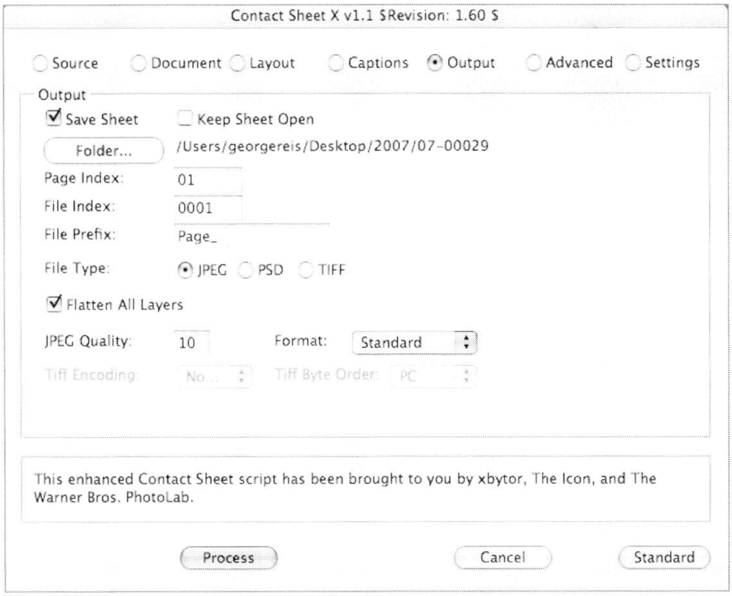

Figure 10.12 The Output tab for in Contact Sheet X

Summary

The process of making contact sheets is simple: just choose the Contact Sheet command from Bridge or Photoshop (or the Contact Sheet X script). If you're using Photoshop's feature, print or save the contact sheets once they are complete. If you're using Contact Sheet X, the files will be saved with the naming options set.

PDF Presentations

In addition to making prints for court, detectives, or other interested parties, sometimes it is necessary to project the images from an LCD projector or to deliver images on a CD, DVD, or other media. PDF Presentation is a feature that can create a multipage PDF document from a set of selected images and place password security on the file to reduce the risk of unauthorized viewing, editing, or printing. The resulting PDF file can be viewed using the free Adobe Reader software.

11

Chapter Contents

Creating Presentations

The advantage of the PDF format is that virtually everyone with a computer can read these files with the free Adobe Reader software (available from www.adobe.com/products/acrobat/readstep2.html). Regardless of the file format of the original image files, the PDF document can be opened with Reader or Acrobat without the need for any additional software.

The PDF presentation is an excellent way to distribute images, as mentioned earlier, but it is not a substitute for providing copies of the original images for analysis. If images are to be submitted to a colleague for a technical review or to an attorney for an independent analysis, original images as well as copies of any enhanced or modified images should be provided in the formats in which they currently exist. A PDF presentation may be provided in addition to, but is not a substitute for, the original data provided for technical review or independent analysis.

PDF Presentation can be invoked from either Photoshop or Bridge. In Bridge, choose the images for the PDF presentation by clicking the first image and then clicking the last image while holding down the Shift key. Then choose Tools > Photoshop > PDF Presentation (Figure 11.1). Or this feature can be chosen directly in Photoshop by choosing File > Automate > PDF Presentation.

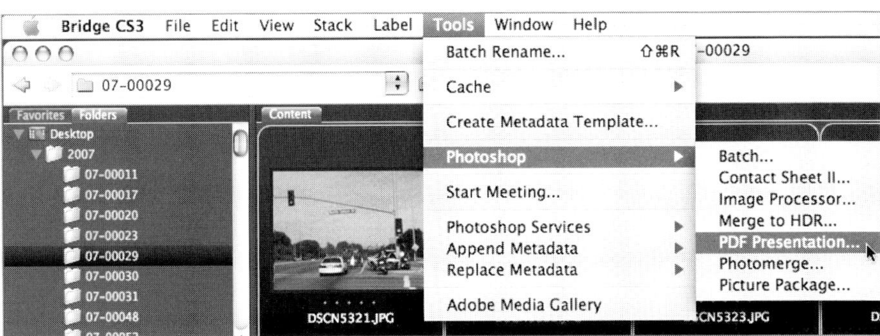

Figure 11.1 Selecting images in Bridge and choosing Tools > Photoshop > PDF Presentation is one way to invoke this filter.

This opens the PDF Presentation dialog box (Figure 11.2), which has several options available, including options to create a slide show with transitions between images and to create a multiple-page PDF document—with one image placed on each page. I'll show you how to create a multipage PDF.

The slide show option creates a full-screen presentation without the visible navigation tools normally seen in Acrobat. The images will change based on the parameters set for the slide show if that option is selected. The slide show can be viewed as a multipage PDF by pressing the Esc key on your keyboard after opening the file.

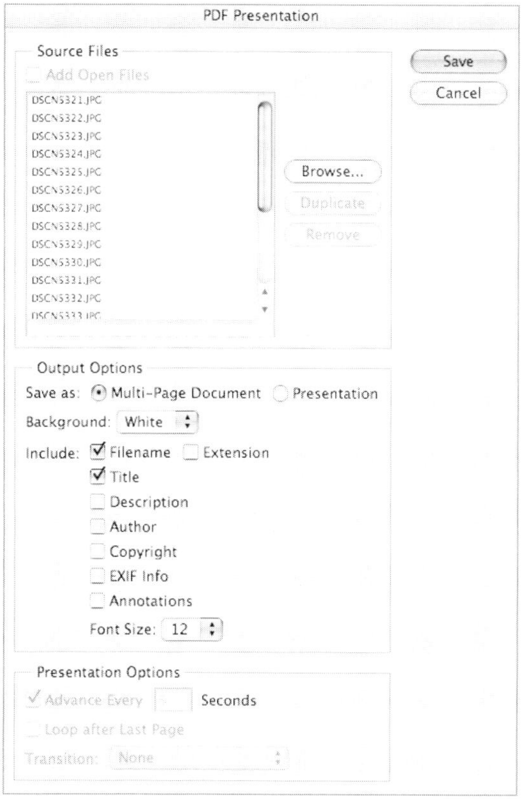

Figure 11.2 The PDF Presentation dialog box has a new feature in Photoshop CS3, which is the ability to add caption information by checking boxes in the Output Options section of the window.

The first section of this window displays the files that were selected in Bridge. Additional images can be added to the presentation, selected images can be removed, or the order of the images can be changed by selecting and dragging them within the window.

The Output Options section is where you choose whether to create a multipage PDF document or a slide show presentation. If the slide show option is chosen, transition timing and effects can be selected in the Presentation Options section. In Photoshop CS3, you can also choose to have a caption below each image by checking boxes to display various types of metadata. I previously added the case number as the title for these images (see Chapter 3), so I am choosing to display the filename and title under each image.

Once you verify that the correct images are selected and in the correct order, click the Save button to open a new window prompting you to name the file and choose a location in which to save it (Figure 11.3).

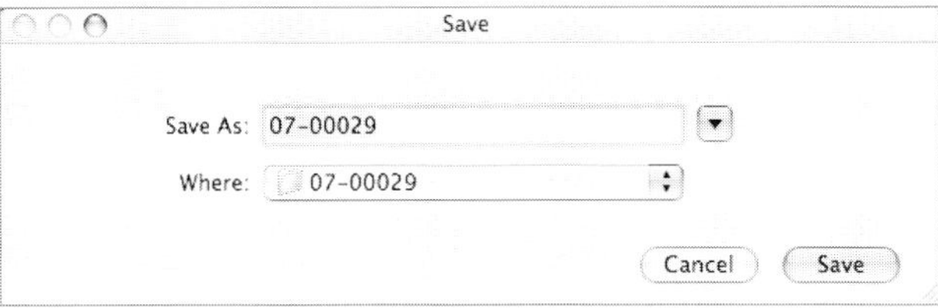

Figure 11.3 In this window, you can name the PDF document and choose where to save it. I typically name the file with the case number and save it with the case images.

Make these choices and click Save, which will open a third window, the Save Adobe PDF window (Figure 11.4), providing options for image quality, color profiles, and password security, among other things. This window starts out displaying the General options panel. On the left side, other panels can be selected and displayed.

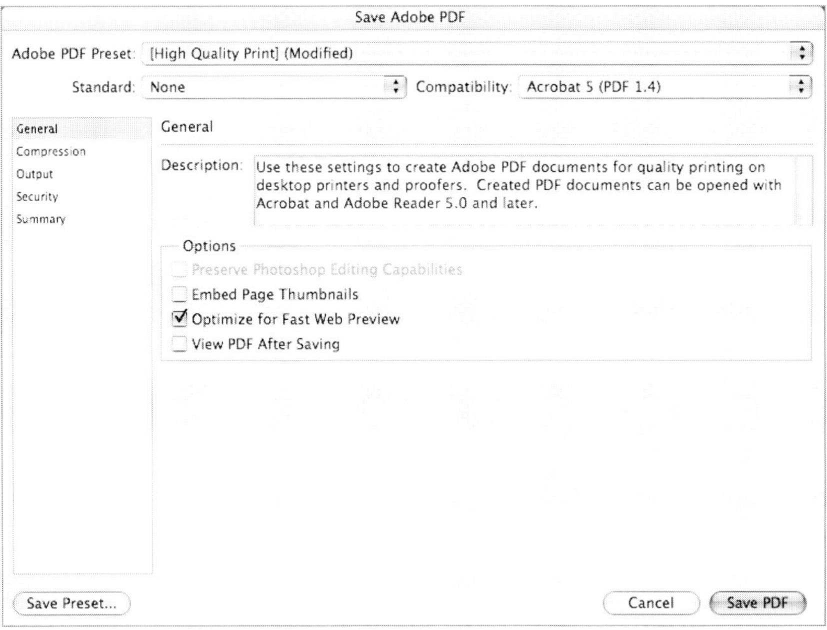

Figure 11.4 This is the main window for setting the resolution, color profiles, and security for the PDF presentation.

The Presets pop-up menu allows you to choose a preinstalled preset or one that you have created. I have chosen the High Quality Print preset but will make changes to several options and then save a preset based on those changes.

I have left the Options section set to the default settings. Checking Embed Page Thumbnails would provide a Preview icon for the document. I leave the Optimize For Fast Web Preview box checked in case this document will be viewed over a server or with a web browser. I generally don't want to view the PDF after creating it, so I leave that box unchecked.

The next tab is the Compression tab (Figure 11.5). It provides options for reducing the image resolution of large files and for compressing images. If high-quality images are required, choose Do Not Downsample and None for the compression type. The resulting file may be large, but the images will retain their full quality, and when you zoom in, they have the same detail as the original images. The Zip compression option is a lossless compression method and will reduce the file size without reducing the quality of the images in the PDF file.

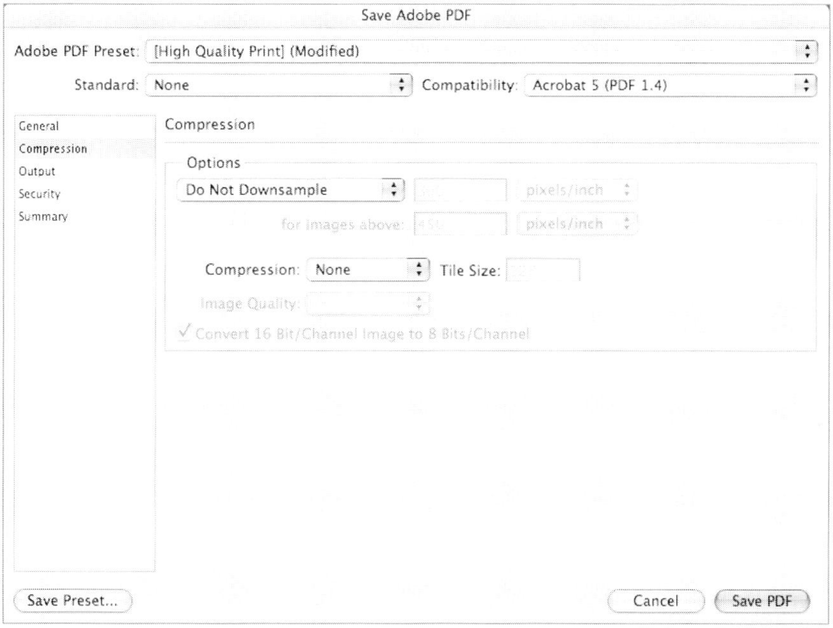

Figure 11.5 The Compression panel provides options for image resolution and compression settings.

If I were creating this file to display on a monitor as full-frame images only, then I may have chosen to downsample the images to 72ppi and to use JPEG or Zip compression. Downsampling reduces the file size and can make changing from one image to another much quicker—but it does reduce the image resolution as well. JPEG compression will also result in lower image quality. Choosing to downsample or to use JPEG compression should only be done if the images will not be enlarged significantly and if the full quality of the original images is not required. If the images may be enlarged or zoomed while being viewed, or if they are going to be printed, it is better to avoid the downsampling and the lossy JPEG compression options.

Clicking the Security tab (Figure 11.6) presents the security options for the PDF file, which include the option to require a password to open the file and a separate password to print or edit the file. The PDF Presentation security options support 40-bit or 128-bit encryption. If you're delivering sensitive images on CD or DVD or via email, requiring password protection can help prevent unauthorized individuals from viewing the images.

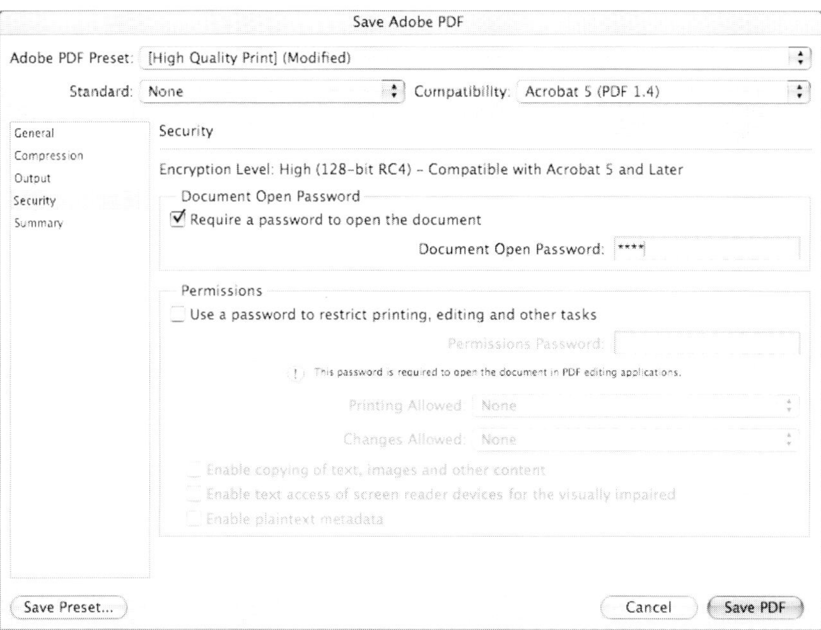

Figure 11.6 The Security panel provides password protection for opening the file or for modifying or printing the file.

In this example, I have chosen to require a password for opening the file. Checking the box makes the Document Open Password field active. You must type a password in this box before continuing.

Click the Save Preset button to create a preset for PDF Presentation with all the settings chosen for this setup (Figure 11.7). Choose a name that will identify this as your standard setting or as an uncompressed, lossless compressed, or high-Quality setting. The next time you want to use this setting, you can select it from the Presets drop-down menu without having to choose each setting individually.

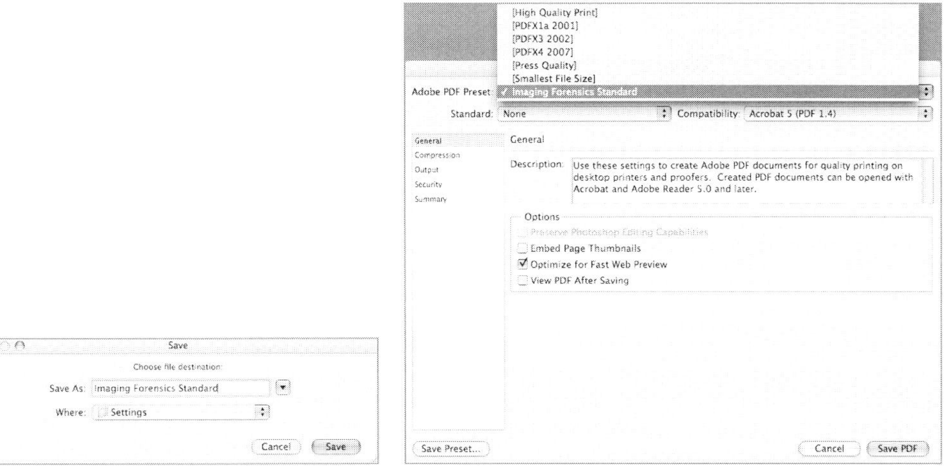

Figure 11.7 Clicking the Save Preset button brings up the window on the left. Choosing this preset (right) will enable all settings so you won't have to choose each of them.

Click Summary in the Window section to show all the options set in the other windows for review. If you click Save PDF, you'll see prompts (Figure 11.8) to reenter the passwords that you set for both opening the file and editing the file (if these options were selected).

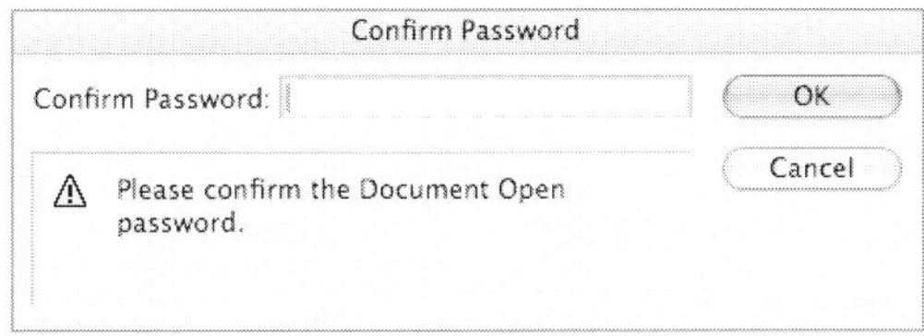

Figure 11.8 Password confirmation dialog box

Opening and Viewing PDF Presentations

When you attempt to open the PDF, a password window like the one in Figure 11.9 appears, requiring you to enter the proper password before the file can be displayed. Simply enter the main security password for the document and click the OK button and the PDF file will open.

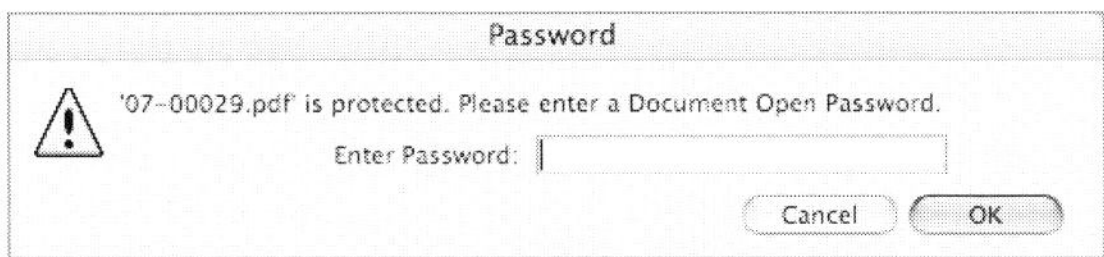

Figure 11.9 Password prompt in Adobe Acrobat

The PDF window can be configured in many ways—I have chosen to display thumbnails on the left for easy navigation (Figure 11.10). Clicking any thumbnail will display it in the main window. There are also navigation controls at the bottom of the page. PDF files can also be displayed full screen and keyboard shortcuts can be used to move from page to page.

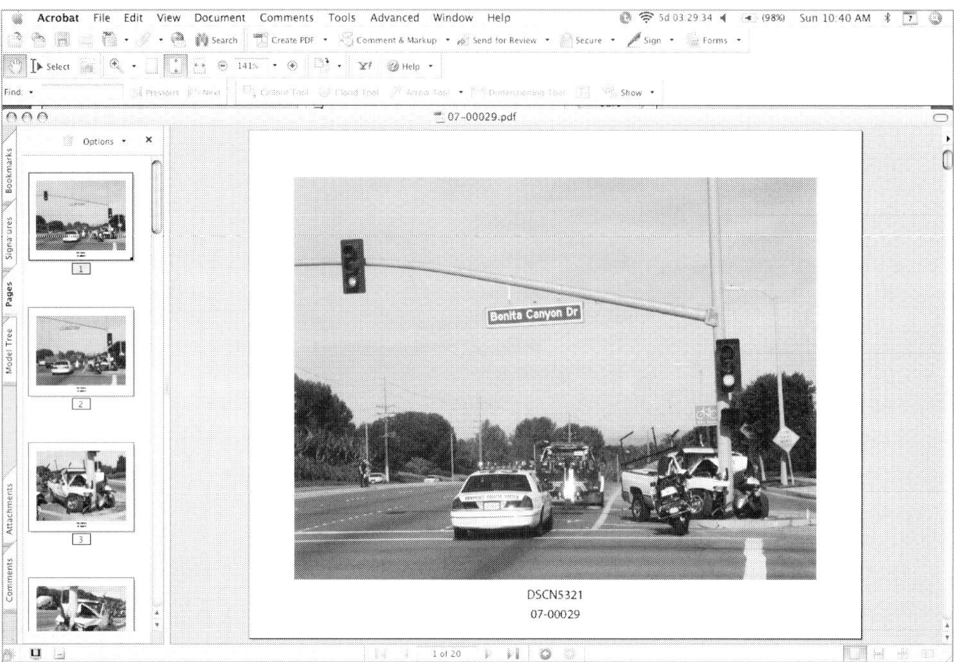

Figure 11.10 The PDF presentation opened in Adobe Acrobat with thumbnails on the left

Also notice that each image has the filename and case number as a caption. The ability to automatically add captions to the PDF presentation was added in Photoshop CS3.

Summary

The PDF Presentation feature provides an excellent option for delivering images to a prosecutor, insurance company, or other interested party to the case. It can be used for court presentations in place of programs like PowerPoint. Options are available to retain the full quality of the original images or to reduce their resolution or apply compression when a small file size is more important than retaining the full image quality.

The multipage PDF document can be viewed by anyone who has the free Adobe Reader.

Preparing Court Exhibits

Court exhibits can be enlarged poster-sized prints or projected images that might include some type of annotation. The annotation can be as simple as lines pointing to objects of interest in the image or as complex as animated or multi-page comparison charts that show magnified sections to illustrate similarities or differences in fingerprints, handwriting, toolmarks, and so on.

The court exhibits themselves can be simple or complex. We'll look at some basic methods for preparing exhibits in Photoshop in this chapter. These concepts and techniques can be expanded upon to create interactive displays of much greater complexity.

12

Chapter Contents

Using Court Exhibits

Traditionally, static court displays to depict the findings in a comparative analysis have been created by mounting large prints onto matte boards or foamcore, with Chartpak tape used to identify points of comparison. It was not unusual for such a display to take several hours to an entire day to create—from making enlargements and mounting prints to applying the Chartpak tape and letters. If a display was damaged, it would have to be created again from scratch.

Creating court displays in Photoshop has made the process much faster—a typical court display can be made in 30 minutes to an hour. Court displays can be presented as large prints or projected with an LCD projector. They can be static displays, made to look similar to the traditional displays, or they can be interactive, running in a slide-show-type format, showing different features with each image. In addition, if a print of the court chart is damaged, one simply needs to make another print from the file.

In this chapter, we'll review the method for creating a static display that is similar to a traditional court chart. It should not be difficult to think of how this can be expanded and combined with the PDF presentation to create more dynamic displays. It should also be noted that if one is making court displays frequently, it may be more efficient to make them in a page layout application such as Adobe InDesign.

Creating Court Exhibits

The court display in Figure 12.1 is created with a few simple steps. First the two prints are scanned to show the same area. They are then pasted into a new document and placed next to each other, and then lines are added with the Line tool. Finally, the letters, title, and captions are added with the Text tool. The same techniques would be used for displays showing comparisons of a suspect or vehicle from a video, tool marks, tire or footwear impressions, and questioned documents. Expanding on this technique, separate images (or layers) can be made showing Galton points, creases, ridge flow, individual ridges, and so forth.

The two images in this example (Figure 12.2) were scanned at 350 percent at 240ppi. This made each image about 3×4 inches, which fit well onto an 8×10 inch canvas.

Because these images have no color values of importance, I desaturate them so that no color shift is present. This can be done by selecting one image and pressing Shift+Ctrl+U/Shift+Cmd+U or choosing Image > Adjustments > Desaturate.

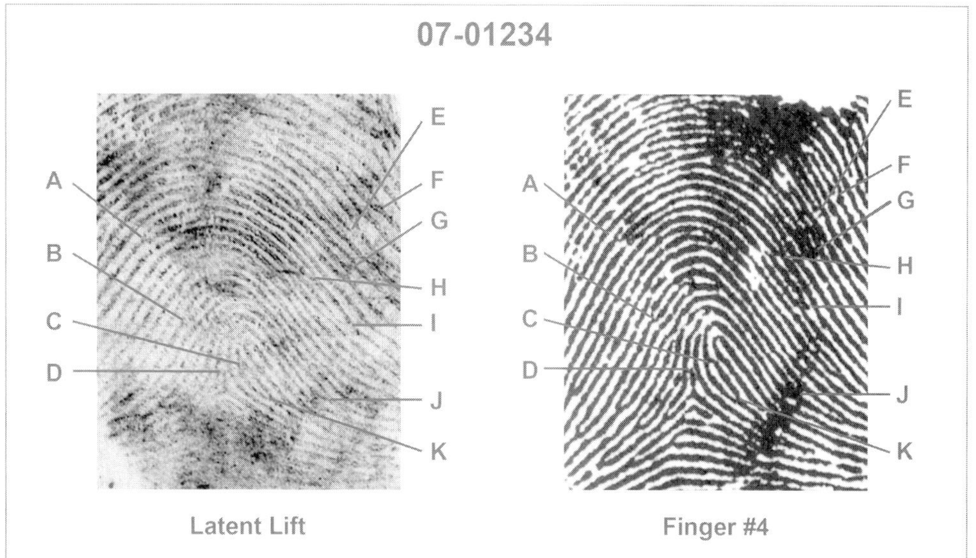

Figure 12.1 This is a typical static court display. Without much additional effort, a number of variations can be created, including showing ridge flow, tracing each ridge one at a time, using layers to illustrate one feature at a time, and enlarging areas.

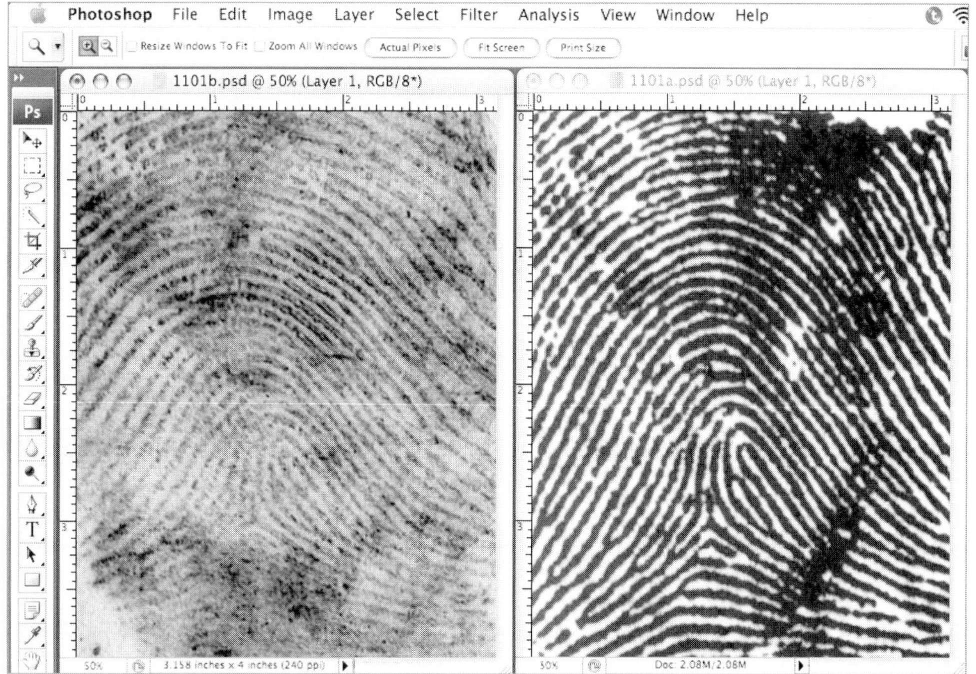

Figure 12.2 The two prints, scanned at 350 percent

The next two steps will be to create a new canvas and paste these two images onto it. This canvas is the equivalent of the mounting board used in traditional court displays.

Create a new canvas by choosing File > New. This brings up the dialog box seen in Figure 12.3. Set the canvas size, resolution, color space, and canvas color in the canvas settings area—in this example, I chose 10×8 inches (for a landscape orientation) at 240ppi in RGB color space with a white background color. If you anticipate using these parameters frequently, you can choose Save Preset and have quick access to these settings through the Preset pop-up menu. Otherwise, click OK to dismiss the window and create the new canvas.

New
Name: Untitled-1
Preset: Custom
Size:
Width: 10 inches
Height: 8 inches
Resolution: 240 pixels/inch
Color Mode: RGB Color 8 bit
Background Contents: White
Advanced
OK
Cancel
Save Preset...
Delete Preset...
Device Central...
Image Size:
13.2M

Figure 12.3 The new document window

Paste the two fingerprint images into the new canvas by selecting one image, selecting all, copying, selecting the new canvas, and pasting. Then repeat this with the second image. Or you can drag and drop. To do this, first select the Move tool from the toolbar by clicking it, or press the V key on your keyboard. Also check the Auto-Select Layer box on the Move tool options bar (Figure 12.4); in Photoshop CS3, be sure the pop-up menu is set to Layer and not Group. This enables Photoshop to automatically select the layer under the cursor when you're moving objects with the Move tool and there are multiple layers.

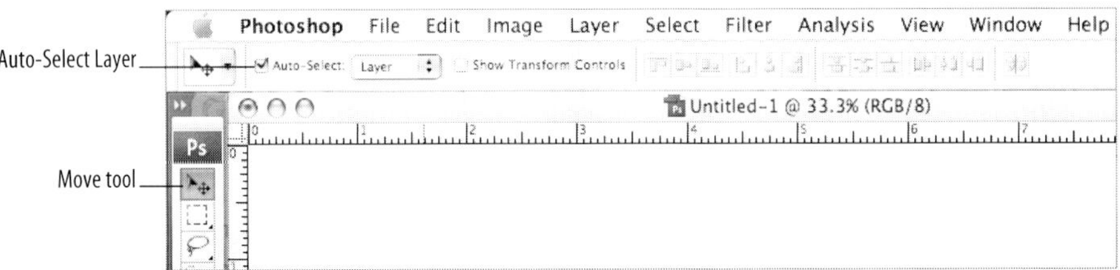

Figure 12.4 The Move tool and Move tool options

With the Move tool, click one of the fingerprint images to make it active, and then click and hold down the left mouse button while dragging it onto the new canvas. In the example shown in Figure 12.5, I clicked the latent print and dragged to the new canvas—the cursor changes shape, and an outline of the image should show on the new canvas, as seen in Figure 12.4. Once this has been dragged into place, let go of the mouse button. Now the latent print can be closed, and the same thing can be done with the inked print. The next step is to align the prints on the canvas.

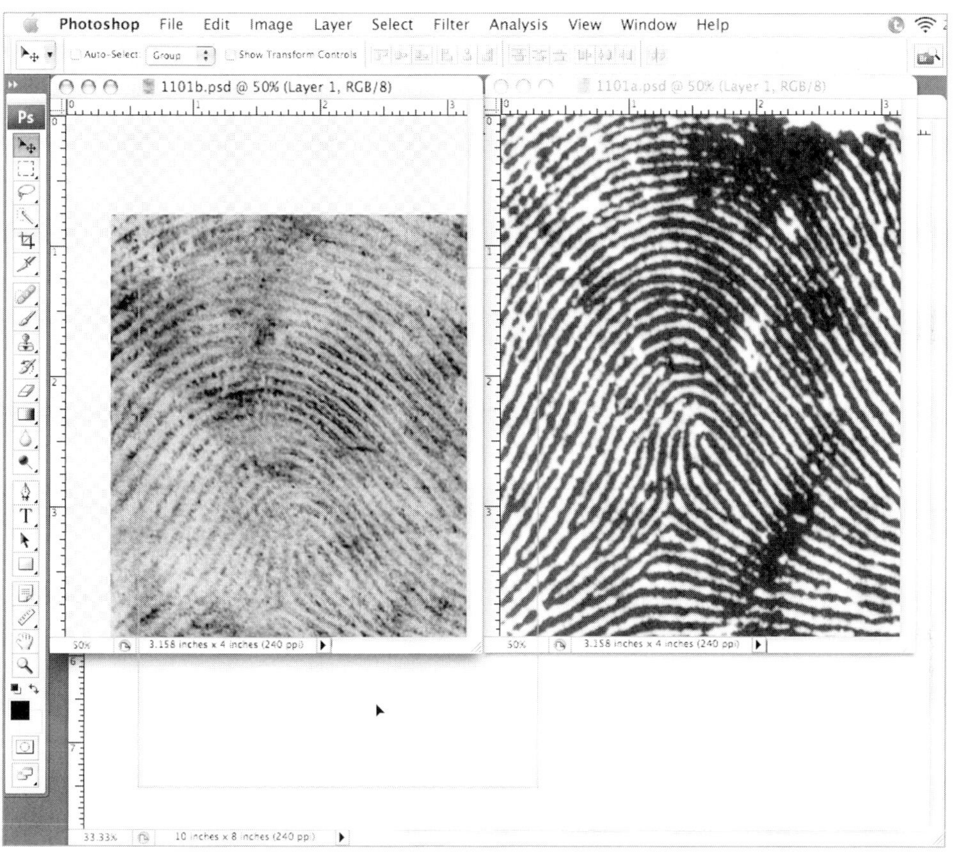

Figure 12.5 Dragging the images onto the new canvas. Notice the cursor shape and image outline in the new canvas.

To align the images using guidelines, I first move one image into place by clicking and dragging with the Move tool. I then drag guidelines to relevant spots across that image. Figure 12.6 shows that I placed vertical guidelines one inch from the left and right edges and a horizontal guideline at the core of the fingerprint. In order to drag a guideline into place, Photoshop's rulers must be visible; if they are not, choose View > Rulers, which will place a check mark next to Rulers in that menu and will place the rulers on the top and left edges of the image window. Now, with the Move tool, move the cursor into the ruler area and click and drag and a guideline will be placed when you release the mouse button. It can be moved with the Move tool to reposition it at any time.

Once the guidelines are in place, move the other print into alignment using the guidelines for proper placement.

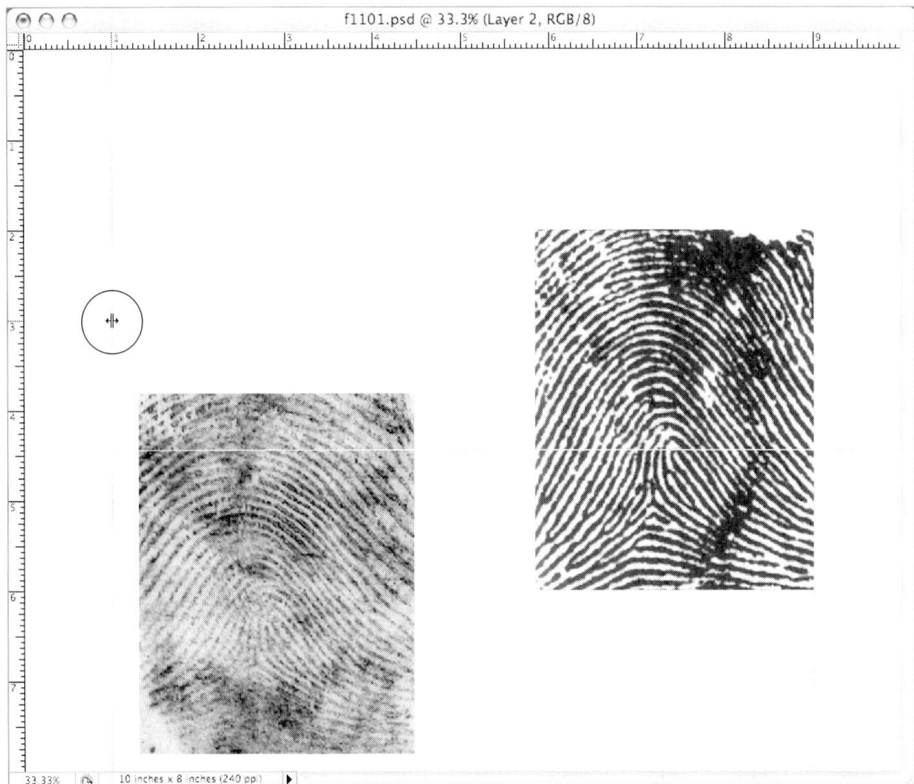

Figure 12.6 To create guidelines in an image, drag the cursor from Photoshop's ruler area into the image.

Images on multiple layers can also be aligned with the alignment tools in the Move tool options bar. To use this feature, select the layers you want to align in the Layers palette (Shift+click to select a group of layers). Next, choose the alignment type from the Move tool options bar and the layers will align based upon that criteria.

Labeling Exhibits

The image is now equivalent to having mounted two prints onto a mount board, as shown in Figure 12.7. The remaining steps are to place the lines, letters, titles, and captions.

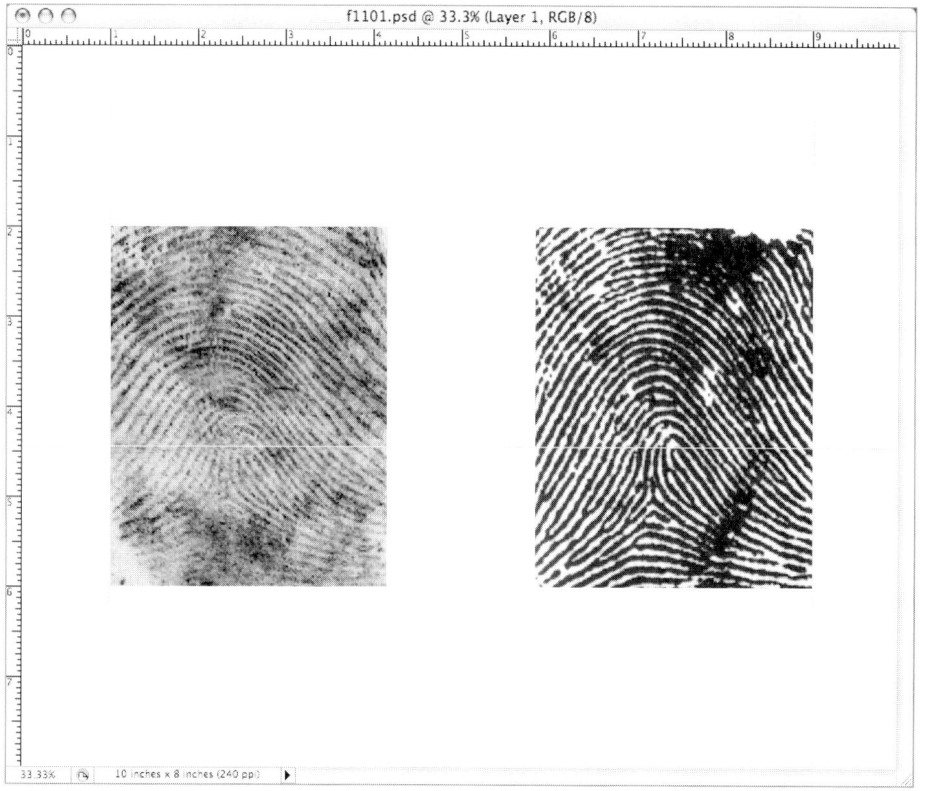

Figure 12.7 The two images aligned on a single canvas

Before creating lines, you need to create a new layer for placing your lines so that they can be easily erased if you make a mistake in placing them. To create a new layer, click the New Layer icon at the bottom of the Layers palette and a new layer will be created "above the layer that is currently active, as in Figure 12.8.

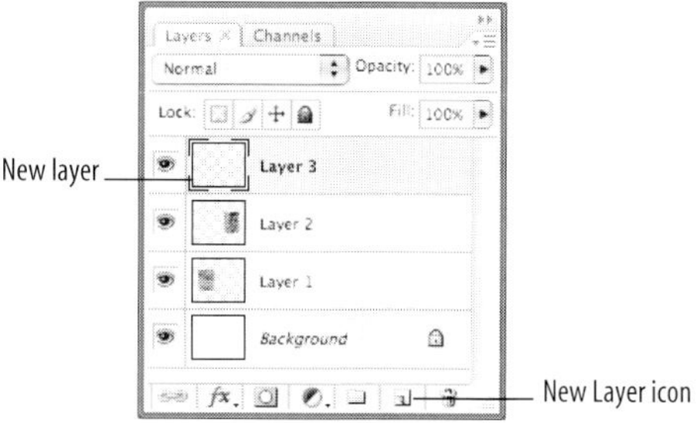

Figure 12.8 The Layers palette and the New Layer icon

To create lines, you need to do several things: choose the color to make the lines, select the Line tool, and set a couple of parameters for the Line tool.

To select a color, choose the Swatch palette and click on your color of choice. As you can see in Figure 12.9, I chose the first color in the default swatches, which is a bright red.

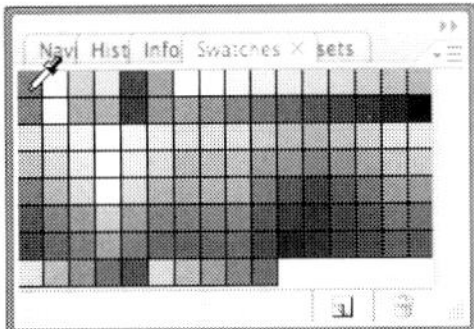

Figure 12.9 The Swatches palette

The Line tool (Figure 12.10) is one of the Shape tools and can be chosen by clicking and holding the mouse button while selecting the Shape tool, highlighting the Line tool, and releasing the mouse button. In the Shape tool options bar, click the Fill Pixels icon and choose a line weight that creates a line with the thickness you prefer—4 to 8 pixels will usually provide a strong visible line that doesn't interfere with the details of the underlying image. The thickness of the line will depend on personal preferences as well as the resolution of the image; a 4-pixel thickness on a 240ppi document is the same as a 6-pixel thickness on a 360ppi document.

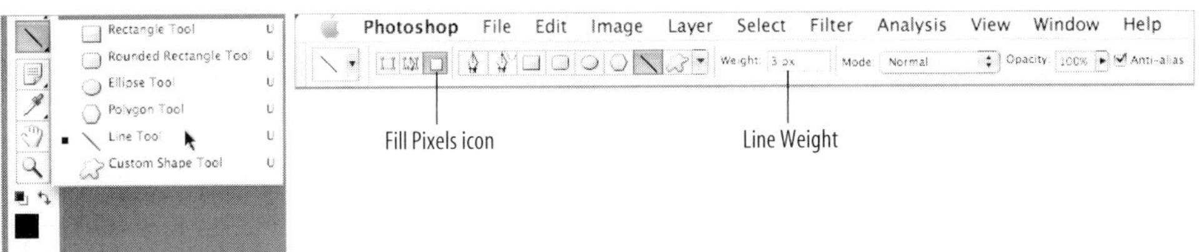

Figure 12.10 The Line tool is part of the Shape tools in the toolbar. The Line tool options include the Fill Pixels option and the ability to set the line thickness or weight.

To use the Line tool, simply drag and drop lines where you want them placed. Before you place the lines, you can place guidelines to keep the ends of the lines evenly aligned, as seen in Figure 12.11.

There are many options for building this part of the chart, three of which are shown in Figure 12.12. Instead of using lines, you could create circles around groups of features, draw lines with the Pencil or Brush tool along ridges or shapes of features, or copy and enlarge sections of the image to show more detail.

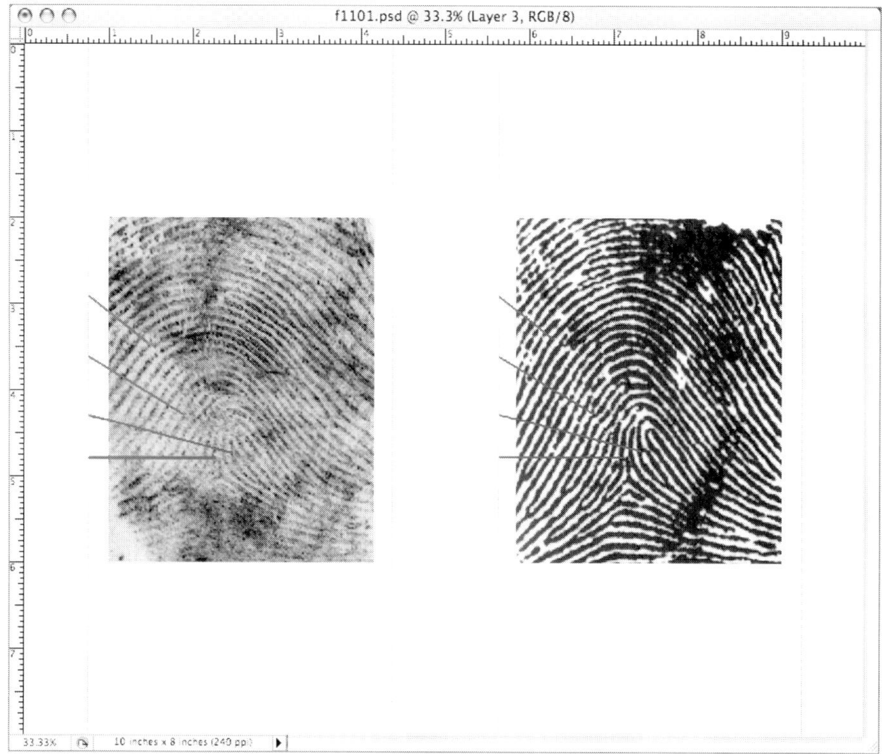

Figure 12.11 Click and drag the Line tool to draw lines on the image.

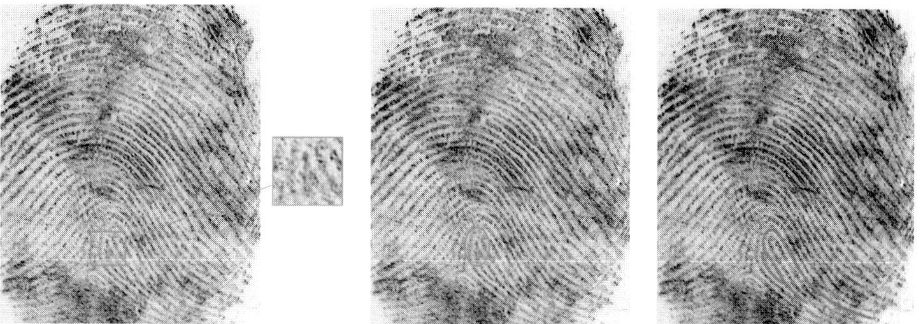

Figure 12.12 Three samples of different approaches to creating a court chart

The next step is to place your letters, title, and captions. Select the Text tool, and choose the font, text color, and font size in the Text tool options bar (see Figure 12.13). Then click in the chart where you wish to place a letter, title, or caption and type. Finish each entry by either pressing the Enter key on the number portion of the keyboard or by clicking the check box on the option bar. Each use of the Text tool creates a new layer, and you can edit it by clicking it to activate it.

Figure 12.13 The Text tool and Text tool options

To complete the chart, I prefer to combine several of the layers that have been created into layer groups to make it easy to turn on or off the visibility of each layer or group of layers (Figure 12.14).

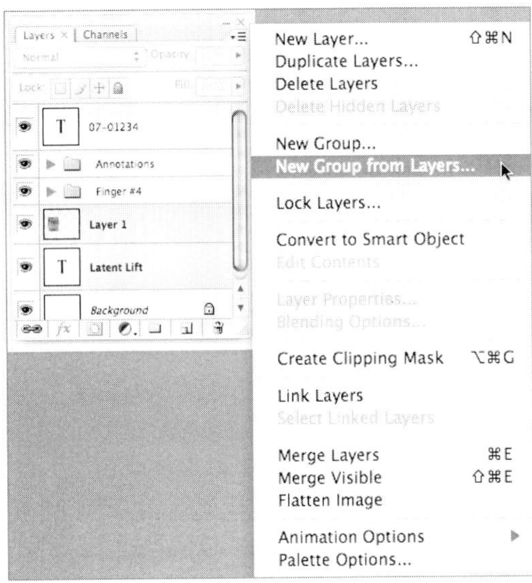

Figure 12.14 Selecting New Group From Layers from the Layers palette flyout menu

An easy method for combining layers is to turn off the visibility icons on the layers that are not be combined and then choose Layers > Merge Visible. You can click on the name of each remaining layer and change it to easily identify the content of each layer.

Summary

Creating court exhibits is frequently just a matter of copying one or more images onto a blank document and adding some annotations. These exhibits may be printed as poster-sized images or projected on a screen with an LCD projector. Even if the courtroom presentation is done with projected images, it's important to make printed copies so that they are available to the jurors during deliberation.

Photomerge

13

Combining multiple photographs using the Photomerge feature can provide a way to increase the apparent resolution of your photographs or show a wider view than your equipment will otherwise allow. In both cases, the technique is relatively simple: take multiple, overlapping photographs and stitch them together in Photoshop using the Photomerge feature.

Chapter Contents

Adjacent or Panoramic Photographs

When photographing large areas, or even small subjects with fine detail, a single photograph may not contain the resolution needed to retain the level of detail required for analysis. This is true whether the photograph is from film or a digital camera. It is wise to be familiar with your equipment and know its resolution limitations.

When you're in situations where this resolution limitation is likely to occur, you can combine several photographs to increase the resolution while still showing the entire subject area.

This is also helpful when the subjects won't fit in a single frame because you're too close. This can occur when in a confined place or when an object (such as a tree) is blocking part of the main subject.

Traditionally, multiple photographs were carefully aligned and mounted together as a single image. The process was difficult at best because often lens distortions would make alignment precarious. In addition, getting the color and density in each print to match was often much more difficult than expected.

In Photoshop CS and above, the Photomerge tool can make this process very simple. Multiple, overlapping images can be easily combined and blended together, creating a single image of the entire subject. This can be important in footwear and tire impression photography where a single image may not provide enough resolution to resolve the fine details needed by the examiner.

Photoshop CS3 also has some new blending features that help create even better panorama images than in earlier versions, which will be explored in this chapter.

Figure 13.1 shows the single file taken with a wide-angle lens, the series of images taken from a single position, and the final image made by combining this series of images into a single image. There is a change in perspective because the single file was not taken from the same position as the series of images—this was due to cars and trees that restricted the view.

As can be seen, the exposure from each image is consistent, as is the focus. These images were handheld, which illustrates how this technique works with real-world scenes, not requiring the camera to be on a tripod and rotated on the optical center of the lens (as is preferable with QuickTime Virtual Reality panoramas).

As can be seen in the cropped images in Figure 13.2, the resolution is greatly increased by combining the images through Photomerge.

Single shot

Multiple shots for Photomerge

Completed Photomerge

Figure 13.1 The top image is a single frame showing most of the shopping center, next is the series of six frames used to create the Photomerge, and the completed Photomerge image is at the bottom.

Cropped area from single frame

Cropped area from Photomerge

Figure 13.2 The image on the left is cropped from the wide angle photo—notice the lack of sharpness at this magnification. The image on the right is cropped from the completed Photomerge—notice the increased sharpness.

Photographing the Scene

For three-dimensional subjects, it is best to photograph the series of images from a single point. For flat objects—such as blood spatter on a wall or a tire impression—the camera or subject can be moved, keeping the subject-to-lens distance equal and the camera back parallel to the subject. In both cases, the photographs should also be taken in manual exposure (with the same exposure for each image) and manual focus (with the same focus distance for each image). This will make blending work much more smoothly.

With either approach, it is wise to photograph the images in a logical order (from left to right or top to bottom, for example). With photographs like the example in Figure 13.2, it is easy to see the correct sequence of the images, but if the subject is a plain wall with blood spatter, the proper sequence is not as obvious. Photomerge does an excellent job of properly combining the images in the correct sequence most of the time. But with some subject matter, even Photomerge may not be able to correctly organize the correct sequential order. Having notes of the order in which the images were taken can help if the files need to be manually sorted.

Take the photos with manual exposure, with the same exposure for each, to keep the tonality at the edges of overlapping areas consistent, making blending of images much smoother. If the photos are taken with automatic exposure, the images should be corrected to get the closest tonal match before they are merged.

Use manual focus to prevent a shift in the focus point from one image to the next. If the subject matter varies in distance throughout the set of images, use a small aperture for maximum depth of field.

Merging the Images

It is best to move the images to be merged into a separate folder so that they are easy to identify for this process.

To begin, select the sequence of images to be combined into the composite image in Bridge by selecting the first, then holding the Shift key and clicking on the last image of the series. If the images need to be rotated, click one of the Rotate icons in the upper-right corner of the Bridge window (Figure 13.3). Then select Tool > Photoshop > Photomerge. This will launch Photoshop and each image will be opened and copied into the Photomerge window.

In Photoshop CS3, some new alignment and blending features have been added. Selecting Photomerge will open the dialog box shown in Figure 13.4, which provides several alignment options. The alignment choices are Auto, Perspective, Cylindrical, Reposition Only, and Interactive Layout. If Auto is selected, Photoshop will attempt to use the best of these three methods:

Perspective is the best choice when merging a set of images that are of a limited angle and the objects at the ends of the stitched image appear too small.

Cylindrical is for full 360-degree stitching.

Reposition Only is for flat objects in which the camera, scanner, or subject was moved (keeping the camera back and subject plane parallel) rather than rotated.

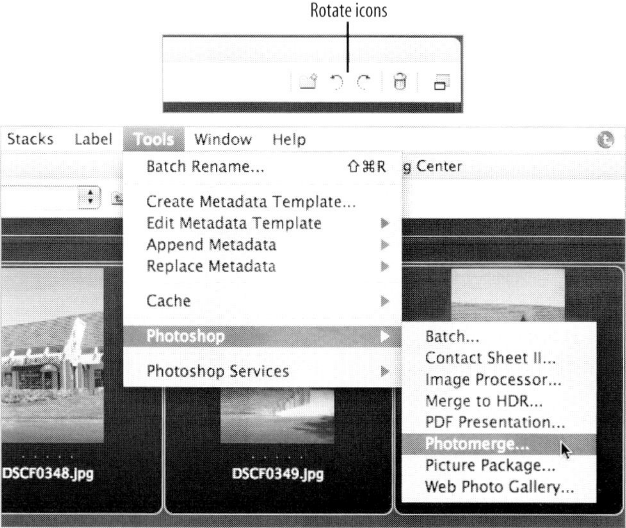

Figure 13.3 The Rotate icons are located in the upper-right corner of the Bridge window. To access Photomerge from within Bridge, choose Tools > Photoshop > Photomerge.

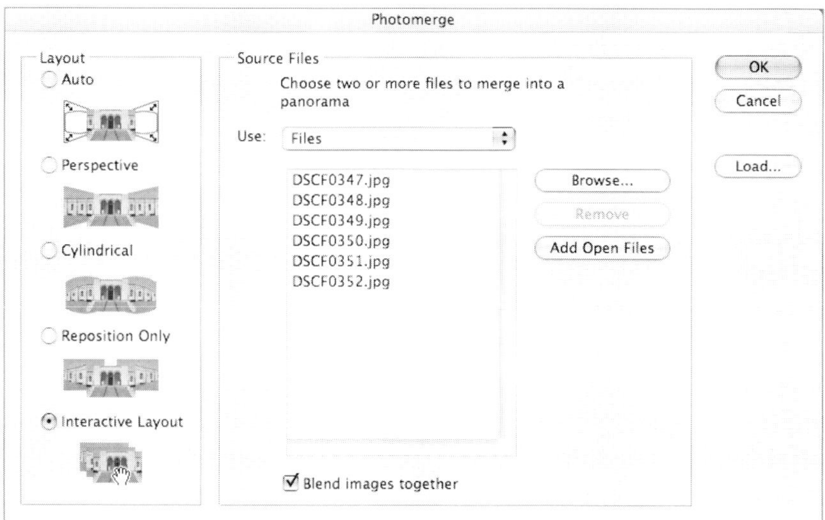

Figure 13.4 In Photoshop CS3, this is the first dialog box that opens. Choosing the Interactive Layout option will open the images into a similar environment as in Photoshop CS2. Choosing other layout options will create merged images with less user interaction.

Choosing any of these options will result directly in a multilayer stitched image. Choosing Interactive Layout will, instead, open a new window, shown in Figure 13.5.

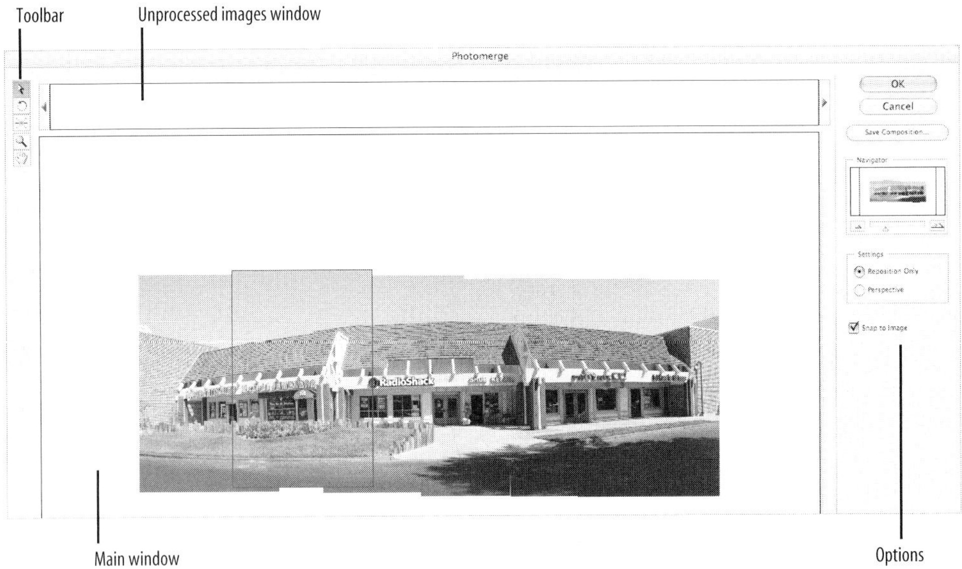

Figure 13.5 The interactive layout in Photoshop CS3 is very similar to that in Photoshop CS2 and enables the user to drag unprocessed images into the layout, reposition images in the layout, and correct for perspective issues.

The Photomerge window has four main sections: the toolbar, the unprocessed image window, the main window, and some optional settings.

When the images are brought into Photomerge, Photoshop attempts to automatically place and align them in the main window.

Choose the Select Image tool on the toolbar to reposition any misplaced or misaligned images by clicking and dragging them into position. The Rotate icon will rotate images, and the Zoom and Hand tools are for navigating in the image. The Photomerge Vanishing Point tool provides some perspective capabilities.

If Photoshop was unable to determine the proper placement of any images, they are placed in the Unprocessed Image window; from there, the user can place them manually. To do so, simply click any images in this window and drag and drop them into place in the main window.

The Options section offers several controls to make adjustments to the image. The Perspective button corrects perspective issues, and the Advanced Blending check box (in Photoshop CS2) will improve the blending of the image. There is no Advanced Blending in Photoshop CS3's window because advanced masking will automatically be applied with this feature.

As can be seen in Figure 13.6, selecting the Perspective button corrects for the perspective distortion in the image caused by the frames on the end being at a greater distance from the camera.

Figure 13.6 The image after applying the Perspective button

Clicking OK then completes the process, and the full resolution image will be opened in Photoshop.

When the image is opened in Photoshop, it can be cropped to the subject and to eliminate the ragged edges, as shown in Figure 13.7.

Figure 13.7 Applying a crop to the completed Photomerge

To crop the image, select the Crop tool in the toolbar by clicking it or by pressing the C key. Click and drag the cursor to the area desired, and press the Enter/Return key to complete the crop.

The image can now be saved or prepared for printing.

Summary

In many applications in forensics, combining multiple images can be a useful tool. The sample image in this chapter illustrates by using a large scene that was photographed in sections to provide a wide perspective image with high resolution. In confined locations (bathroom, walk-in closet, storage room), you can stitch images to show a floor-to-ceiling view.

The advantage of this feature is that a detective, prosecutor, examiner, or juror can see the entire object or scene in the full image area as well see the fine detail in separate photographs.

III

Image Analysis and Enhancement

This section deals with methods for working with image in a comparative analysis workflow. Frequently, an image may not natively show all of the detail that it contains. Clarifying this detail can improve the way in which the image is displayed and make analysis more effective.

The techniques in this section include methods for precise sizing of an image and for measuring objects in an image. We'll look at most of the adjustments you'll typically need to make—changes to color, blur, and even image defects such as lens barrel distortion—and at printing.

14 Compositing Images

There are several ways to combine images for different purposes. In Chapter 12 we looked at methods for combining multiple images into a court chart, and in Chapter 13 we looked at combining a sequence of images to create a single, high-resolution image. Chapter 23 includes a section on combining images to reduce image noise. In this chapter, we will look at how we can combine multiple photographs of the same image to show differences in lighting in the images.

Chapter Contents

When to Composite Images

The primary application for this technique is to show a well-lit scene or object with a laser bullet trajectory or to show a piece of evidence with a fluorescing stain.

Typically, photographs of fluorescing stains or laser trajectories have very dark backgrounds because of the need to show the laser or fluorescence. To show the scene or object under "normal" lighting requires a second photograph.

By combining the images, you can see the overall scene or object and the fluorescence or laser in the same image. With film, this could be done in the darkroom, by exposing a sheet of photographic paper with two negatives—one of the overall object or scene and one of the fluorescence or laser. However, this can be difficult because the two images must be exactly aligned and the two print exposures must be made by trial and error.

Information from multiple images can become important in a case when you need to show the exact position or size of a fluorescing stain in a crime scene, the exact position or size of a fluorescing bodily fluid on an object, the exact path of a bullet trajectory in a scene, and so on.

In Figure 14.1, the overall scene is the top-left image, the bullet trajectory is the bottom-left image, and the image on the right shows the combined information from them both. This allows us to see the scene in full illumination and see the bullet trajectory in the same image.

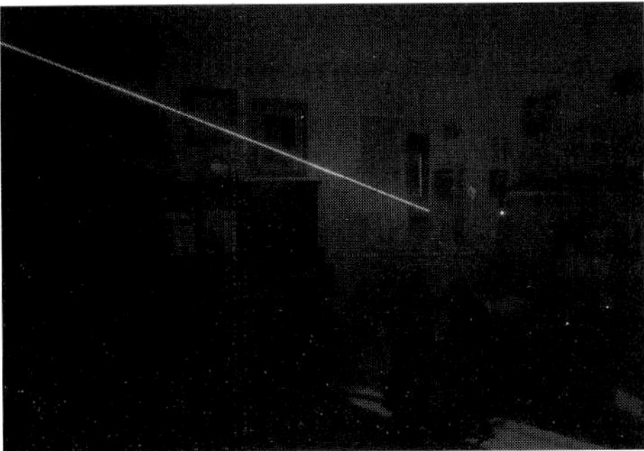

Figure 14.1 On the left are the two original images, with the combined image on the right, showing the effect of the Lighten mode.

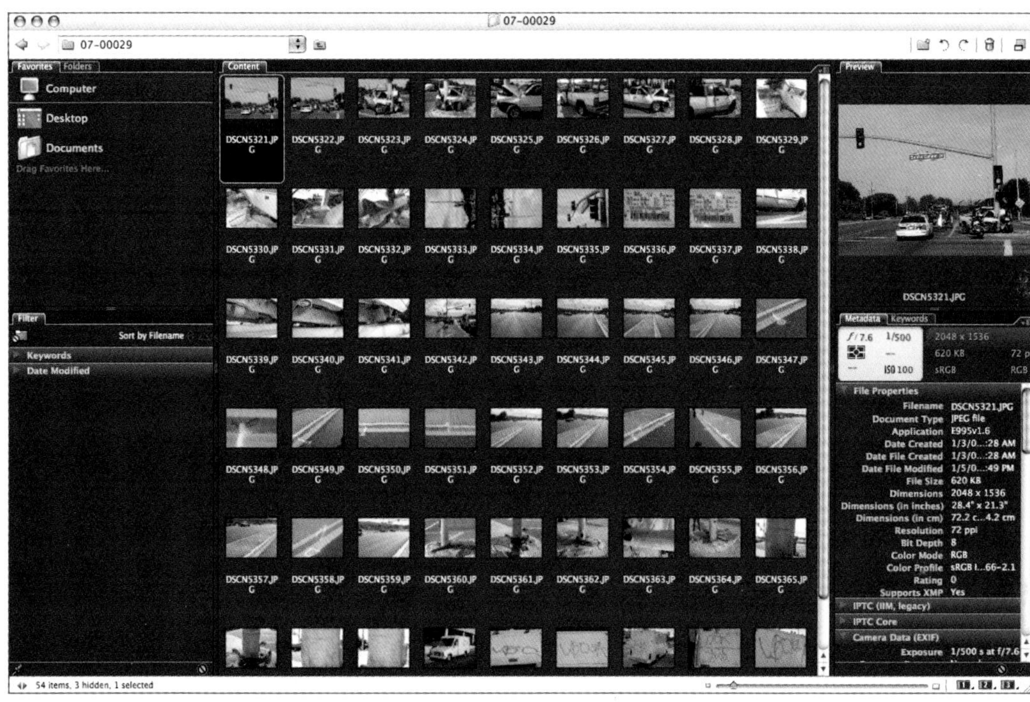

When Bridge is set to display high-quality thumbnails, the thumbnails and the preview image show accurate color.

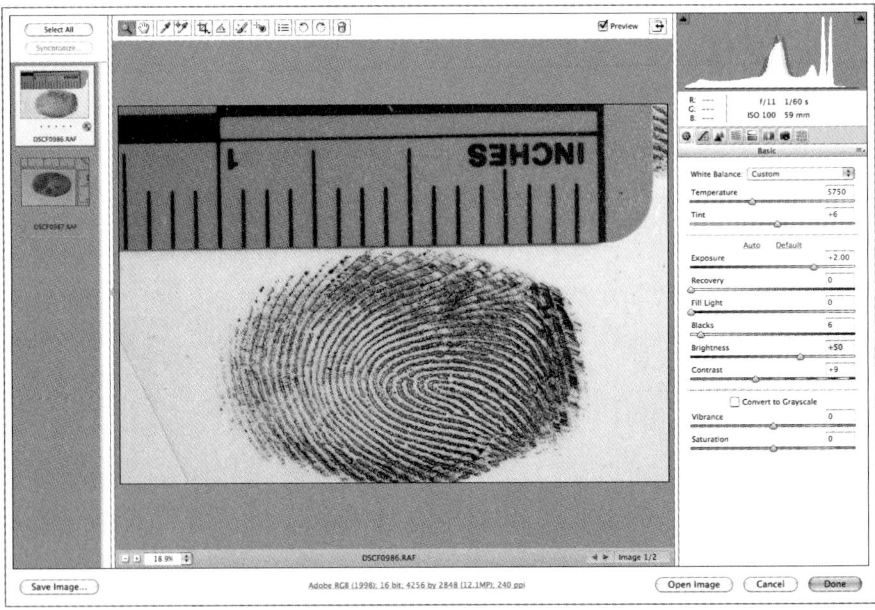

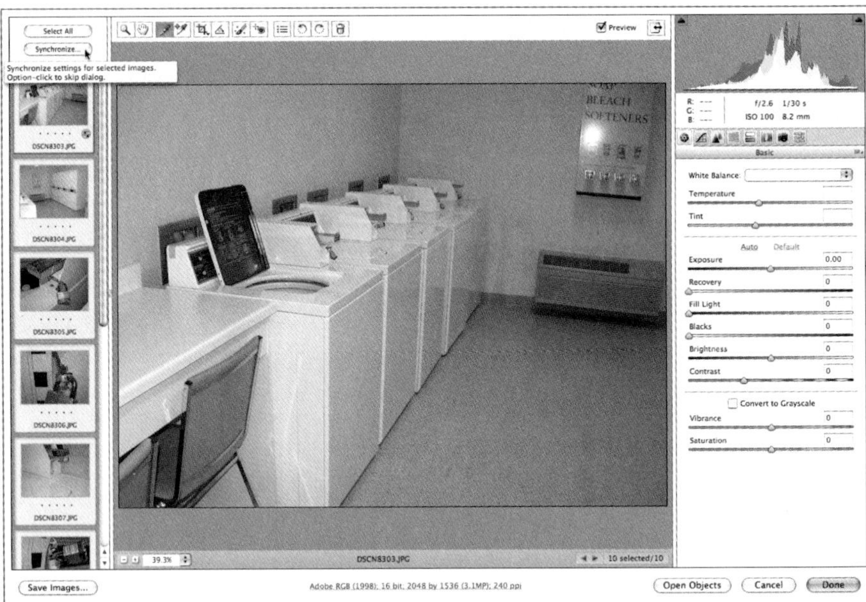

Adobe Photoshop Camera Raw provides a high-quality preview image. The thumbnail images are updated as adjustments are made, with uncorrected images displaying their default values. The histogram displays the pixel values of each color channel.

Bridge's filmstrip view will display very large, high-quality preview images when the preference is set to display high-quality thumbnails.

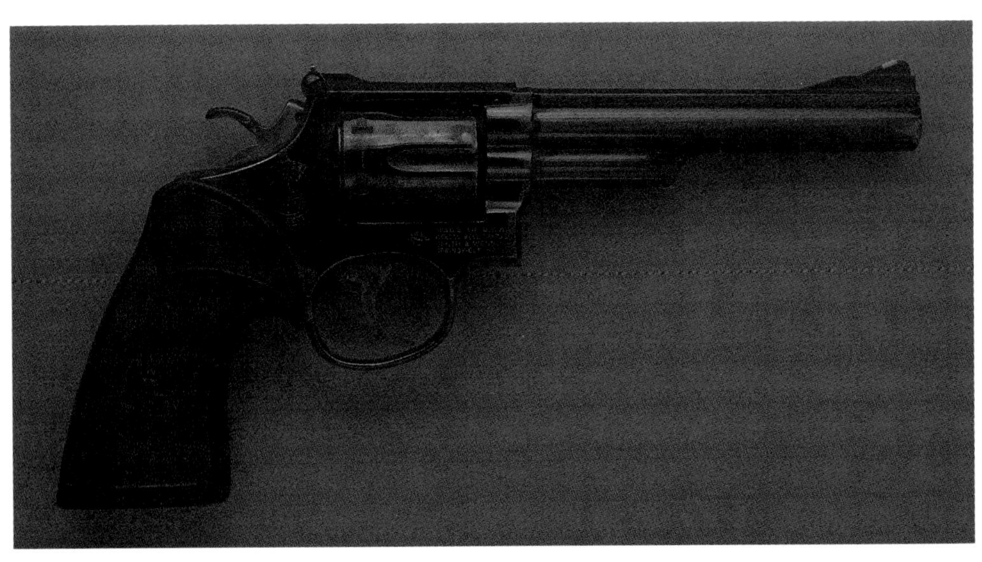

MADE IN U.S.A
SMITH & WESSON

Adjustments to brightness, contrast, and color can be quite dramatic. Each of these pairs illustrates an image with exposure and/or color shift issues and the corrected version.

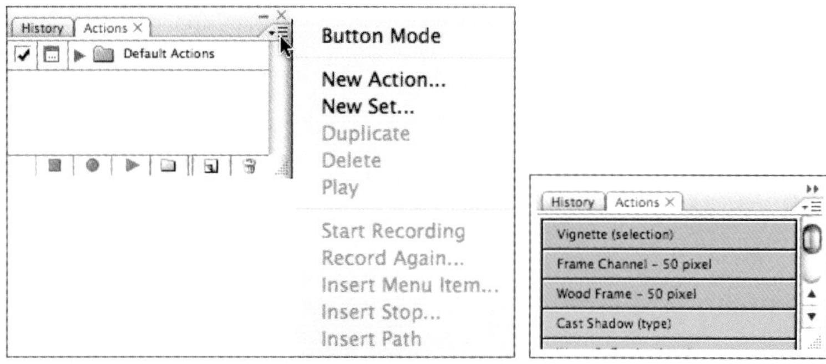

With the Actions palette in Button mode (top right), you can make use of colors to separate different types of actions—for instance, actions for fingerprint enhancement can be one color, actions for video enhancement another, and actions for printing can be a third color.

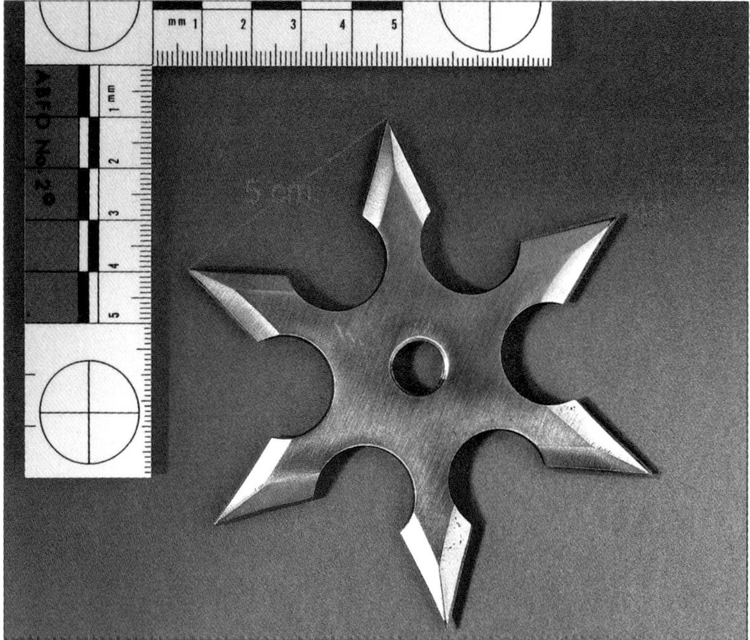

Using a contrasting color for text and lines makes it easy to identify the areas marked on this image. Because these annotations are on separate layers, the visibility can be turned off to show only the photo.

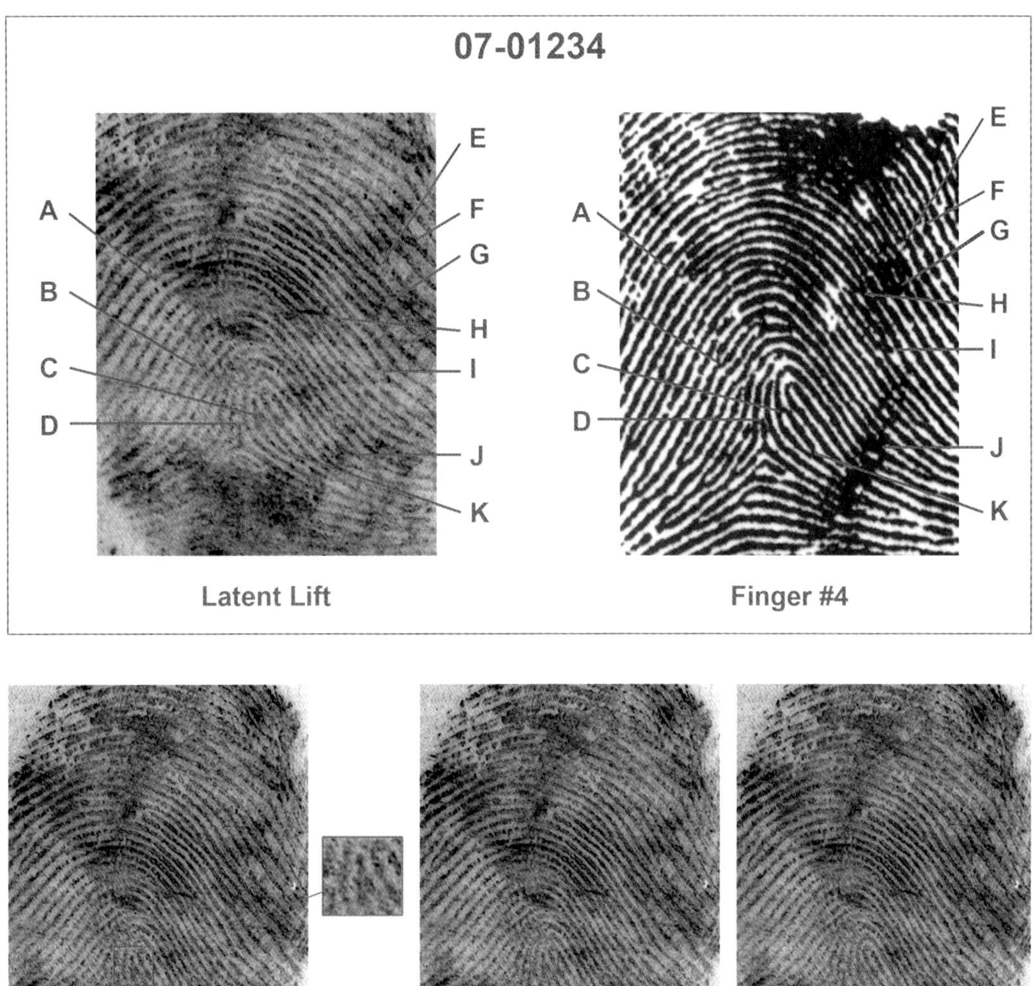

Top: A typical court chart showing a fingerprint comparison. **Bottom:** Various methods that can be used in static court charts (from left, magnification, highlight, and ridge tracing).

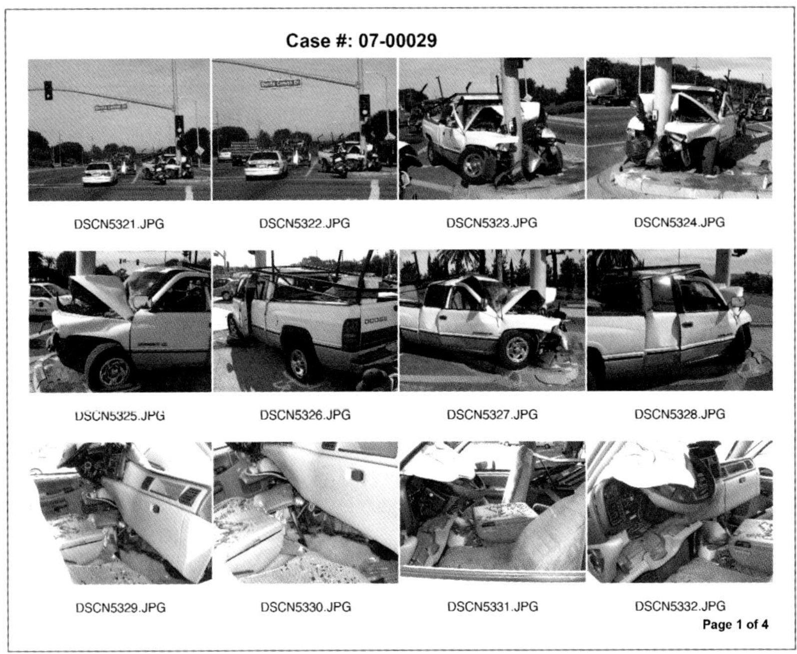

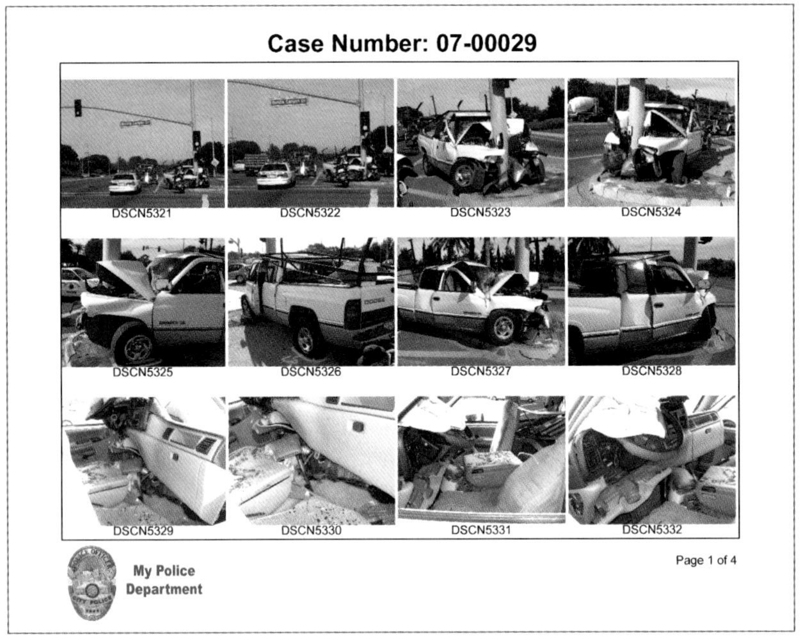

The top image shows a contact sheet using Photoshop's built-in contact sheet tool; the bottom image shows a contact sheet made with the Contact Sheet X script that is included on the companion CD.

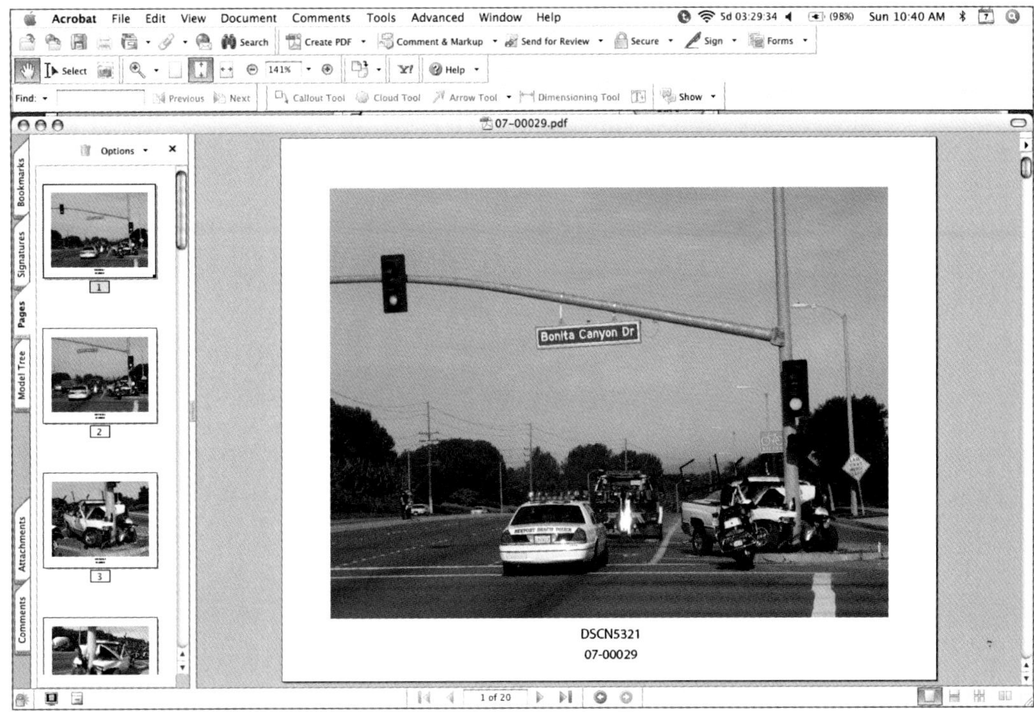

PDF Presentation creates a multipage PDF document that can be opened in Adobe Acrobat Reader. The Acrobat window can be organized to show thumbnails representing each page.

Single shot

Multiple shots for Photomerge

Completed Photomerge

The illustration on this page shows a single photo of this shopping center taken with a wide-angle lens, the six photos used to make a panorama, and the completed panorama made using Photoshop's Photomerge feature. The image on the opposite page compares the resolution from the single wide-angle photo to the same area from the panorama.

Cropped area from single frame

Cropped area from Photomerge

Using the Lighten blend mode in layers will only display the lightest pixel in a given spot. In this illustration, the laser trajectory image is copied and pasted as a new layer onto the living room photo. The layer blend mode is set to Lighten, which displays the lightest pixel in each pixel position—showing the living room and the laser trajectory.

The Lens Correction filter can correct the barrel distortion of wide-angle lenses, as shown here with the original image on top and the corrected image on bottom.

Removing noise in a single image will always be a compromise between the amount of noise removed and the amount of detail retained. If there is substantial color noise, using a method to remove only the color noise can retain more sharpness than removing all noise.

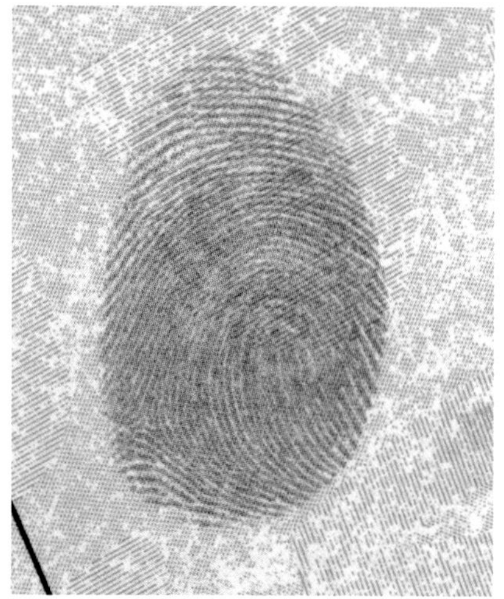

Color isolation techniques can be used to subdue or enhance objects in an image to show details better. In the fingerprint image, this technique can eliminate the green security printing to make the fingerprint easier to see. In the endorsement signature, the purple endorsement printing can be greatly reduced to separate the signature from the background.

Photoshop can be used to work with video images as well as still images. The top image illustrates images that need to be deinterlaced. On the bottom is an example of frame averaging within Photoshop.

Photographing the Scene

The first step for combining images of this type is to properly do the photography. Two exposures need to be taken—one for the laser or fluorescing stain, the other for the overall scene or object.

These exposures must be made on a tripod, copy stand, or other stable surface so neither the camera nor the subject moves between exposures. If photographing stains on clothing, do not reposition the clothing between exposures. When the two images are merged, they must be in alignment for best results.

Both photographs must be properly exposed. The overall scene or object must be exposed to show the scene or object as it appears under "normal" lighting. It is important not to overexpose this image or it may be impossible to see the fluorescence or laser from the other photograph. Bracketing your exposures can help guarantee that you'll have images that work well for this technique. The photograph of the stain or laser should be made so that the stain or laser has very bright values and the rest of the subject is subdued.

Combining the Images

Open both images in Photoshop, and tile them so that they either overlap or are next to each other on your monitor. The steps to combine them will be simply to copy one onto the other and change the layer mode to show only the lightest pixels from each image.

To combine the two images, one of the images can be copied and pasted or dragged onto the other.

- To copy and paste, select one image by clicking on it or its title bar, choose Edit > Select All or press Ctrl+A/Cmd+A, then copy it by choosing Edit > Copy or pressing Ctrl+C/Cmd+C. Select the other image and paste by choosing Edit > Paste or pressing Ctrl+V/Cmd+V.
- To copy by dragging and dropping, first select the Move tool by clicking it on the toolbar or by pressing the V key. Click one image to select it, click and drag it until your cursor is over the second image (Figure 14.2), then press the Shift key and release the mouse. Pressing the Shift key will center the image that is being copied; otherwise, it may be placed out of alignment and need to be moved into place.

Once one of the images has been copied onto the other, you will see that the resulting image has two layers, as shown in Figure 14.3. The bottom layer is the original scene image, and the second layer is the pasted image of the laser in this example. Because this layer is set to 100 percent opacity and its visibility is on, we cannot see the data from the bottom layer.

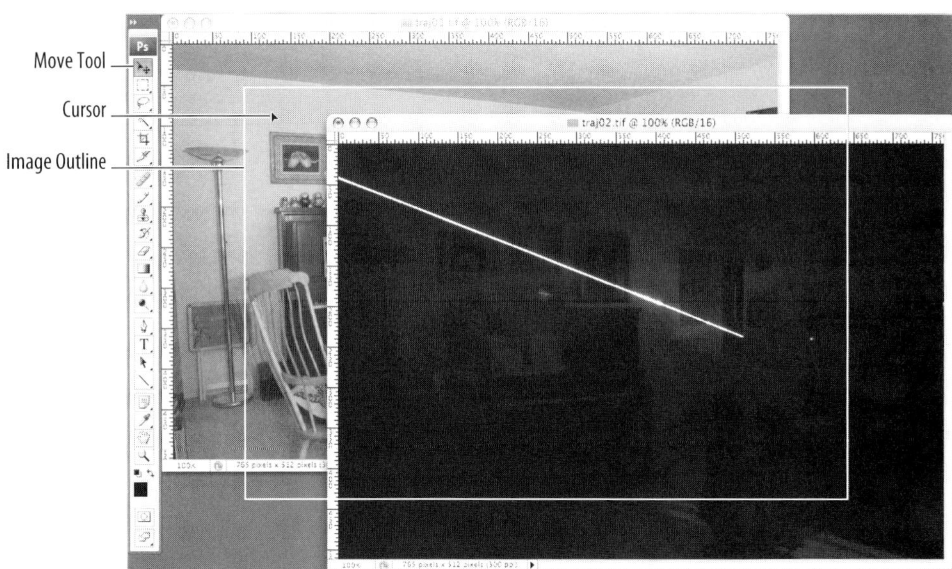

Figure 14.2 One image needs to be pasted onto the other. One method is to simply drag and drop the image using the Move tool, as shown here.

Figure 14.3 After one image is copied onto the other, the Layers palette shows that the image now has two layers, with only the top layer visible in the image.

Our next step is to see the brightest pixels from each image, which will show the laser from the top layer and the overall scene from the bottom layer.

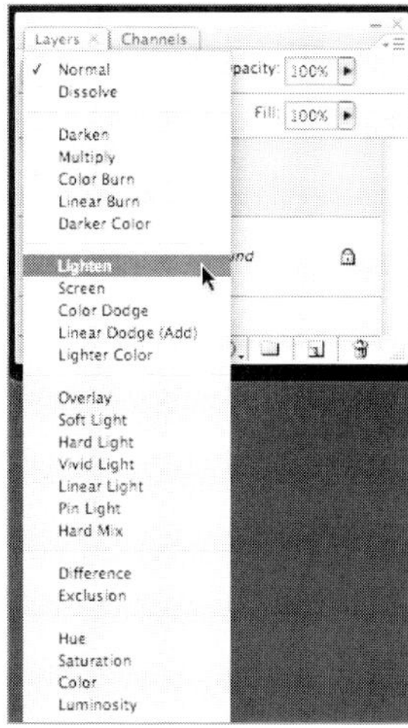

Figure 14.4 Choose the Lighten mode from the pop-up menu in the Layers palette to show only the lightest pixel in any position.

To combine the images to see only the lightest pixel from each layer, click the Mode pop-up menu and choose Lighten. Now the image should show the full scene or object with the dye, stain, or laser also fully visible.

Summary

Combining images to show more than can be seen with a single exposure can be important in many instances. Using layer modes to show the brightest pixels from two separate layers enables an image to show an object or scene as well as a laser light or fluorescing stain. This provides excellent illustrative evidence to show size or position of objects that would be otherwise difficult to illustrate.

Layer modes go beyond just this application, however. The Difference layer mode is useful in aligning multiple images and for image subtraction, the Darken mode will show only the darkest pixel at any given position, and several layer modes can be used on duplicate layers to lighten or darken an incorrectly exposed image.

The key to the application of layer modes in this chapter is to correctly expose the two images, keep the alignment the same for both (if alignment is off, the top layer can be moved with the Move tool), and then, after combining the two, simply change the mode to Lighten for the top layer.

Precise Image Sizing

Printing images at an exact size is a common requirement in forensics. Here are just some examples:

- *Printing enhanced fingerprints for AFIS entry*
- *Printing footwear or tire impression images for comparison*
- *Taking measurements in blood spatter images*

The method you will use to make your images exactly 1:1 (or any exact size) in Photoshop is relatively easy but not very intuitive. This chapter will step through the process for making an image 1:1, 3:1, or any other exact size.

Chapter Contents

Viewing Images at the Proper Magnification

When you're doing any critical work, it is essential that the image is displayed at a screen magnification that will not introduce any frequency interference, such as 50, 100, or 200 percent. The magnification amount can be viewed in the image title bar (Figure 15.1).

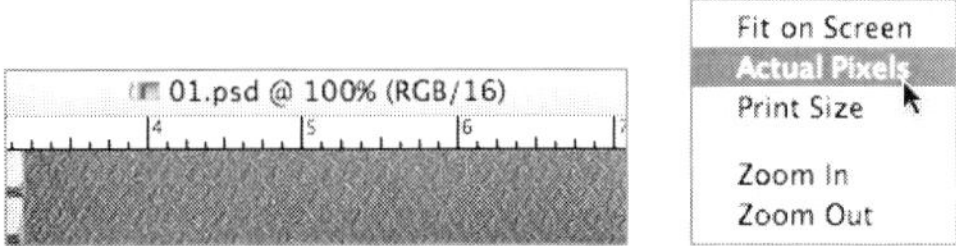

Figure 15.1 On the left is the image title bar showing the image magnification. On the right is the contextual menu for the Zoom tool.

If the image is not displayed at 100 percent, zoom into it to view at 100 percent (or a factor or multiple of 100). A quick way to display an image at 100 percent is to select the Zoom tool, right-click/Control-click, and choose Actual Pixels from the contextual menu. Or, simply click with the Zoom tool to increase the magnification, and Alt/Option+click to reduce the magnification.

Verify that Photoshop's rulers are visible on the top and left sides of the image (Figure 15.2). If the rulers are not visible, choose View > Rulers or press Ctrl+R/Cmd+R.

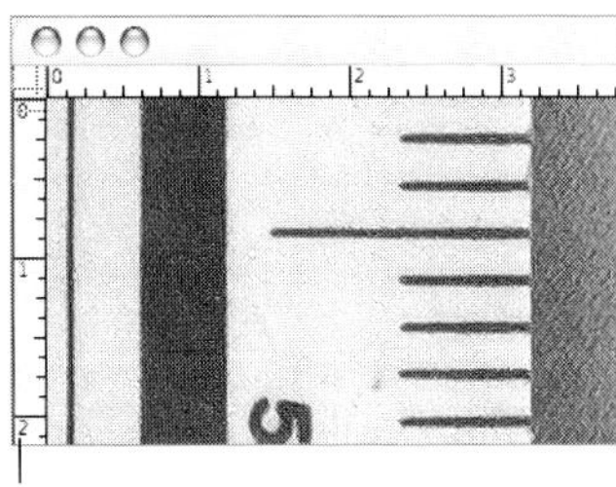

Photoshop's rulers

Figure 15.2 Photoshop's rulers are visible on the left and top of the image window.

The rulers may display units in pixels, inches, centimeters, millimeters, points, picas, or percent. You can change this setting by right-clicking/Control-clicking in the ruler area itself (Figure 15.3). The units should be in pixels; if they aren't, right-click/Control-click in the ruler area and select Pixels from the contextual menu.

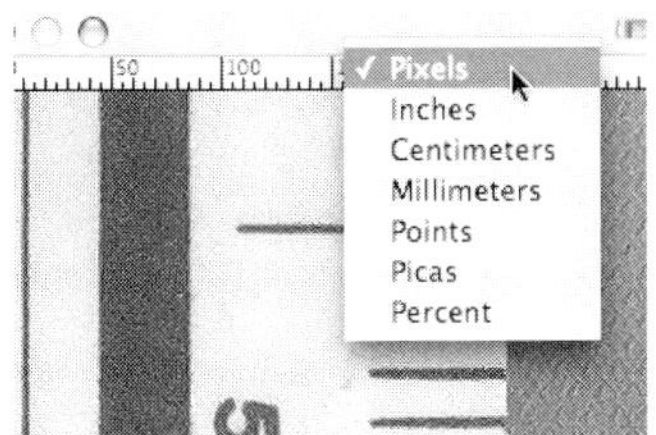

Figure 15.3 Right-click/Control-click in Photoshop's ruler area to bring up the contextual menu to choose Pixels as the unit.

You can also change Photoshop's rulers to pixels in the Units And Rulers Preferences panel. Choose Edit > Preferences > Units And Rulers (Windows) or Photoshop > Preferences > Units And Rulers (Mac OS) and choose the appropriate setting. The advantage to using this method is that it can be recorded as an action, but it can't if you use the contextual menu method.

Photographing for Accurate Measurement

For any image to be accurately sized, it is essential that a few general rules are followed:

- The object should be photographed with a ruler in the image.
- The object and the ruler should be on the same plane.
- The plane of the object and the focal plane of the camera should be parallel.
- Or, more simply, the ruler and subject should be on the same flat surface and at the same angle as the camera.

Following these three criteria is essential if one is to achieve the best results for precisely sizing an image.

Calibrating Image Size

To calibrate an image, you must measure a known distance within the image and enter the data from this measurement into the Image Size dialog box.

For this image, we will measure a length of 1 centimeter on the ruler. Zoom in tightly with the Zoom tool to display a 1-centimeter length in the ruler (Figure 15.4). Zooming provides more accurate placement of the Measure tool, providing a more precise result. The zoom magnification percentage should be an exact multiple of 100 (e.g., 200, 300, 400, and so on) to prevent frequency interference artifacts in the image.

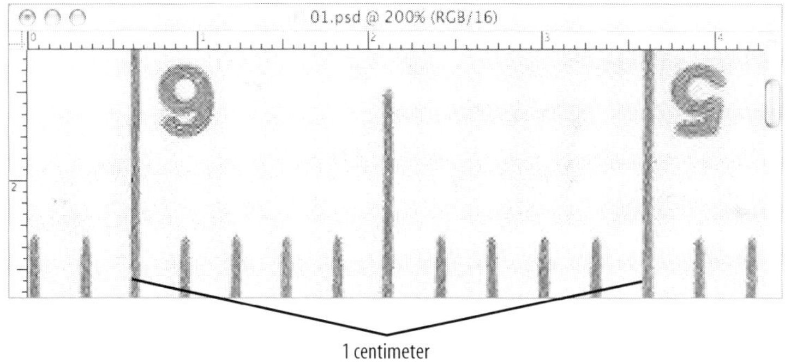

Figure 15.4 One centimeter on the ruler starts and ends on the same position of the ruler line as shown here.

Now select the Measure tool (it is in the same place as the Eyedropper tool and in CS3 is now named the Ruler tool). With the Measure tool selected, click and draw a line the length of 1 centimeter along the ruler in the photo, as shown in Figure 15.5. If the line you draw with the Measure tool begins on the right edge of a ruler mark, the end of the line should also be on the right side of the ruler mark. The angle of the ruler is unimportant—that is, it doesn't have to be parallel to a side of your image, although it does need to be on the same plane as your subject and parallel to your camera back.

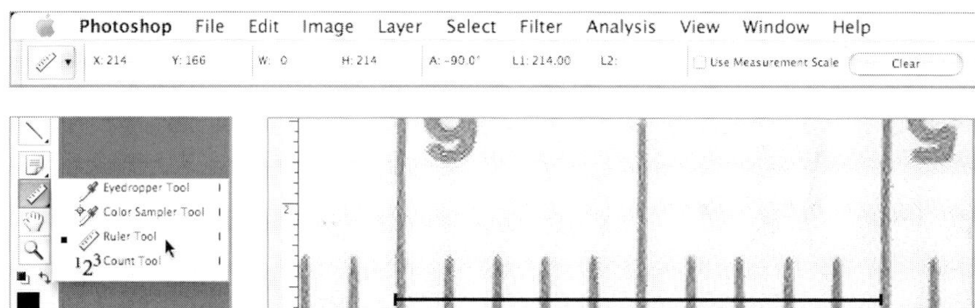

Figure 15.5 On the left is the Measure tool (the Ruler tool in Photoshop CS3); at the top are the tool options, and on the bottom right is the line drawn with the tool. Note that the measurement starts and ends on the same side of the ruler lines.

The distance measured in this example is 1 centimeter, but it is also a certain number of pixels. This distance, in pixels, is displayed in the Measure tool options bar as L1 in CS3 and D1 in earlier versions of Photoshop. In CS3, be sure to uncheck the Use Measurement Scale box so that the value in L1 will be based on the unit set for Photoshop's rulers.

The distance displayed as the L1 or D1 value will need to be entered in the Image Size dialog box in the Pixels/Centimeter field. In this example, my measurement shows 214, and that is the value I will enter (Figure 15.6). To access the Image Size dialog box, choose Image > Image Size. There are three settings to make in the Image Size dialog box, as shown in Figure 15.6. First, uncheck the Resample box; this retains the full image quality by not changing the number of pixels in the image. Next, set the Resolution units of measurement pop-up menu to pixels/inch or pixels/cm, depending on the units of the ruler in the photo. Last, enter the L1 or D1 value in the Resolution text box. In this example, I have changed the resolution units to pixels/cm and entered 214 in the Resolution text box. Click OK and the image will print 1:1.

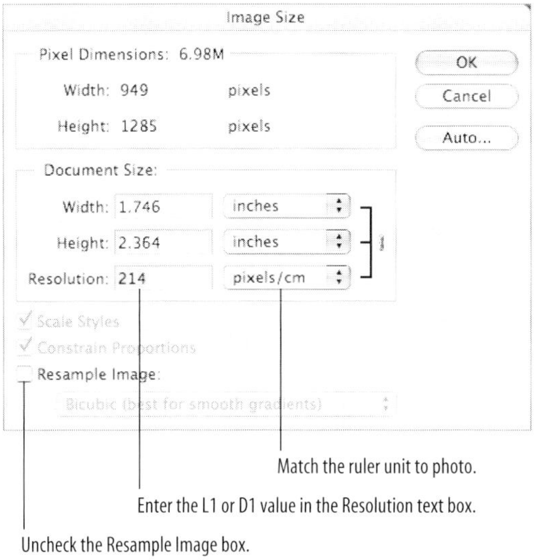

Match the ruler unit to photo.

Enter the L1 or D1 value in the Resolution text box.

Uncheck the Resample Image box.

Figure 15.6 Changing the resolution setting in the Image Size dialog box

This process was nondestructive in that no pixel resampling was done. That is, the image has the same number of pixels now as it did when it was opened—it simply will now be described to the printer differently. This image is also calibrated so that you can make measurements of objects in the image as described in Chapter 16.

Now the image is sized exactly 1:1. If you print it, it will print life size. If you take measurements from the image, they will be accurate. You can verify the accuracy of your calibration a couple of ways. You can print it and measure the ruler, or you can align your ruler with Photoshop's ruler for comparison, as shown in Figure 15.7. This is done by scrolling the image so that the lines of the ruler in the photograph are aligned with Photoshop's rulers. If everything was done correctly, there should be an exact correspondence between them (although the lines in the rulers may not be in the same places, the relationship and spacing should be the same).

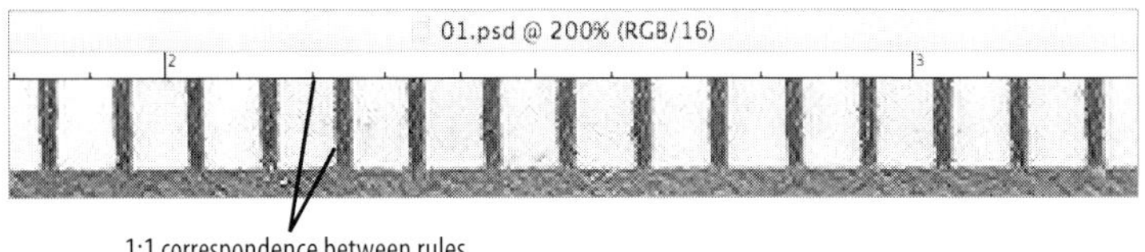

Figure 15.7 With Photoshop's rulers set to centimeters, they line up in exact proportion to the lines in the ruler in the photo, showing that this image is 1:1.

Getting the Greatest Precision

For even greater accuracy, a larger distance can be measured with the Measure tool. For instance, if 4 centimeters are visible on the ruler, more precision can be achieved if the Measure tool is drawn along 4 centimeters on the ruler. This measurement would be four times the length of measuring 1 centimeter, so the L1 or D1 value would need to be divided by four (or the number of units measured) before being entered into the Resolution text box.

For example, if you photographed a footwear impression and have a 12-inch ruler visible, measure the full 12 inches. Suppose that is 3048 pixels. Dividing 3048 by 12 gives us 254, so you would enter 254 Pixels/Inch in the Image Size dialog box.

It is also important to note that there is significant variance in the thickness and the spacing of the lines in some rulers. This can have a direct effect on the accuracy of your measurements. Replace any rulers that have significant variances in line thickness or spacing—the better your ruler, the more precise your measurements will be.

Sizing and Printing

Some images may need to be calibrated to 3:1, 5:1, or even smaller than life size, such as 1:2. In these instances, after the initial calibration, you will need to return to the Image Size dialog box. Change the unit pop-up menu to Percent and type the required percentage in the text field. For instance, type 200 to get a 2:1 or 50 for a 1:2 size image. As long as the Resample Image box is unchecked, this will change the enlargement/reduction without resampling—maintaining the full quality of the image. If this step is done with the Resample Image box checked, it will change to the desired size ratio but the image quality will be slightly affected because of the image resampling. As a general rule, the amount of resampling in this step is not likely to be visible in the print output as long as it is a minimal amount.

An image calibrated using this method can be printed to most printers without any other adjustments. Some printers, however, may require very specific output resolutions. Some mini-lab printers and some dye sublimation printers may require images to be printed at 300ppi or 500ppi, for instance. To print to such a printer and maintain the same image size, open the Image Size dialog box and check the Resample box. Now enter the proper resolution for your printer, such as 300ppi or 500ppi. The image will now be properly printed. It should be noted, however, that this resamples the image and will cause some level of image degradation. Because of this, the image should be saved prior to this step to maintain the full image quality.

It is also possible that resampling for printing to a laser printer or an ink-jet printer may give better results. Different brands and models of printers use different methods to determine how to apply toner or ink to paper. Printing might also be improved if the images are resized to 300 or 360 pixels per inch. It would be wise to print several tests to determine the best approach to printing with your specific equipment and workflow. Test files for determining optimal printer resolution are included on the companion CD. For more information on printing also see Chapter 8.

Summary

It's important in forensics to make images exactly 1:1 or calibrate them to other size ratios when you're working with fingerprints, footwear, tool marks, blood spatter, tire impressions—that is, anything for which comparisons might be needed. This simple process can be done natively in Photoshop with a great deal of precision—especially if the subject is photographed as described in this chapter.

Chapter 16 is about measuring objects in photos. The first step for that process is to calibrate the image using the technique described in this chapter.

16 Measuring Objects

If an image has been calibrated using the method described in Chapter 15, any object on the same plane as the ruler can also be measured. The two key issues are that the calibration must be done with precision and the object must be on the same plane as the ruler.

Chapter Contents

The Importance of Measurements

When an image has been calibrated, the diameter and distance between bullet holes in a wall, the size of a knife blade, or the distance between features in a tool mark or tire impression may be measured.

In addition to measurements of length, angles can be measured.

Annotations of these measurements can be made in a separate layer and used for later calculations or as part of a court display.

Note: In macro photography, if an object is only a centimeter closer to the lens than the ruler, measurements can be significantly off. That same centimeter difference in distance may not show a measurable difference in general scene photography. The rule of thumb is that the closer the objects are to the camera, the more critical it is that the ruler and subject are on the same plane.

In Figure 16.1, there are annotations to show the distance between two points on the star, the diameter of the hole in the center of the star, and the angle of one point. The steps to make the measurements and annotations areas follows:

1. Calibrate the image view using the techniques in Chapter 15.
2. Create a new layer and draw the annotations with the Line tool.
3. Use the Measure tool (in CS2) or Ruler tool (in CS3) to measure the distances and/or angles.
4. Finally, place those measurements using the Text tool.

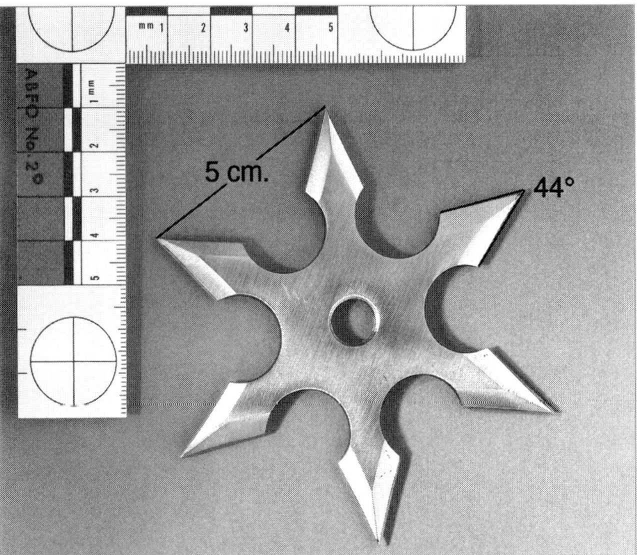

Figure 16.1 Image with measurements and annotations of length and angle.

Note: Photoshop CS3 Extended introduced some new measurement tools and functionality that enable measurements of perimeter, area, and several other values in addition to length and angle. Because this chapter only addresses length and angle measurements, only features that are in Photoshop CS3 and also in earlier versions of Photoshop are used. See the sidebar at the end of this chapter for more information on the additional measurement features in Photoshop CS3 Extended.

Annotating Images

Create a new layer by clicking the New Layer icon on the bottom of the Layers palette (Figure 16.2). This layer will hold the annotations made to the image.

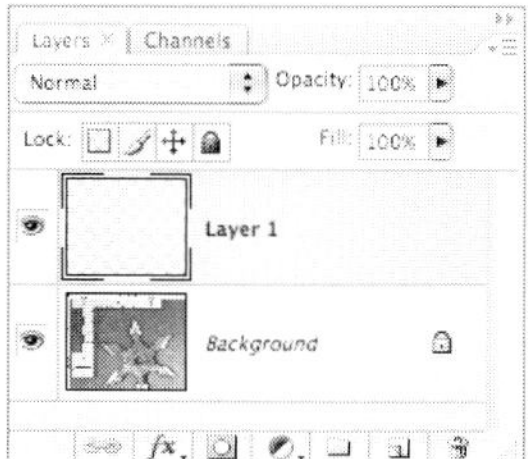

Figure 16.2 A new, blank layer can be created by clicking the New Layer icon in the Layers palette, by choosing Layer > New > Layer, or by pressing Shift+Ctrl+N/Shift+Cmd+N).

To select a color for the annotations, click a color in the Swatches palette, as shown in Figure 16.3.

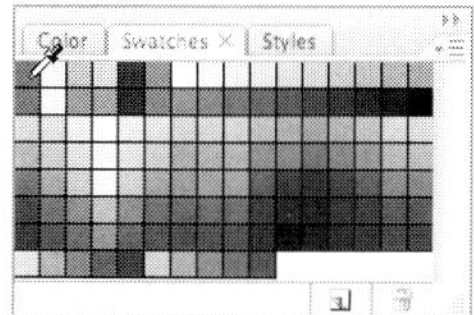

Figure 16.3 Picking a color in the Swatches palette

The next step is to draw lines to illustrate what will be measured, using the Line tool (Figure 16.4) as described back in Chapter 12 (clicking the Fill Pixels icon and setting the line weight at 4 to 6 px). It is important to draw lines as accurately as possible and not to obscure the underlying image. One method to accomplish this is to set the opacity of this layer to something less than 100 percent so that the background layer can be seen through annotation lines. To reduce the opacity of a layer, select that layer in the Layers palette and click and drag on the word Opacity or enter a percentage value in the Opacity field. I did not do that in this example to make it easier to see my lines in the printed book.

Figure 16.4 Setting the Line tool so lines don't interfere with the image

Measuring Objects

After drawing these lines with the Line tool as described earlier, select the Ruler/Measure tool and draw measurement lines representing the distance measured, as shown in Figure 16.5. The lines drawn with the Ruler/Measure tool are used for measuring objects, but they do not print, which is why we made our annotations in the previous section. The distance of the line drawn with the Ruler/Measure tool is shown as the L1/D1 value in the Ruler/Measure tool options (L1 in Photoshop CS3 and D1 in earlier versions).

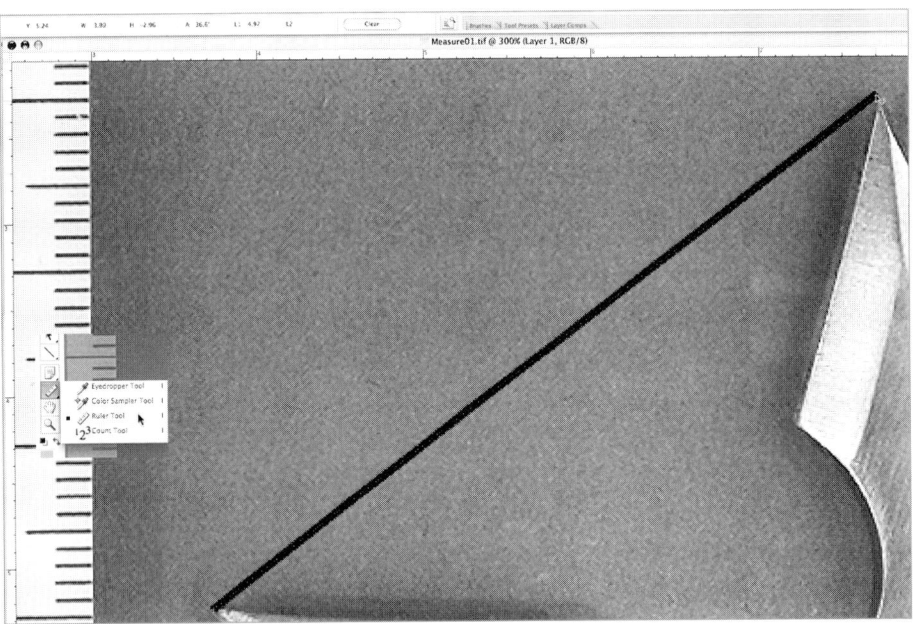

Figure 16.5 Draw with the Ruler/Measure tool over the line drawn with the Line tool.

To get the value for an angle, draw a line with the Ruler/Measure tool along one edge of the object (Figure 16.6), then lift up on the mouse, press and hold the Alt/Option key, click the mouse button again, and continue drawing the second line with the Ruler/Measure tool. The value for the Angle is displayed as the A value in the Ruler/Measure tool options.

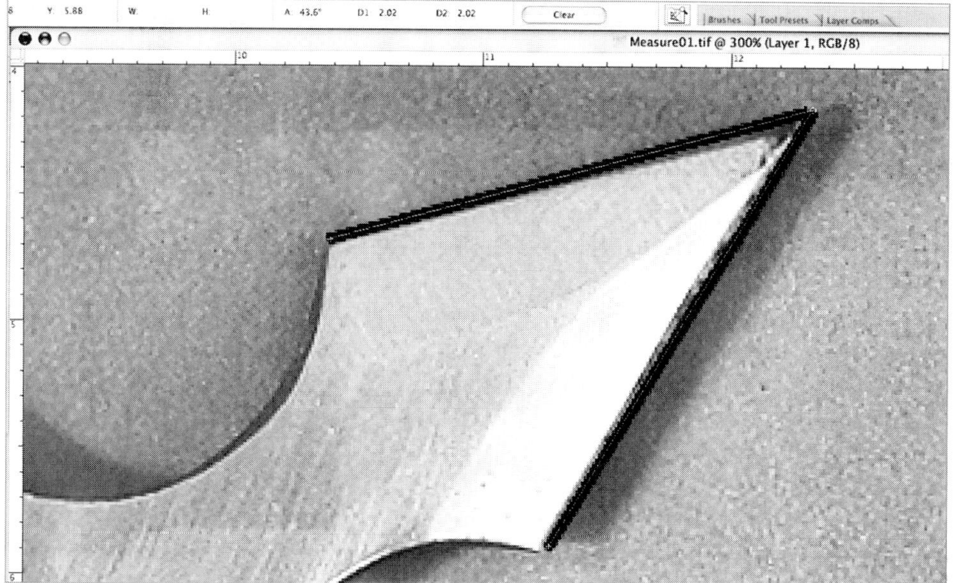

Figure 16.6 To measure an angle, Alt/Option+click at the end of the first line before continuing with the line forming the second part of the angle.

The next step is to choose the Text tool and type the values for the measurements made, as shown in Figure 16.7. If the text covers a line, that can be fixed later—it is important to place the text where you want it placed.

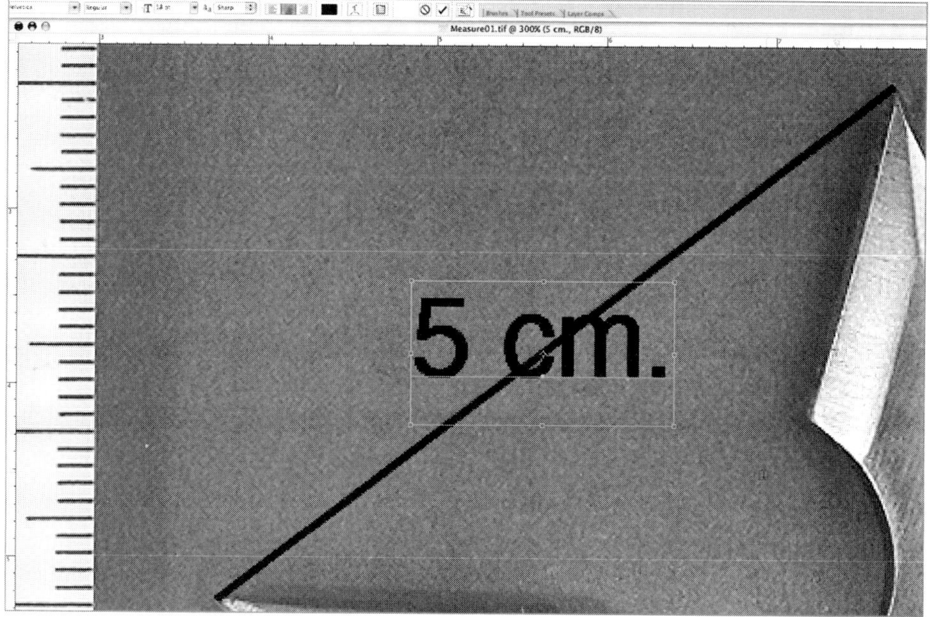

Figure 16.7 Type the distance with the Text tool.

As shown in Figure 16.8, to delete any section of the line that appears under text, choose the layer that has the lines, and with the Marquee tool, select the area to be deleted and press the Delete key on the keyboard.

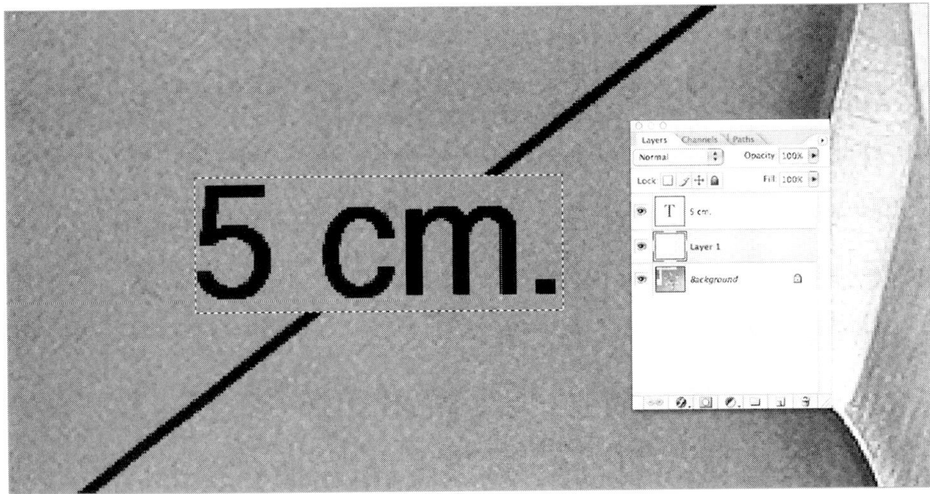

Figure 16.8 By selecting the annotation layer, you can delete the line where it intersects with the text.

Grouping Layers

If several items were annotated and text added, the total number of layers in the image can be significant. Multiple layers can be grouped together as shown in Figure 16.9. This places them into a single folder in the Layers palette. To combine the annotation layer with the text layers, click the topmost layer, hold the Shift key down, and then click the lowest layer that should be included in the group. Click the flyout menu and choose New Group from Layer. The new group can then be renamed by double-clicking its name and typing in a new name such as Annotation Layers.

Grouping layers in this way gives organization to the image, and it also makes it easy to control the visibility of multiple layers in a court exhibit or for printing multiple versions of the image (one with and one without the annotation, for instance). The more complex the image, the more important this becomes. In questioned document analysis, for example, a single image may include dozens of writing samples with separate annotations for different groups—the ability to control visibility of each group separately can make it much easier to keep focus on each separate sample while presenting this evidence in court.

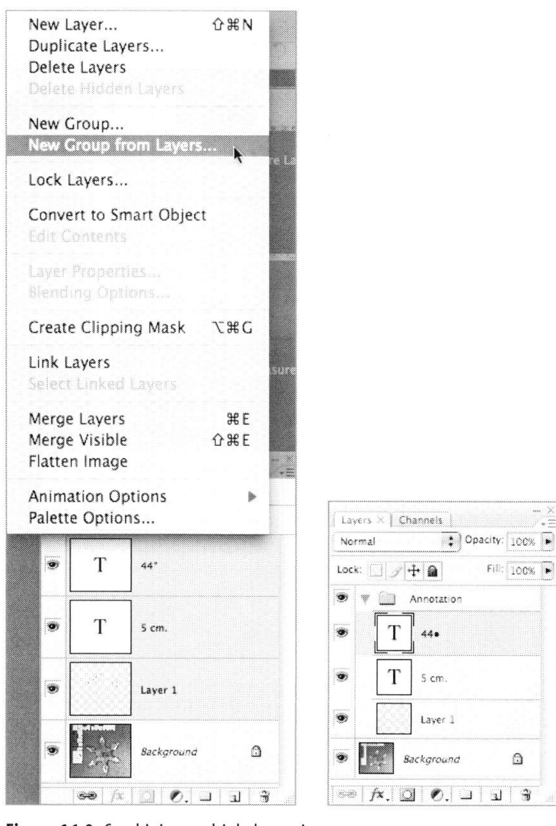

Figure 16.9 Combining multiple layers into a group

Photoshop CS3 Extended Measurement Features

The Extended version of Photoshop CS3 has added an Analysis menu item, a Measurement Log palette, and a Count tool.

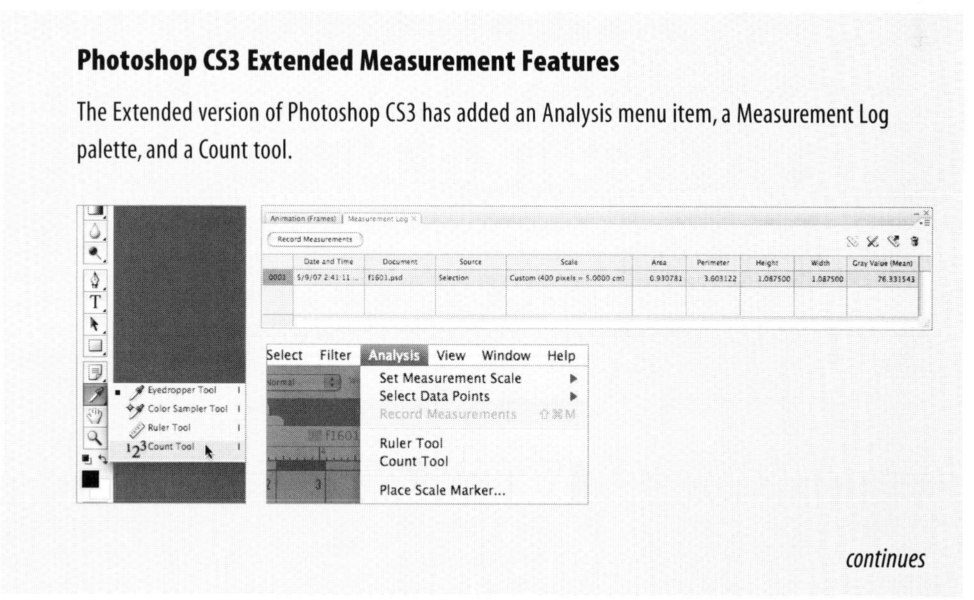

continues

Photoshop CS3 Extended Measurement Features *(continued)*

The Count tool is used to mark features on an image, such as Galton points on a fingerprint. Select the Count tool from the toolbar and click where you wish to place a point. Each click will produce a new dot with a sequential number beginning with the number 1. The color of the label can be changed by clicking on the color swatch in the options bar. Clicking the Clear button will delete all count labels. Clicking and dragging on an existing point will move it.

The Analysis menu works with the Measurement Log palette to calibrate an image and to make a variety of measurements including height, width, perimeter, diameter, area, gray value, and more. The measurements can be based on a selection or on a line drawn with the Ruler tool.

To calibrate an image, choose Analysis > Set Measurement Scale > Custom. This opens the Measurement Scale dialog box, in which you can manually enter data for a pixel length, logical length and logical units.

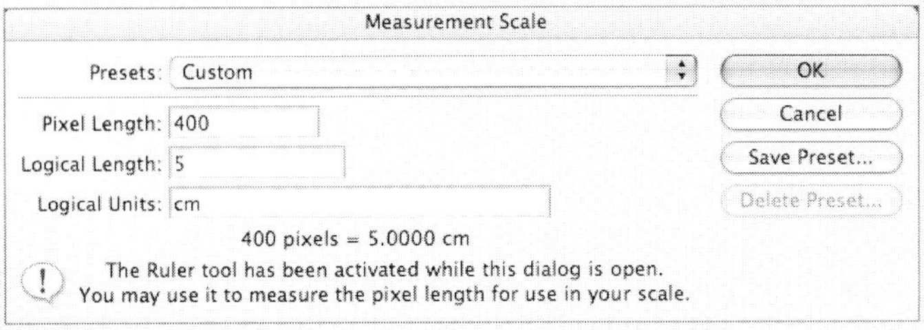

Measurement Scale
Presets: Custom
Pixel Length: 400
Logical Length: 5
Logical Units: cm
400 pixels = 5.0000 cm
The Ruler tool has been activated while this dialog is open.
You may use it to measure the pixel length for use in your scale.
OK
Cancel
Save Preset...
Delete Preset...

You can also partially automate this process using the Ruler tool. To do this, draw a length with the Ruler tool of a known distance, 5 cm, for example. The pixel value of this line is automatically entered in the Pixel Length field. Enter the length drawn in the Logical Length field (5 in this example) and the scale unit in the Logical Unit field (cm in this example) and click OK. This calibrates the image for additional measurements but not for printing. To calibrate an image for printing, use the method described in this chapter.

You can now draw a line with the Ruler tool or make a selection with any of the selection tools and make a measurement. First, open the Measurement Log palette by selecting Window > Measurement Log. Selecting Select Data Points > Custom from the menu or from the Measurement Log flyout menu provides a list of measurements that can be made. Check the boxes for the features to measure and dismiss the dialog box by checking OK. Last, click the Record Measurements button in the Measurement Log palette and the measurements will be displayed as shown in the screen shot earlier in this sidebar.

Summary

There are many instances when it may be important to measure objects in images—whether as simple as measuring the length of a knife blade or as complex as showing the angles of each droplet in a blood spatter photograph. With a calibrated image (as described in Chapter 15) and using Photoshop's Ruler/Measure tool, lengths of objects and angles can be easily measured and annotated in a text layer.

It is important to note that the precision of the measurements are dependent on the resolution of the image—measurements from a 3 megapixel photo of a footwear impression will not have as much precision as measurements from an image at a higher resolution (all other things being equal).

17 Distortion Correction

Several types of image distortion can affect the appearance of your photographs. The two most common are barrel distortion from wide-angle lenses and perspective distortion from photographing an object at an oblique angle. Because these are so common, we often mentally correct for these when viewing photographs.

This chapter primarily addresses the issue of wide-angle lens distortion, with a discussion of the issues of perspective distortion at the end of the chapter.

Chapter Contents

The Limits of Distortion Correction

Wide-angle lenses are quite common and are often the default focal length in point-and-shoot-style cameras. Barrel distortion appears as curved objects in the edges of the images and can make straight lines appear to be curved.

A number of third-party plug-ins for Photoshop have enabled the correction of lens distortion, and Photoshop has included this capability without the need for a plug-in beginning with CS2.

It should be noted that this process is destructive—meaning that it changes the pixel values in the image. I generally work on a duplicate layer with destructive processes so that the original image data can be compared with the results of processing on two layers of the same image.

As with all processes used in image analysis, all work should be done on a copy of the original. It is also recommended that the History Log be set to record all adjustments made to the image. See Chapter 1 for more information about using a valid forensic workflow.

Correcting Wide-Angle Distortion

In the sample images in Figure 17.1, you can see the curved edges in the original image and then the corrected view. This feature enables you to create preset corrections and then apply them to images individually or to multiple images in a Photoshop action.

Figure 17.1 The original image on the left shows obvious barrel distortion, which has been corrected with the Lens Correction filter.

The first step is to photograph a test chart with a specific camera and lens combination to create the preset that you will later apply to your images. I created a test chart in Photoshop, printed it, then photographed it with my Fuji S2 camera using an 18–35mm lens at the 18mm focal length.

With the test chart open, choose Filter > Distort > Lens Correction (Figure 17.2). This will open the image into the Lens Correction filter and allow you to make several adjustments. This filter allows you to correct barrel distortion, pincushion distortion (from telephoto lenses), lateral chromatic aberration, lens vignetting, and perspective distortion. This chapter covers only the lens distortion correction features.

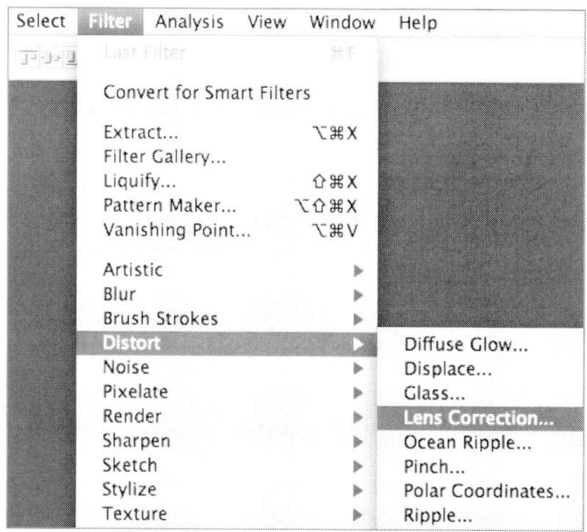

Figure 17.2 The Lens Correction filter is available, in Photoshop CS2 and CS3, from the Distort submenu in the Filter menu.

The Lens Correction window (Figure 17.3) displays the image on the left side of the window, a toolbar in the upper-left corner, preview and grid options on the bottom, and the adjustment tools on the right side.

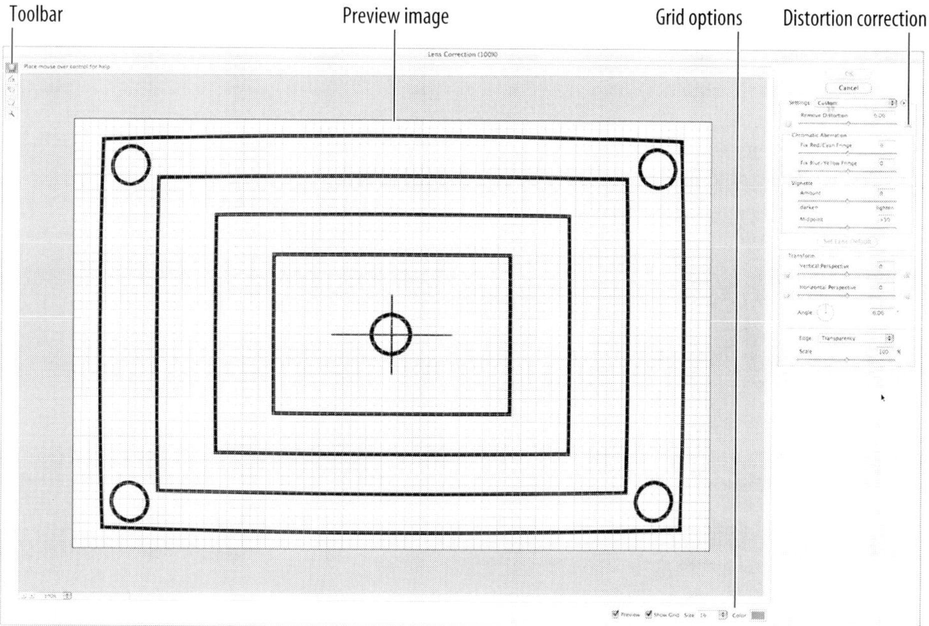

Figure 17.3 The Lens Distortion window provides tools for correcting distortion as well as chromatic aberration and perspective distortion.

The toolbar has a Straighten tool to straighten an image, a Zoom tool to magnify the image on the screen, a Hand tool for navigation, and a Hand tool to move the grid.

The Preview toggle changes the view between the original image and the image viewed with the current settings. The grid options can toggle the grid on and off as well as set its color and spacing.

There are several options available in the adjustment settings area for perspective correction, image rotation, lateral aberration correction, and lens distortion correction. The lens distortion correction setting is a single slider control. Moving this to the left puts a negative value in the text field and adds convexity to the image, which can correct pin-cushion distortion from some telephoto lenses. Moving the slider to the right places a positive number in the text field and adds convexity to the image, which can correct barrel distortion from wide-angle lenses. The Custom setting in the Settings menu allows you to name a correction, save it, and apply it later to one or more images.

In this example, I am using the test chart to provide an accurate correction for a specific lens at a specific focal length setting. I will then save this setting and apply it as needed to crime scene, evidence, or traffic collision images.

The photo of the test chart in Figure 17.4 allowed for easy alignment of the grid to the lines in the image, and a setting of +3.90 corrected the barrel distortion. In instances where precision is needed when making adjustments, the arrow key can be used in place of the slider. In this case, you would click once in the text field and use the up or down arrow on the keyboard to change the value by 10ths of a unit or hold the Shift key while clicking the arrow keys to change the value in whole units.

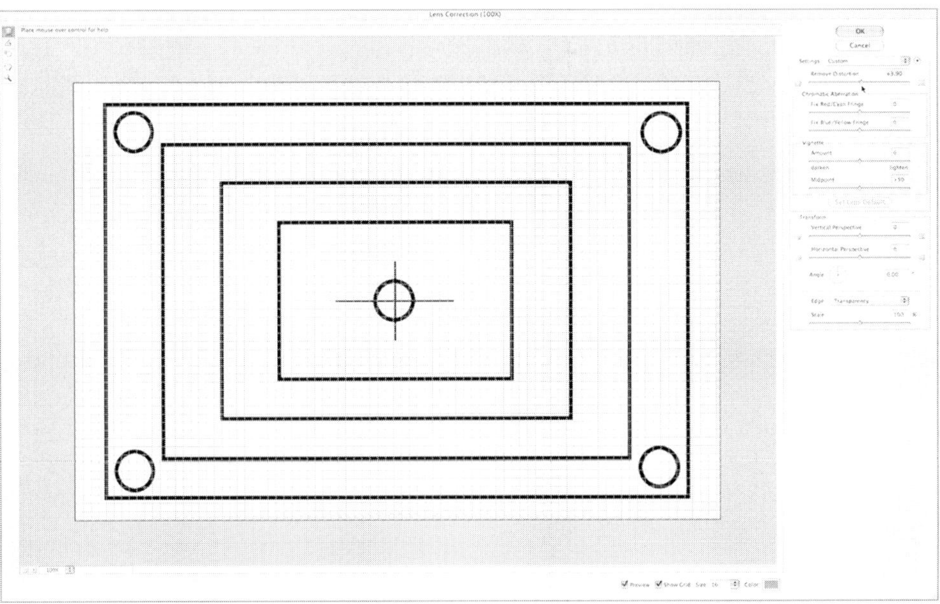

Figure 17.4 The corrected preview test image

Saving and Reusing Distortion-Correction Settings

Once you have calibrated this camera and lens combination, this setting can be saved and then later applied to images taken with this same combination.

To save the settings, click the Settings flyout menu button and choose Save Settings (Figure 17.5). This opens a dialog box in which this setting can be saved for future use. Give the setting a sensible name—I chose 18mm Lens for this example—and click Save.

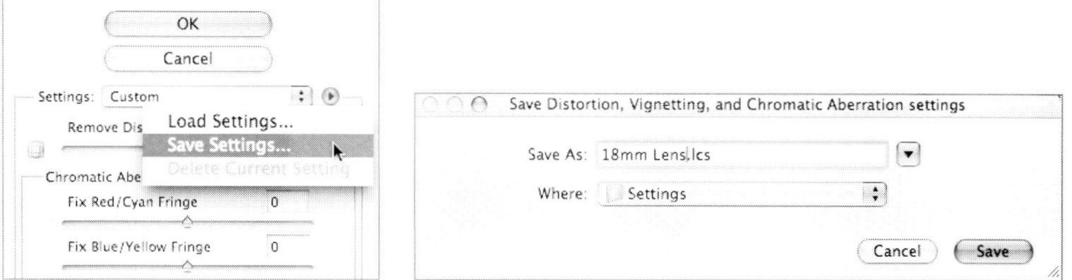

Figure 17.5 Settings can be saved for each lens or focal length and then loaded on future images.

To apply this correction to an image, open the image, create a duplicate layer, open the Lens Correction filter, and apply the appropriate settings. The corrected layer can be renamed and the image can be saved.

After opening the appropriate image, duplicate the image layer by pressing Ctrl+J/Cmd+J on the keyboard (Figure 17.6). Then double-click the layer name and give it a descriptive name—in this example I named this layer Dist Corr 18mm Fuji S3.

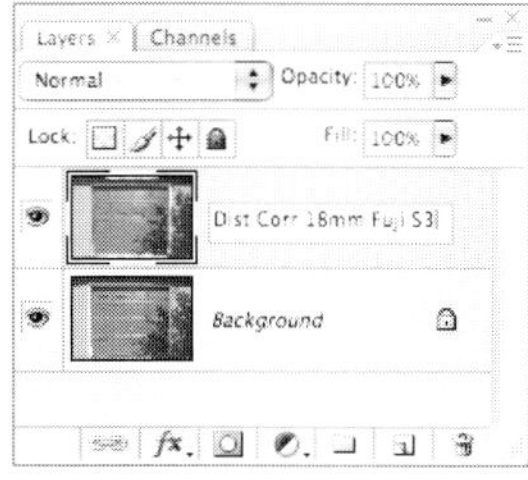

Figure 17.6 Applying the filter to a duplicate layer and renaming the layer.

With the duplicate layer active, choose Filter > Distort > Lens Correction. In the Lens Correction dialog box (Figure 17.7), choose the appropriate setting from the Settings pop-up menu—in this example, 18mm. This applies the saved settings to the preview image, which should show the lens distortion corrected. Adjust the grid size, the position or image magnification, and the position or rotation if needed, and verify that the correction is correct. If so, click OK.

Figure 17.7 Here is the saved 18mm Lens setting applied to the working image.

Turning on the visibility of this layer will show the corrected image; turning off the visibility will show the original image. It should be noted that this correction causes a pinching of the outside edges of the image and some of the original image may show when the top layer is visible. The way to correct this is to display the top layer with the bottom layer off. A quick way to toggle between views is to Alt/Option+click the visibility icons. This reverses the visibility state for all layers: layers that were off will be on and vice versa.

This image can now be saved.

Correcting Perspective Distortion

There are two issues with perspective in images that have been photographed at an angle—one is keystoning and the other is foreshortening. Keystoning is the effect of objects that are farther from the camera appearing smaller—this is commonly seen in photographs of tall buildings in which the tops of the buildings are smaller in the photograph than the bottom. Foreshortening is the effect of an object or group of objects becoming compressed along the depth of the image.

In forensics, perspective distortion can make comparative analysis more difficult, and is the reason why photographing footwear, tire impressions, blood spatter, and other subjects that will be measured and/or compared with the camera back parallel with the subject. When this isn't possible, it may be necessary to correct the perspective distortion. Unfortunately, Photoshop's two features for correcting perspective distortion may result in an incorrect width-to-height ratio. Because of this, it is essential that any correction made be considered as approximate, or that measurements be made along all edges of the subject to verify or modify the correction.

The two features for correcting perspective distortion in Photoshop are the Perspective Transform and the Transform options in the Lens Correction filter. In the Lens Correction filter, simply adjust the slider to correct the horizontal or vertical perspective in the Transform options section of this window.

To access the Perspective transform, first either unlock the background layer or create a duplicate layer (transforms will not work on a locked layer, and the Perspective Transform will not work on a Smart Object). Next, choose Edit > Transform > Perspective. Handles will be present at each corner of the image, and can be dragged to correct the perspective distortion.

With either method, measure known distances along each edge of the image or subject to verify or correct for any remaining foreshortening, keystoning, or width-to-height ratio issues.

Summary

In many cases, the small amount of distortion caused by wide-angle lenses is insignificant. However, when measurements are important or when distortion can give a false impression of evidence, it is important to correct this defect. The Lens Correction feature in Photoshop CS2 provides a simple interface for correcting barrel and pincushion distortion.

The Perspective Transform and the Transform options in the Lens Correction filter can help correct perspective distortion, but are likely to still have some amount of distortion or aspect ratio issues remaining. If using these tools to correct perspective distortion it is important to measure known objects in the image to verify the results.

18 Noise Reduction

Image noise in digital and video images is similar to grain in film. Low-light surveillance video will frequently be noisy, and this noise is often referred to as snow. The overall image degradation created by image noise may reduce the visibility of fine details.

Noise is caused by several factors in a digital environment. The most common contributors to noisy images are poor-quality components, long exposures, underexposure, and high ISO settings. Underexposure doesn't actually increase noise, but it reduces the signal-to-noise ratio, making the noise a larger percentage of the image data.

Chapter Contents

Noise Reduction Methods

There are two general methods for reducing noise: processes that work on a single image and processes that work on a group of images (such as multiple frames of a video). This chapter will explore methods that work on individual images. The method for working with multiple images is a frame averaging technique, which will be covered in Chapter 23.

Of the methods available for reducing noise in individual images, some can reduce both the luminance and color noise in the image, and some can be applied specifically to the color noise in an image. If noise is primarily color noise (it affects one or more color channels rather than the brightness values in the image), the noise can be greatly reduced while retaining most of the detail in the image. If the noise affects the overall brightness values in the image, most noise reduction methods will cause overall blurring and loss of fine detail to the image. Frequently, this blurring is acceptable because the image noise is worse than the resulting blurriness.

Photoshop CS2 introduced the Reduce Noise filter, which can be applied to the overall image noise or specifically to the color noise. In earlier versions of Photoshop, color noise can be reduced by using the Median filter with layer blending modes. In this chapter, we'll look at both of these methods of noise reduction.

Reduce Noise Filter

The Reduce Noise filter will work on single images and can be set to reduce noise while maintaining some level of image detail, as shown in Figure 18.1.

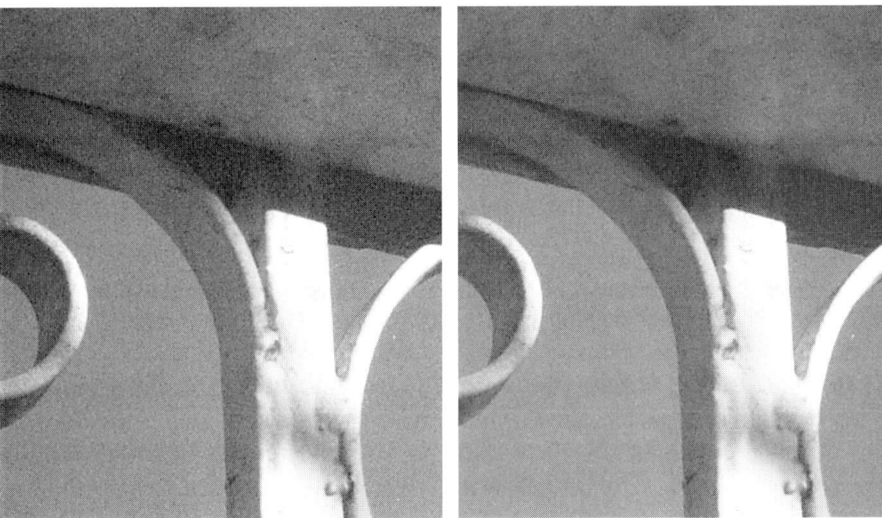

Figure 18.1 A cropped portion of the original image on the left with substantial image noise, the same image on the right with reduced noise but retention of detail after the Reduce Noise filter was applied.

To use this tool, choose Filter > Noise > Reduce Noise; this will open the Reduce Noise Filter dialog box (see Figure 18.2). If the image has been converted to a Smart Object in CS3, the filter will be applied as a nondestructive Smart Filter. If the image hasn't been converted to a Smart Object, the filter can be applied to a duplicate layer of the image file for a nondestructive workflow.

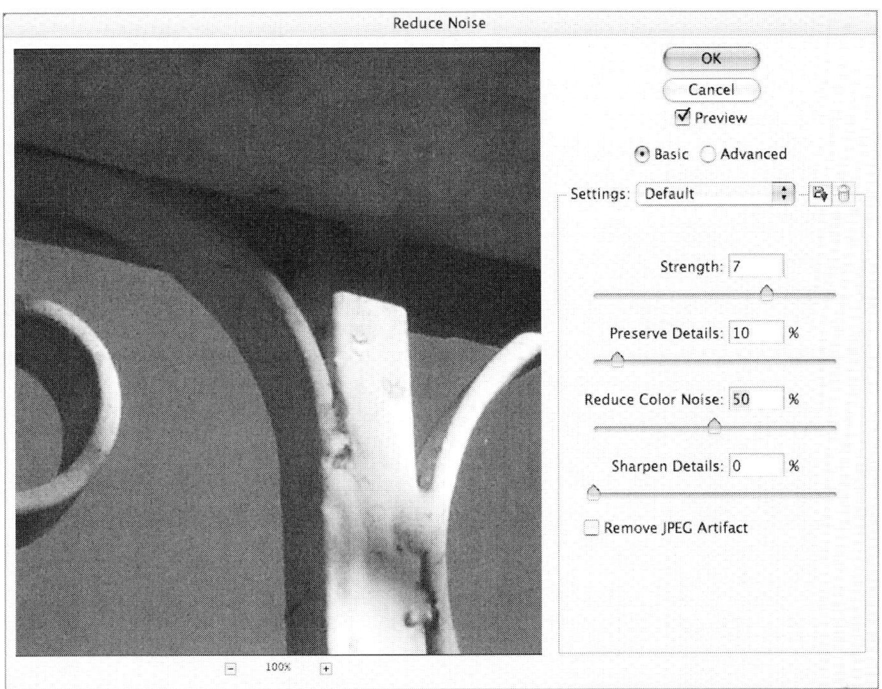

Figure 18.2 The Reduce Noise filter dialog box in the Basic mode

The Advanced button will bring up a tab to allow adjustments to be made separately to the individual color channels. This image is very noisy, with both color noise and luminance (brightness) noise, so we'll stay in the Basic mode and work on all channels together. Frequently, noise is the worst in the blue channel, so working in that channel alone can help retain overall image sharpness while eliminating a majority of the noise.

In the Adjustments section of this dialog box, four sliders provide control in reducing noise while retaining image detail.

The **Strength** slider refers to the overall strength of the filter to all color channels together (luminance noise). The higher the setting, the greater the noise reduction. It is important to note that higher settings also result in a loss of overall sharpness.

The **Preserve Details** slider will preserve fine details in the image, but too high of a setting can prevent much noise from being reduced. A balance between the Strength setting and the Preserve Details setting can reduce a substantial amount of noise while retaining good detail.

Reduce Color Noise eliminates noise on the color channels separately—this is important because some noise affects all color channels equally, and that noise will be reduced with the Strength slider, and some noise is specific to separate color channels, which Reduce Color Noise will reduce. Objects that have edges with contrasting colors will often show a blurring of color along those edges with a high setting of the Reduce Color Noise slider.

Sharpen Details applies a sharpening filter to the image. Although there can be more control for image sharpening using Smart Sharpen or the Unsharp Mask dialog box, using this feature within this filter enables a better visualization of the combination of noise reduction with sharpening. I will frequently apply some sharpening as a preview, then bring this setting back to zero, apply the filter, and follow it up with an Unsharp Mask or Smart Sharpen filter.

When applying this filter, I frequently will click the + button below the preview window to enlarge the preview image to 200 percent or more. The area displayed within the preview box can be adjusted by clicking and dragging on it. Clicking the preview image also displays it as it appeared before applying the filter, so I will frequently click and release my mouse button on the preview image to get a better idea of how much this filter is reducing noise versus how much it is blurring the overall image.

When noise is modest, this filter does an excellent job of reducing it while preserving detail. When noise is more substantial, there will be some loss of detail when applying the filter with enough strength to significantly reduce the noise.

Median Filter

In Photoshop CS or earlier, the Reduce Noise filter isn't available. The Median filter (Figure 18.3) reduces noise by replacing one or more pixels in small neighborhoods (3×3 or 5×5 pixel areas, for example) with the median pixel value from that group. Because noise will generally be small and will have a different value than surrounding pixels, this works well for reducing noise. The downside to the Median filter is that small details and edges of objects also have different values than surrounding pixels, so they lose detail as well. If the noise is primarily color noise, the Median filter can be applied to a duplicate layer and be applied to only the color value with the color blending mode.

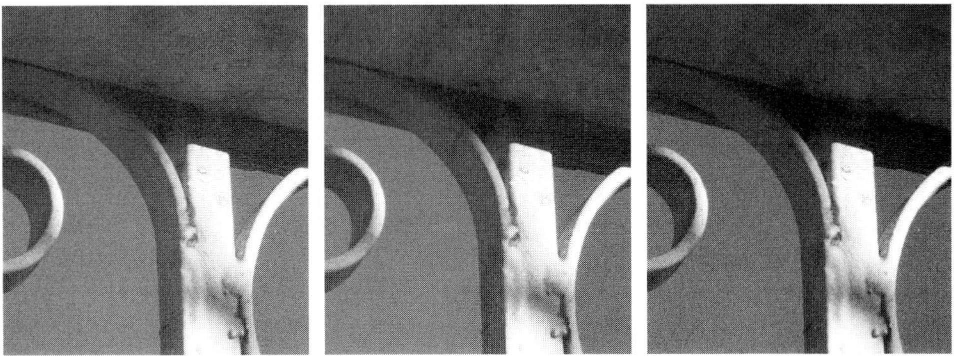

Figure 18.3 A cropped portion of the original image on the left, with a Median filter applied in the center, and with the Median filter in color blending mode on the right.

To use this filter, choose Filter > Noise > Median, which will open the Median filter dialog box (see Figure 18.4). The filter has only one variable, which is the Radius setting. If all noise is 1 or 2 pixels in size, a setting on 1 should work well. If noise is larger, either a larger Radius setting can be used or the filter can be applied multiple times. Applying the filter at a low Radius setting multiple times will tend to retain more detail in the image while still reducing more noise than a single application of the filter.

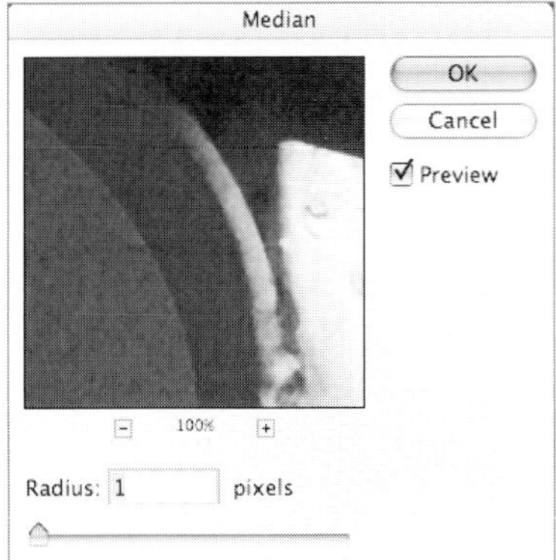

Figure 18.4 The Median filter dialog box

After applying this filter to a duplicate layer, I like to rename the layer with the filter name and radius setting used, such as Median 1, for example.

If the noise is primarily color noise rather than luminance noise (it shows as color speckles rather than light spots), then the Median filter can be applied with a much larger Radius setting and applied to only the color information in the image.

This is done by using a duplicate layer of the image (press Ctrl+J/Cmd+J or choose Layer > Duplicate Layer from the menu). Once the filter is applied, change the layer mode to Color in the Layers palette (see Figure 18.5). This applies this filter only to the color information in the image.

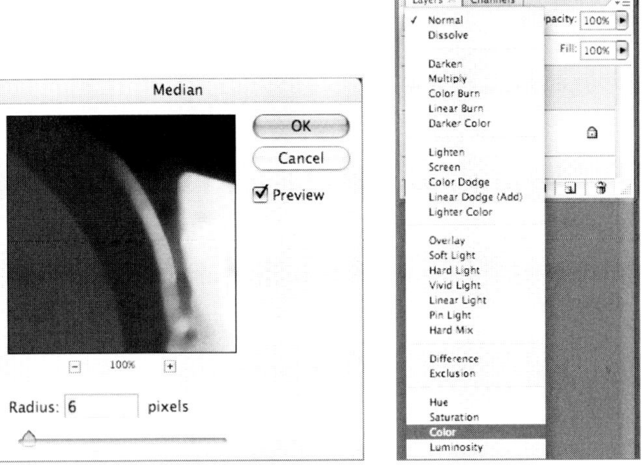

Figure 18.5 The Median filter with a large Radius setting, and setting the layer blending mode set to Color

Summary

When faced with underexposed images, low light, or long exposures, you may find that image noise significantly degrades image quality. If only one image of the subject is available, the Reduce Noise filter can reduce the impact of noise while retaining image detail. If you're using a version of Photoshop that doesn't have the Reduce Noise filter, the Median filter can be applied, although it will cause blur in the image, even with a small Radius setting.

19 Deblurring and Sharpening

Although deblurring *and* sharpening *seem to imply the same thing, I am using the two terms separately to describe two different processes. Deblurring refers to a process called deconvolution, which corrects a defect, such as focus blur or motion blur. Sharpening refers to a general process of increasing contrast in edges of objects to give the appearance of greater sharpness. Photoshop has features for both sharpening and for deblurring and this chapter will cover both of these as well as the use of a Photoshop plug-in filter.*

Chapter Contents

A Variety of Sharpening Tools

In this chapter, we will look at three different filters: Photoshop's Unsharp Mask, the new Smart Sharpen filter in Photoshop CS2, and a filter called Interactive Deblur from the Ocean Systems plug-in ClearID. Unsharp Mask is a general sharpening filter that adds contrast to edges of objects and works well for many images. The Smart Sharpen and Interactive Deblur filters are deconvolution filters, and work best for focus blur and motion blur, especially if you can estimate the amount of blur in the image.

I have used the same original image to show the results of these three filters and to show how both focus blur and motion blur can be corrected. Because of this, these images have artificial blurring in them to best provide a proper comparison of the filters.

As with all processes in this book, it is assumed that valid forensic procedures are followed and that all work is done only to copies of originals, not to the originals themselves. These issues are covered in Chapter 1, "Best Practices."

For more information on the Ocean Systems plug-in, see the end of this chapter and also Chapter 22.

The top-left image in Figure 19.1 shows the fingerprint blurred with a Gaussian blur, which is similar to a focus blur. The top right shows the same print with a motion blur applied, which is similar to the motion blur that may be due to subject or camera movement. The Unsharp Mask and Smart Sharpen images show the results of using these filters on the Gaussian blur print. The Interactive Deblur image shows the results of using this tool on the motion blur image.

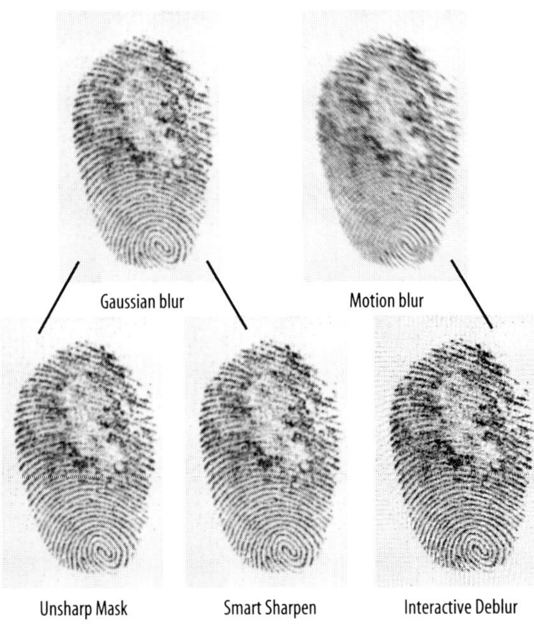

Figure 19.1 The original and clarified versions of a fingerprint image

Unsharp Mask

If you're using Photoshop CS3, the first step is to convert the image to 16 bit and then to a Smart Object (see Chapter 7). If using an earlier version of Photoshop, duplicate the image layer so that the filter can be applied to the duplicate layer and then compared to the original data in the background layer. You duplicate the image layer by selecting the layer and pressing Ctrl+J/Cmd+J on the keyboard. With the new layer highlighted, the filter can be applied.

To access this filter, choose Filter > Sharpen > Unsharp Mask (Figure 19.2). This opens the Unsharp Mask dialog box (Figure 19.3), which provides three variables that can be set to achieve the best results. This filter works by increasing the contrast along edges of objects, and the parameters are used to control the way this added contrast will be applied to the image.

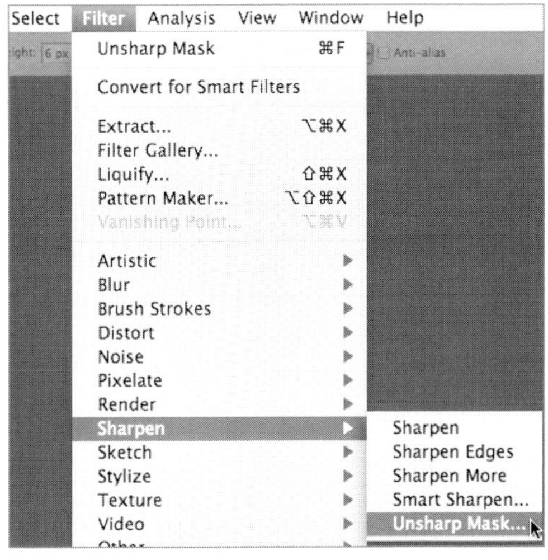

Figure 19.2 Accessing the Unsharp Mask filter from the Filter menu

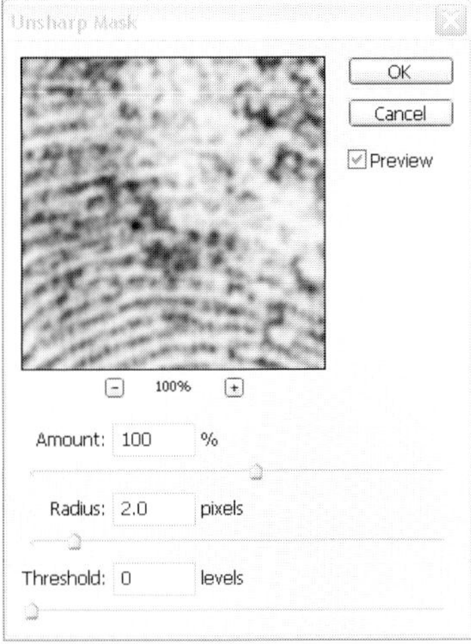

Figure 19.3 The Unsharp Mask dialog box

The Amount slider controls how strongly the additional contrast will be applied. Higher numbers will provide stronger contrast along the edges of the subject—that is, the darker side of edges will be darker and the lighter side will be lighter. The Radius slider controls the width of the added contrast. Larger numbers will give the appearance of thick lines along the edges of objects and smaller numbers will have thinner lines. The Threshold slider will allow you to apply the sharpening only to areas of high contrast. The value you set with this slider controls how much tonal variation there must be for the filter to determine that there is an edge and then the filter is applied.

While making adjustments it helps to toggle the Preview check box on and off. This allows you to see comparisons between the original image and the applied corrections.

As a general rule, Amount will usually be set between 100 and 300 percent for comparative analysis. For images of people or more photographic subjects, settings of 50 to 150 are more likely. The Radius setting is dependent on the subject, resolution, and amount of correction needed, but settings of 0.8 to 3.0 pixels are typical. Setting very large numbers can cause the adjustments to spill into each other, so it's best to keep this setting less than the width of any feature. For comparative analysis (fingerprints, footwear impressions, toolmarks), I generally leave the Threshold setting at zero but will slightly increase it for images of a more photographic nature (crime scenes, traffic accidents, departmental portraits).

Once the adjustments are made, click OK to apply them. In Photoshop CS3, when you're using Smart Objects, this will show up as a Smart Filter below the Smart Object in the Layers palette (Figure 19.4). In earlier versions, I rename the layer with the settings used for this filter to have a quick reference to this information. This information is also stored in the History Log. The file is now ready to be saved.

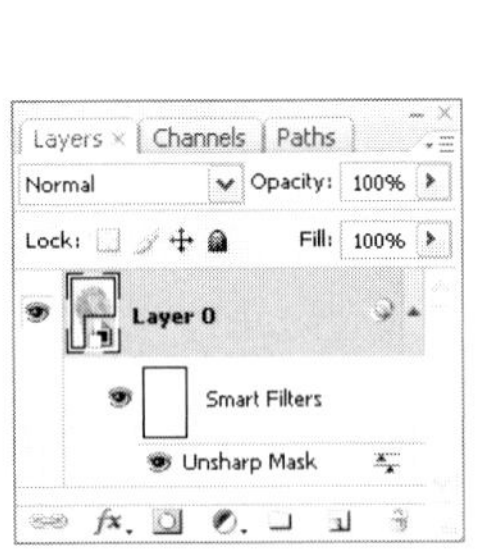

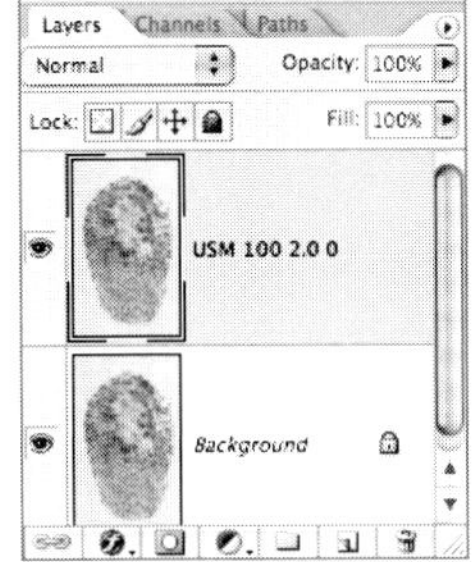

Figure 19.4 The Layers palette in CS3 showing the Unsharp Mask as a Smart Filter on the left and in CS2 as a duplicate layer that's renamed on the right.

Smart Sharpen

This filter was introduced in Photoshop CS2 and works a bit differently than the Unsharp Mask. Smart Sharpen works to correct the cause of the blur and can be applied to images with a focus blur or with motion blur. In this tutorial, we'll apply it to the image with the Gaussian blur, which is similar to a focus blur.

To access this filter, choose Filter > Sharpen > Smart Sharpen (Figure 19.5). This opens the Smart Sharpen dialog box (Figure 19.6), which provides several parameters to correct for the specific type of blur present in the image (motion blur, focus blur or Gaussian blur).

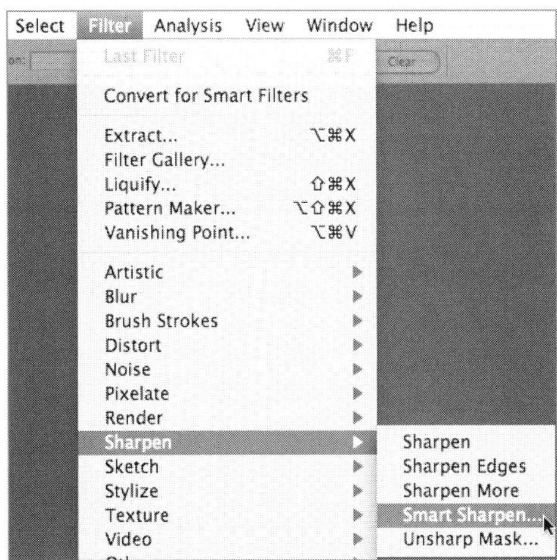

Figure 19.5 Choose Smart Sharpen from the Filter > Sharpen menu.

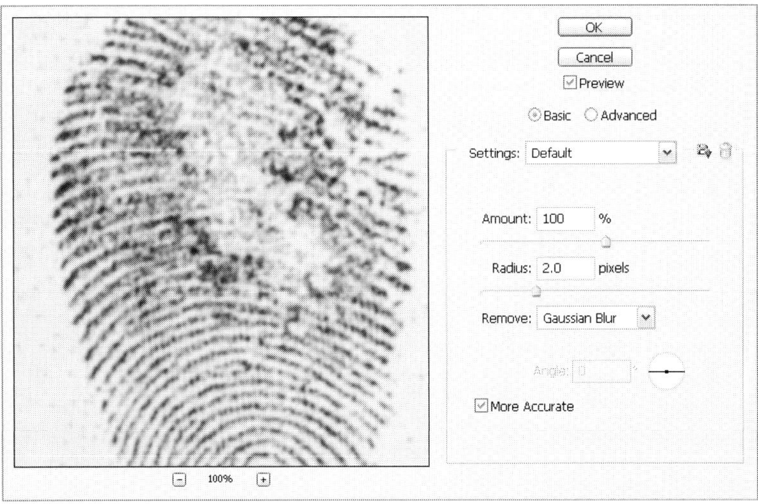

Figure 19.6 The Smart Sharpen dialog box

First, choose the type of blur to correct. The drop-down menu provides a choice of Lens Blur, Gaussian Blur, or Motion Blur. The filter tends to work very well for slight lens blur, which is what we emulated in this example by applying a Gaussian blur. The More Accurate button (at the bottom of the window) should always be checked—it causes somewhat slower processing of the image, but improves the results.

If you select the Advanced button, you can control the adjustments separately for highlight and shadow areas—in most comparative analysis images, the Basic setting will work quite well (I haven't found any instances with comparative analysis images in which controlling the highlight and shadow areas separately has been advantageous). The Amount slider controls how strongly the additional contrast will be applied to the edges of objects. Higher numbers will provide stronger contrast along the edges of the subject—that is, the darker side of edges will be darker and the lighter side will be lighter. The Radius slider should be set to mimic the amount of blur in the image. The Settings drop-down menu allows for specific settings to be saved and applied to additional images.

While making adjustments, it is useful to toggle the Preview check box on and off. This helps to make comparisons between the original image and the applied corrections.

As a general rule, the Amount setting will be between 100 and 300 percent for comparative analysis, as with the Unsharp Mask. The Radius setting depends on the subject, resolution, and amount of correction needed. If there is anything in the image that should appear as a sharp dot, use it as a guide while adjusting this slider.

Once the adjustments are made, click OK to apply them as a Smart Filter. If you're using Photoshop CS2, click OK to save the adjustments to the duplicate layer, and rename the layer with the settings used for this filter to have a quick reference to this information (Figure 19.7). This information is also stored in the History Log. The file is now ready to be saved.

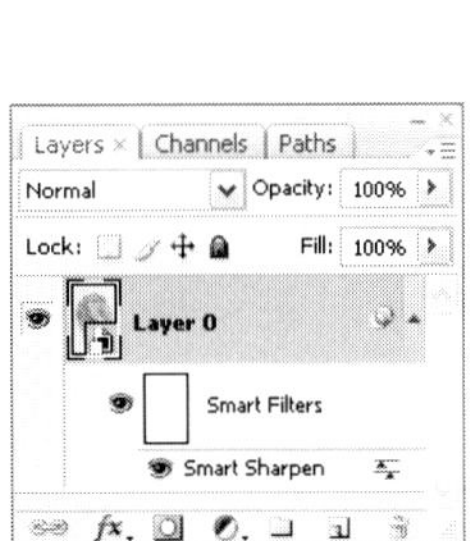

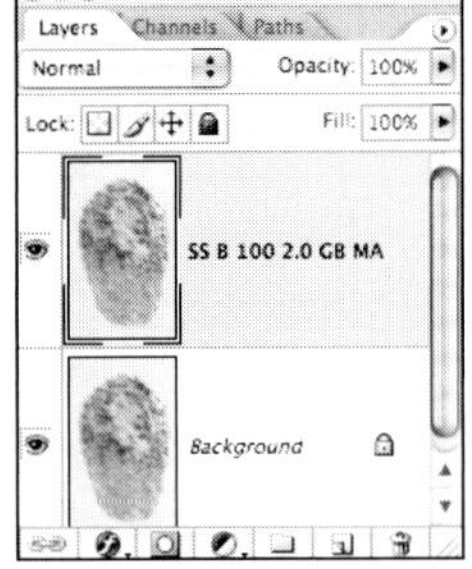

Figure 19.7 The Layers palette in CS3 showing the Smart Sharpen Filter as a Smart Filter on the left, and in CS2 as a duplicate layer renamed on the right.

Interactive Deblur Using Ocean Systems ClearID

This filter is a Photoshop plug-in and works on the same principle as Smart Sharpen—to correct the blur rather than simply adding contrast to the edges of objects. It can be applied to images with a focus blur or with motion blur. This filter is part of the Ocean Systems ClearID plug-in (Windows only), available from www.oceansystems.com. Once installed, the filters can be accessed from the Filter menu or through a JavaScript.

When you use this filter directly from the Filter menu, it opens a dialog box and it functions as any other filter does. When you use this filter from the JavaScript, it will convert the image to 16 bit, create a duplicate layer, apply the adjustment to the duplicate layer, and rename the new layer with the parameters used in the filter. The renaming aspect of this doesn't work with Smart Filters, otherwise it functions well with both Photoshop CS3 and CS2.

We'll run this filter from the script by choosing File > Scripts > dT Fourier Freq > Interactive Deblur (Figure 19.8). This opens the Interactive Deblur dialog (Figure 19.9), which provides several parameters that can be set to achieve the best results.

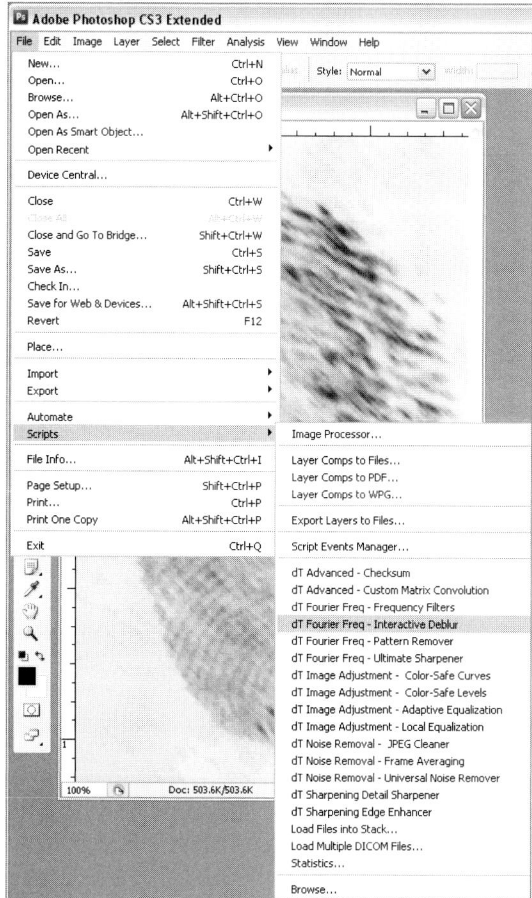

Figure 19.8 Running the Interactive Deblur from the Scripts submenu

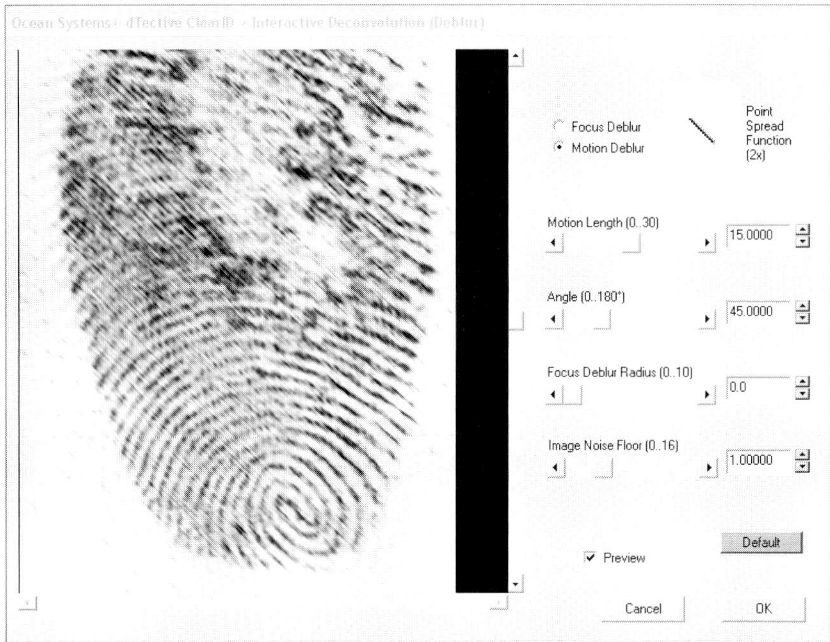

Figure 19.9 The Ocean Systems ClearID Interactive Deblur filter interface

Again, first choose the type of blur to correct. The choices are Focus Deblur and Motion Deblur. In my experience, this filter does an outstanding job with both types of blur as long as the parameters are properly set, which is sometimes difficult. One key is to identify something in the image that should appear as a dot and analyze what type, size, and/or direction of blur it exemplifies.

The **Blur Preview box** shows the shape of the blur, or the point spread function, based on the settings made in this filter. In this case, analyzing the image showed that the blur was at approximately a 45-degree angle, and was about 15 pixels in length—the Blur Preview box provides a visual representation of these settings, which can be compared with the image. It is helpful to refer to the original image and this preview when making adjustments to see if the point spread function matches the type, size, and direction of blur the original image has.

The **Motion Length slider** is only used for correcting motion blur. If Focus Deblur is selected, the Motion Length setting will change to an Astigmatism Ratio setting to correct for blurs that are stronger in one direction. With Motion Deblur, it will accept input from 0 to 30 pixels. Clicking on the slider will move it in increments of 1 pixel. Looking at any edge that is perpendicular to the direction of the blur should provide a good estimate of the length of the blur.

The **Focus Deblur Radius setting** is primarily for focus blur corrections, although there are instances in which an image that has motion blur may have some focus blur as well. It accepts radius settings from 0 to 10 pixels. Clicking on the slider will change the settings in .25-pixel increments. Looking at something that should be a dot in the original image can provide a reference for estimating the blur radius.

The **Angle setting** is used to set the direction of the blur. This can be estimated by looking at something in the image that should appear as a dot or by looking at edges of objects—edges that are parallel to the direction of the blur will be sharpest, and edges that are perpendicular to the direction of the blur will show the most blurring.

The **Image Noise Floor setting** can clean up the graininess in an image and help prevent it from causing artifacts. I usually set Image Noise Floor to a low setting between 0 and 1 to begin the process and adjust the other settings until the results look good. Then I adjust the Image Noise Floor slider until the graininess and artifacts are reduced. I fine-tune the settings until I get the best results possible.

There can be some artifacting with the use of this tool. Moire patterns can be caused by an incorrect angle, and ringing (repeating patterns of the object outlines) can be caused by a Motion Length setting or Blur Radius setting that is too large. Some ringing is normal, but if it seems excessive, try adjusting these settings to improve the results.

Once the adjustments are made, click OK to apply them to the Smart Object as a Smart Filter or to the duplicate image layer (Figure 19.10). The file is now ready to be saved.

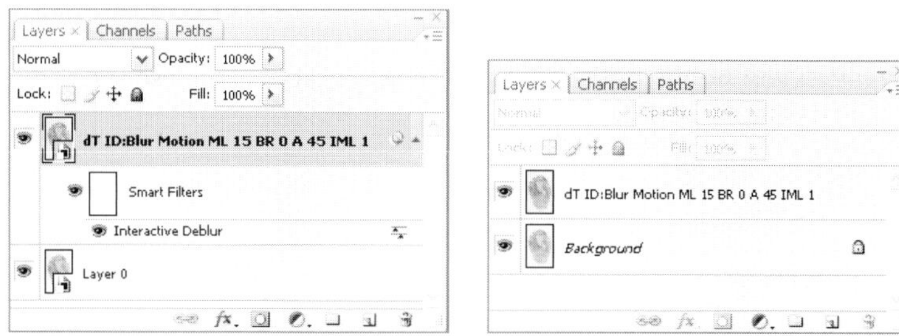

Figure 19.10 The Layers palette in CS3 showing the Interactive Deblur filter as a Smart Filter on the left and as a duplicate layer renamed on the right

Summary

Images that suffer from a lack of sharpness due to focus blur, poor resolution, motion blur, or other factors can often be greatly improved through deblurring or image sharpening. When the factor that caused the image degradation can be identified, the deconvolution method works best either through Photoshop's Smart Sharpen or Ocean Systems's ClearID Interactive Deblur plug-in. For general image sharpening, Photoshop's Unsharp Mask can be used with generally good results.

In all cases, it is best to be conservative in the approach to image sharpening so that artifacts that may obliterate details are not introduced.

20 Contrast Enhancement

Crime scene, evidence, and traffic collision photographs sometimes need brightness and contrast adjustments, and images for analysis can benefit from these same adjustments. And these images may need global or localized adjustments. The method for making these adjustments is also the same: utilizing adjustment layers with a Levels or Curves adjustment layer and isolating local areas with adjustment layer masks.

Chapter Contents

Global Adjustments

Surveillance videos, tool marks, fingerprints, and many other subjects of visible evidence can be improved with basic contrast adjustments. For our global adjustment example, we'll make an adjustment to a fingerprint image, but the concepts will apply equally to blood spatter, video, tool marks, and other types of forensic images.

Note: For all the adjustments described in this chapter, as with all chapters, it is important to use valid forensic procedures, as outlined in Chapter 1—which means working on copies of images, using valid forensic tools, and using techniques that can provide repeatable results.

Figure 20.1 is of a typical black powder fingerprint that is of very low contrast because very little powder adhered to the print. I have converted the image to a Smart Object by choosing Layer > Smart Object > Convert To Smart Object. I also view the image at 100 percent magnification to see the information as accurately as possible.

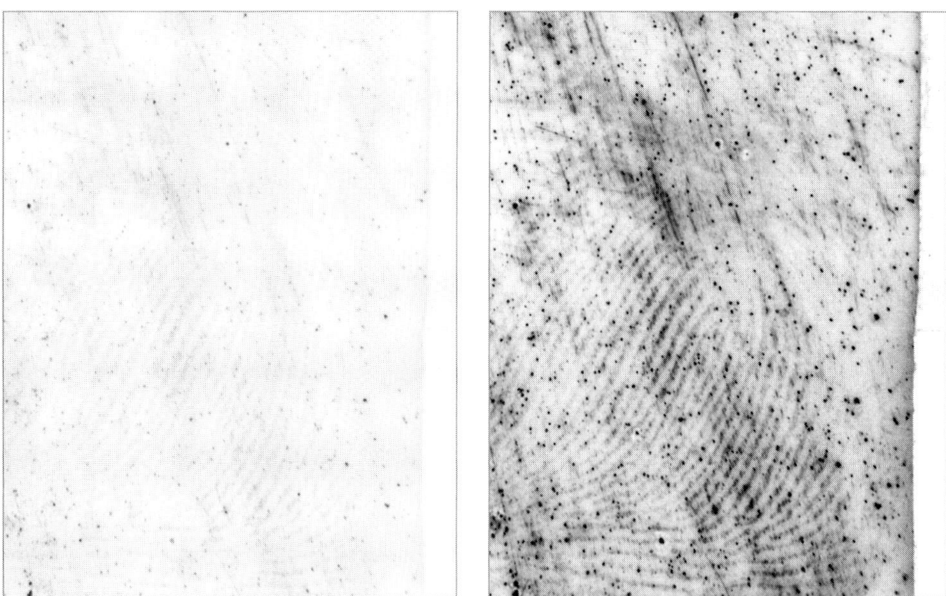

Figure 20.1 A typical low-contrast, light fingerprint image on the left and an enhanced version on the right

When viewing the image, I evaluate it to determine what the worst problem is. In the case of the image in Figure 20.1, there are two problems of equal weight: the image is too light and it has too little contrast. Brightness and contrast adjustments can be done nondestructively using an adjustment layer, as you saw in Chapter 7, as a levels, curves, or brightness/contrast adjustment. For this image, we'll make a levels adjustment by selecting Levels from the Adjustment Layer menu in the Layers palette (see Figure 20.2).

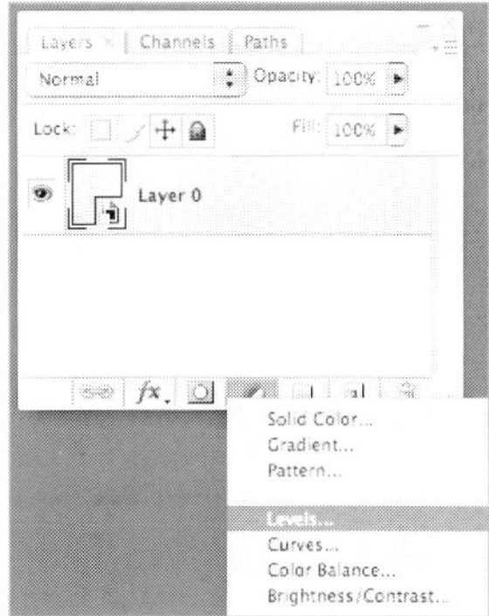

Figure 20.2 Selecting the Levels adjustment layer from the Layers palette

Selecting the Levels adjustment layer opens the Levels dialog box (Figure 20.3). It also automatically creates a new layer. Adjustment layers do not change the values of the pixels in the image, they just display those pixels as though these adjustments were made. After adjustment layers are made, they can be made active or inactive and the adjustments can be reedited if desired.

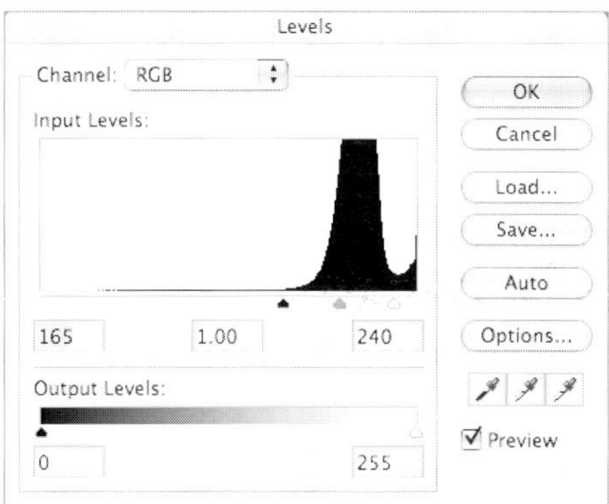

Figure 20.3 The Levels adjustment dialog box

Image Clipping

The Adobe help file describes clipping as follows: "Clipping occurs when a pixel's color values are higher than the highest value or lower than the lowest value that can be represented in the image; overbright values are clipped to output white, and overdark values are clipped to output black. The result is a loss of image detail."

In a forensics workflow, it is important to use caution when clipping in parts of the image that may contain detail important to your analysis because it may cause a loss of image detail in these areas. Judging whether the extended contrast gained when clipping outweighs the loss of some tonal separation is a subjective decision, and it is sometimes best to allow some clipping even if there is a slight loss of tonal separation.

In addition to clipping, some tones can become compressed when the center (midpoint) slider is used. When this slider is moved, it is possible that some tones with different values will be merged to the same value. This will happen more quickly in the 8-bit space than in the 16-bit space—but changing overall brightness should be done conservatively in either case. As with clipping, making adjustments with the midpoint slider will be subjective and some loss of tonality can occur.

In the Levels dialog box, the large graph is a histogram, which displays the tonal range of the image. The darkest pixels are represented on the left, the brightest on the right, with the mid-tone in the center. Understanding the histogram is key to evaluating images and correcting poor exposures. In this image, the histogram shows that most of the pixels are light because most of them are to the right of the midpoint. Moving the Input sliders or changing the values in the Levels Input text boxes can adjust the contrast and/or overall brightness of an image. The left slider is the black point slider: any pixels to the left of it will become pure black (a value of 0). The slider on the right is the white point slider: any pixels to the right of it will become pure white (a value of 255). Sliding these outside sliders (white point and black point) toward the center will increase the contrast and potentially clip the darkest and brightest values, which will cause a loss of tonal variations in those clipped tones. The Output sliders and text boxes at the bottom of the Levels dialog box can reduce contrast in an image, which is rarely needed in images used for comparative analysis.

A general rule of thumb is to move the black point and white point sliders to the edges of the graph in the histogram. This maximizes the tonal values of the image without causing any values to be clipped. In this example, I have slightly clipped the graph on both edges (note the position of the sliders under the histogram in Figure 20.3). Clipping these values can cause some loss of detail. If you hold the Alt/Option key while moving these sliders, the image will show which pixels will be clipped. This is an important step and can enable significant adjustments while verifying that significant data was not lost.

In this example, moving the black point slider to the position illustrated shows a loss of value only in areas that are not part of any ridge detail, as shown in Figure 20.4. All non-white pixels are clipped in one or more color channels. By allowing clipping to nonsignificant portions of the image, I am able to increase the contrast to the maximum amount without losing tonal variations in the ridge detail. Pressing the Alt/Option key while moving the white point slider shows clipped values as non-white, as seen in Figure 20.4. Again, I moved the slider to get the maximum contrast without clipping any significant parts of the fingerprint.

Figure 20.4 The image on the left shows which pixels will be clipped to black, and the image on the right shows which pixels will be clipped to white.

After the adjustments have been completed, click the OK button to apply them to the adjustment layer and to close the Levels dialog box. The adjustments are all contained within the adjustment layer, which can be seen in the Layers palette in Figure 20.5. A thumbnail is visible showing the original image, and another thumbnail represents the adjustment layer. Clicking the visibility icon for the adjustment layer will toggle the adjustment on and off, showing the original image with no changes or showing it with the adjustments applied. Double-clicking the levels icon will reopen the Levels dialog box and show the exact adjustments that were made to the image. The layer can also be renamed to show the adjustments made by double-clicking the layer name and typing in the settings. In this case, I renamed the layer L 165 1.0 240.

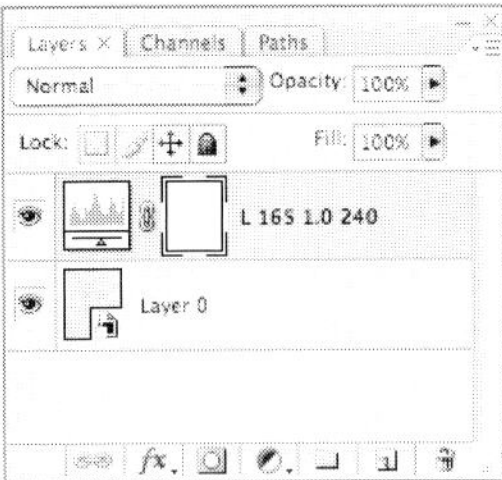

Figure 20.5 The Layers palette after the adjustments were made and the layer was renamed to represent the adjustments made

After making an adjustment, I reevaluate the image to determine if there are any remaining problems. In this fingerprint image, the levels adjustment resulted in a color shift. To eliminate this color shift, I create a Hue/Saturation adjustment layer from the adjustment layer icon in the Layers palette (see Figure 20.6). I use this method because it is non-destructive, keeps the image in the full RGB space, and can be easily demonstrated in court or re-adjusted at another time. There are many methods for desaturating an image, including using the Desaturate command (Image > Adjustments > Desaturate) or converting the image to the Grayscale mode (Image > Adjustments > Grayscale).

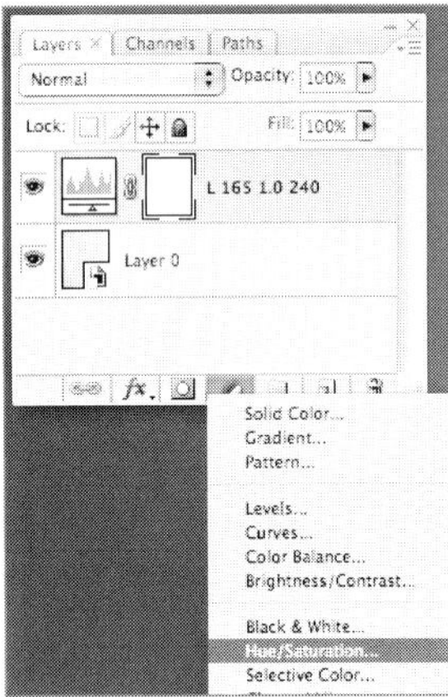

Figure 20.6 Selecting a hue/saturation adjustment from the Adjustment Layer icon in the Layers palette

Adjusting the Saturation slider (see Figure 20.7) to –100 will remove all color values from the image, eliminating the color shift from the image.

After making this adjustment, I rename the Hue/Saturation layer by double-clicking the layer name. In this case (Figure 20.8), I named the layer HS 0 –100 0, which represents the adjustment I made to it.

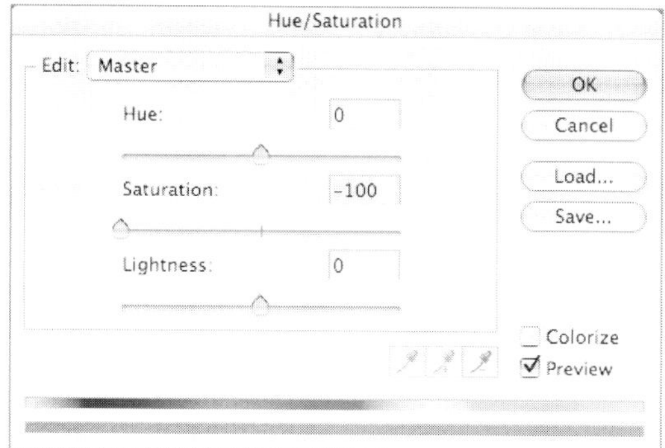

Figure 20.7 The Hue/Saturation dialog box

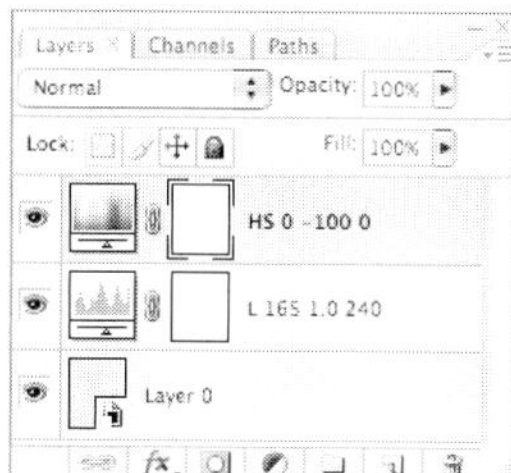

Figure 20.8 The Layers palette with the two adjustment layers

This image can now be saved and closed or sized for printing. If you're saving the image, it must be saved in TIFF or PSD format to retain the separate adjustment layers.

Using Layer Masks for Local Adjustments

When you use adjustment layers to make brightness and contrast adjustments (and other processes) to an image, you can add a layer mask to apply the adjustments only to local areas of the image. The advantages of this method for making local adjustments are that the adjustment layer can be turned off to show the unchanged, original pixel values of the image; the layer mask can be viewed to show exactly where the adjustments were applied; and the Levels dialog (or the dialog from any adjustment layer process) can be accessed to show exactly what changes were made.

A layer mask is a feature that enables an adjustment layer to be applied to specific parts of an image rather than to the entire image. A layer mask is a grayscale image that allows the adjustment to be applied fully where the mask is white, allows no adjustment to show where the mask is black, and allows the adjustment to be applied partially where the mask is gray.

In Figure 20.9, the ridge detail is fairly visible in the areas with the light background but almost indistinguishable in the area with the dark background. Making an adjustment to the entire image would result in a complete loss of ridge detail in the light areas. A layer mask will enable an adjustment to be made to specific areas of the image—in this example, to the dark areas, providing a fingerprint with ridge detail in all areas of the image.

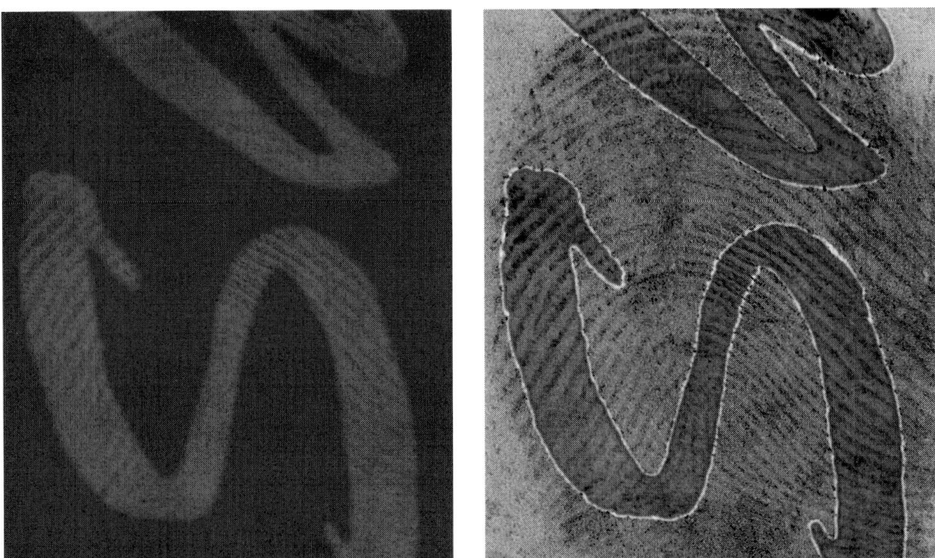

Figure 20.9 The original image on the left and the enhanced image on the right

The process to localize adjustments is the same as outlined in Chapter7—select an area, then create an adjustment layer (which will automatically create a mask based on the selection).

To select only the dark areas of this image, you can use any of Photoshop's selection tools, including the Marquee tools, Lasso tools, and Wand tool. For this image, I used the Wand tool to select the dark areas of the image.

The Wand tool (Figure 20.10) works by making a selection based on tonal ranges in the image. That is, when a pixel is clicked, it is selected, as are any pixels that are adjacent to it with tonal values within the tolerance set in the Wand tool options. Pixels within the set tolerance values adjacent to those are also selected, and so on, until there are no more pixels within the selected tolerance in contact with the selection. If the Contiguous box is unchecked, all pixels in the image within the tolerance setting will be selected whether or not they are in contact with other selected pixels.

Figure 20.10 The Wand tool and the tool options

In this image, I checked the Contiguous box and set Tolerance to 13. This limits the selection to a contiguous area of pixels that are within 13 points of the brightness value of the selected pixel. I clicked a pixel in the main section, then chose the Add To Selection button, and clicked again on an area at the top of the image that was outside of the contiguous area of the initial selection (see Figure 20.11). If I had unchecked the Contiguous box, many of the ridges in the light area would also have been selected in addition to the contiguous dark areas of background.

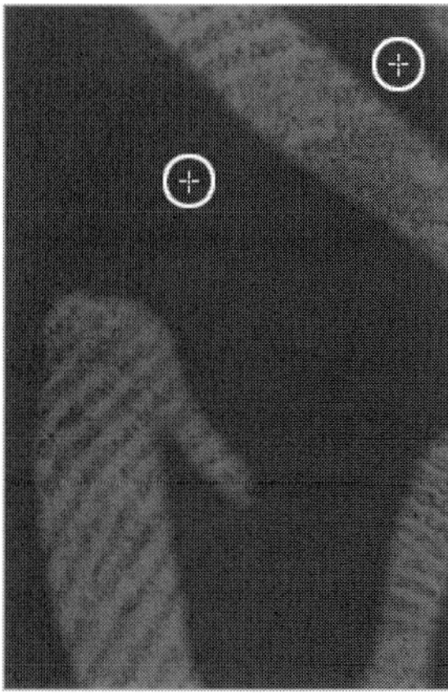

Figure 20.11 Two areas of the image were clicked with the Wand tool as illustrated here.

Before making an adjustment layer, I clicked the Refine Edge button in the Wand options bar and adjusted the selection by setting Smooth to 3, Feather to 1.0, and Contract/Expand to –50 as shown in Figure 20.12. The Contract/Expand setting slightly reduced the size of the selection. The Smooth setting rounded any acute angles, and the Feather setting made a slight transition along the entire selection. The combination will prevent too much of a halo from showing after image adjustments are made.

The next step is to create an adjustment layer. By doing so, a mask will automatically be created based on the selected area in the image. For this image, I created a Levels adjustment layer to increase the contrast in the dark areas of the image.

Figure 20.12 The Refine Edge dialog box

To create the adjustment layer and the layer mask, click the adjustment layer icon on the bottom of the Layers palette and select Levels from the flyout menu.

When the Levels adjustment layer is selected, the Levels dialog box opens, the adjustment layer is created in the Layers palette, and the image shows adjustments as they are made. In this example (Figure 20.13), I adjusted the image so that the ridge detail and background showed enough contrast to distinguish the separate ridges. The input settings were 3, 1.00, 35. This did not clip any significant values in the image, so there is no loss of information.

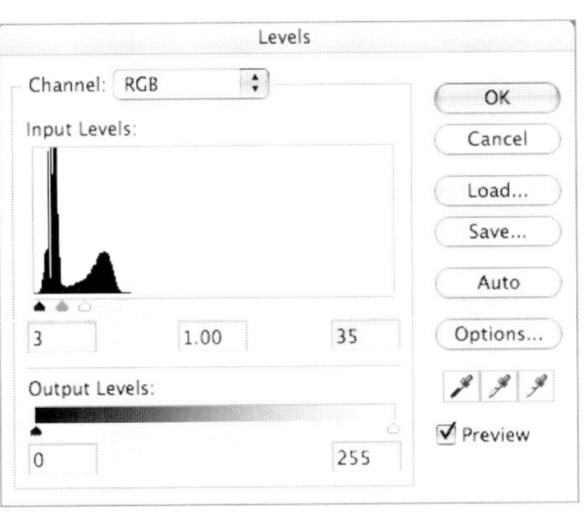

Figure 20.13 The Levels adjustment dialog box and the resulting image

Clicking OK in the Levels dialog box closes the window and makes the adjustments set to the adjustment layer. In my workflow, I renamed the adjustment layer to reflect the adjustments that I made.

Because the overall image is still dark, an additional adjustment can be made to the overall image to increase the contrast between the ridges and background of this print. In this case, the new adjustment needs to be made to the pixels that were not already adjusted—or, put another way, our mask needs to be the inverse of the one we just created. The simplest way to do this is to duplicate the adjustment layer we just made, invert the layer mask, and reedit the Levels settings.

To do this, select the adjustment layer and create a duplicate of it by pressing Ctrl+J/Cmd+J on your keyboard. This duplicates the currently active layer with its layer mask in place. To invert the tonal values of the mask, select Image > Adjustments > Invert, or press Ctrl+I/Cmd+I. Then, to reedit the Levels adjustment, double-click the Levels icon in the Layers palette, which opens the Levels dialog box with the current settings (those we used on the previous adjustment layer).

I adjusted this image to provide better separation of the ridge detail from the background and to attempt to match the values made in the previous layer. I used the Alt/Option key while adjusting the white and black point sliders to verify that I wasn't clipping significant information in the image.

Just as with the previous adjustment layer, this layer can be renamed with the setting used to make the adjustment for a quick reference. Figure 20.14 shows the image with the adjustments made to this point and the Layers palette with the two renamed layers.

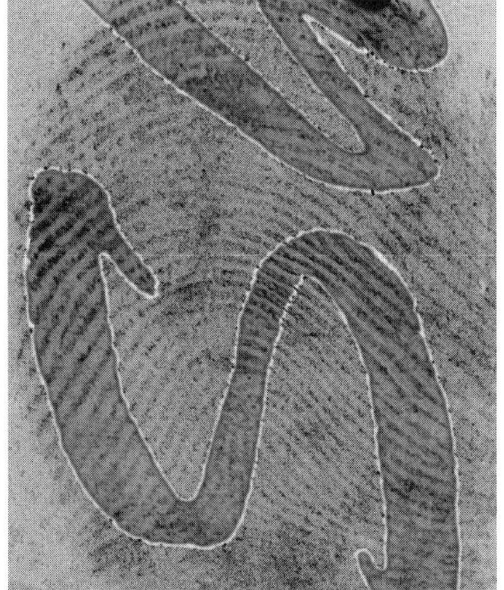

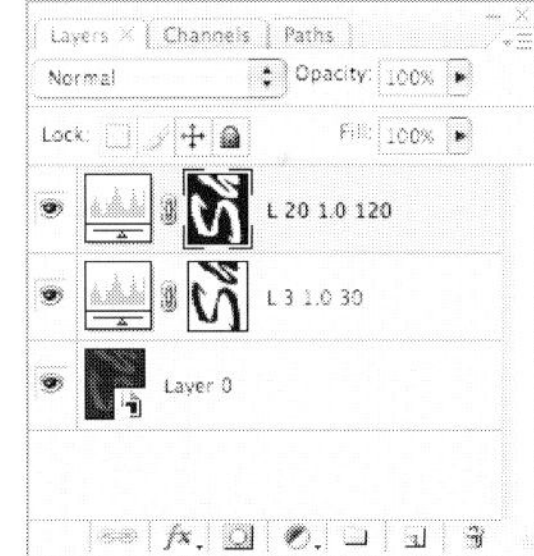

Figure 20.14 The image after applying two adjustment layers

The two sections of the image have different color shifts, so I complete the adjustments to this image by making a Hue/Saturation layer with a Saturation adjustment of –100 to eliminate the color shifts. I rename this layer to illustrate the adjustment. The final image and the Layers palette are shown in Figure 20.15.

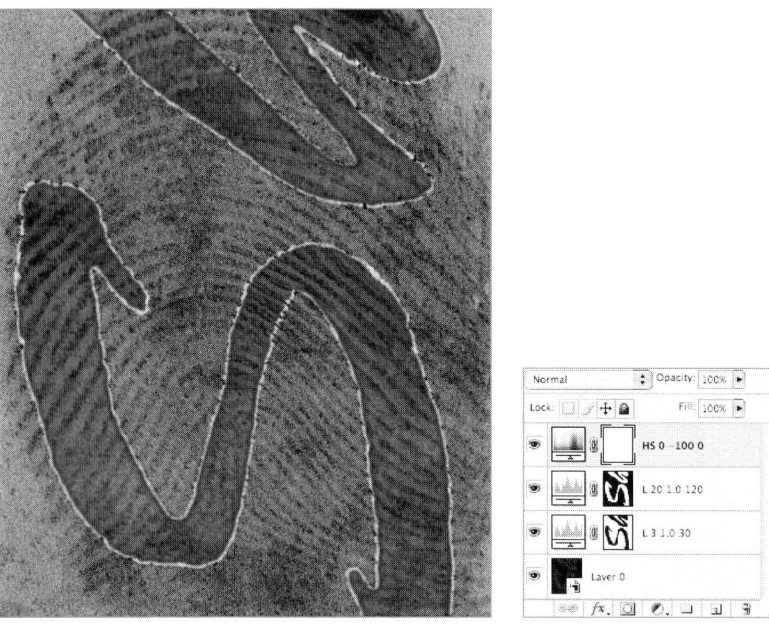

Figure 20.15 The final image on the left and the Layers palette on the right

The visibility for any layer can also be turned on and off by clicking the Visibility icon. To toggle between the original data in the background layer and the corrected image, Alt/Option+click the Background Visibility icon. This will toggle between only the background layer being visible and all layers being visible.

Any individual adjustments can be seen by looking at the layer name, but they can also be seen by double-clicking the adjustment layer icons.

The layer masks can be viewed by Alt/Option+clicking the mask icon. Alt/Option+clicking this icon again will return to the image view.

This image is now ready to be saved and should be saved as a PSD or TIFF image to retain the adjustment layer data.

Summary

A substantial amount of information can be recovered from scans or photographs of fingerprints, questioned documents, tool marks, footwear, and other evidence. Techniques can be used to apply brightness and contrast adjustments to the entire image or to local areas of an image using adjustment layers and layer masks. Although one may need to make extreme adjustments to achieve significant results, if fine detail is involved, it is important not to overprocess the image. The methods described in this chapter should enable one to extract detail in most forensic analysis work.

When image adjustments are made as adjustment layers, the original pixel values in the image remain unchanged. This makes it easy to show others (including a jury) what the image looked like prior to making any adjustments and then showing how each adjustment affected the image. The process is repeatable, as any other technician can see exactly what steps you took in your processing and apply them to a copy of the original.

Using layer masks for local adjustments provides us with a great deal of precision in making image adjustments, plus it provides the ability to show exactly which pixels were adjusted.

Adjustment layers and layer masks provide a nondestructive workflow that meets the needs of the forensics user and makes the technical review process very easy.

Color Isolation

Color plays an important role in the content of many forensic images, including red blood on clothing, the purple of a ninhydrin fingerprint, contrasting colors of a license plate, and ink tints on a questioned document.

Color isolation techniques can be used to take advantage of the color values and reduce the effect of background colors, increase the tonal contrast of different colors, or isolate the colors to extract information from an image.

21

Chapter Contents

Separating Color Channels

When color information is in an image and may be beneficial in extracting image detail, one of the first things I do in my image analysis is to view the image in a variety of color spaces and then isolate each color channel. This often will be all I need to clarify an image; otherwise, it works as an excellent first step. That is, this process can show which color space is best for processing the image or which colors are significant in the image to use when using the Channel Mixer as described below.

Images from digital cameras and scanned negatives, slides, and prints are generally in the RGB color space. This means that the color information of the image is from a combination of red, green, and blue values. In Photoshop, images can be viewed in other color spaces, including CMYK (cyan, magenta, yellow, black) and Lab color (one lightness channel and two color channels). By viewing images in different color spaces, you can separate their channels and frequently isolate specific colors to clarify image detail. The color channels display only the values a specific color has in the image. For example, the red color channel only displays the red pixel values, and the blue channel only displays the blue pixel values.

Figure 21.1 shows an inked print on a check with a green security background. This background makes the print very difficult to see clearly. Converting it directly to grayscale would only change the green values to dark gray, not providing any improvement. Increasing the contrast makes the security background get worse rather than better. However, using color isolation techniques, the color values making up the security printing can be minimized. By following with a Levels adjustment layer, the detail in the print is isolated.

Figure 21.1 Color isolation techniques can be used to separate this fingerprint from the background, as seen in the enhanced image on the right.

In the RGB mode, this technique works very much like using color filters in black-and-white photography—the chosen color is lightened and the complementary color is darkened. In the CMYK mode, the opposite is the case—that is, the chosen color is darkened and the complementary color is lightened. In the Lab color space, the L channel displays the lightness values and the A and B channels display the color information.

The approach to this technique is to work on three copies of the image, one in RGB, one in CMYK, and one in Lab color, then to isolate each color channel. When color contrast contributes to image quality, one or more of the resulting images will generally show more detail.

Figure 21.2 shows the original image used in this example, the image converted to grayscale, and the separate color channels in the RGB, CMYK, and Lab color spaces. The magenta channel in the CMYK color space is the most effective at eliminating the background information from this image.

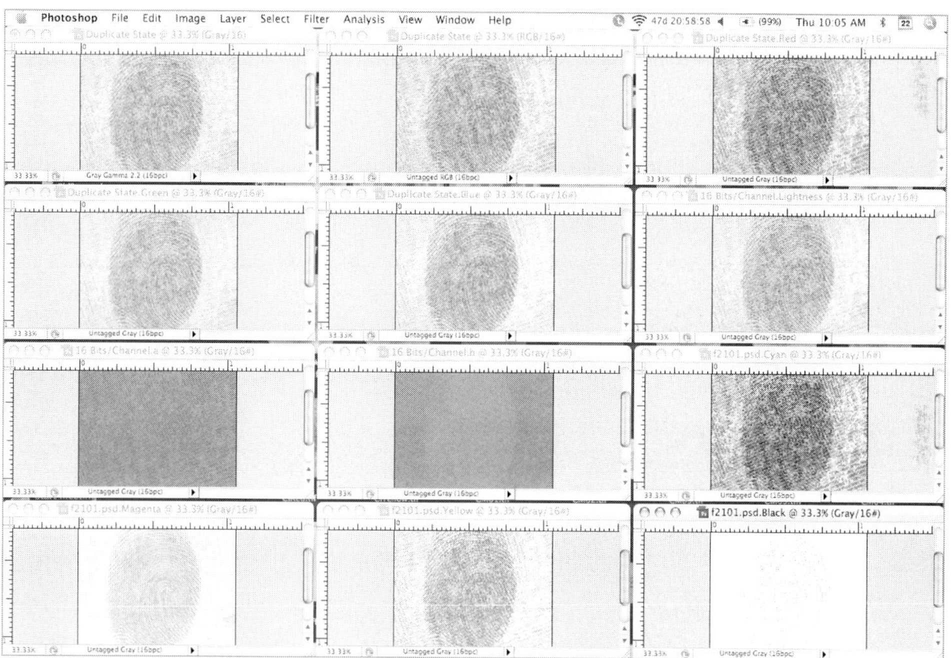

Figure 21.2 After making several copies of the image and separating the color channels, you can compare the images by arranging them using the Tile Horizontally or Tile Vertically command.

There are two primary methods that can be used to view the separate color channels. To begin either one, first open a copy of the image and then make four additional copies.

To duplicate the image, choose Image > Duplicate or click the Create New Document From Current State icon at the bottom of the History palette (see Figure 21.3). If you're using Image > Duplicate to create the duplicates, the image name can be changed or left to the default naming convention. I prefer to just click OK on the dialog box and let Photoshop append the current document name with the word *copy*. Creating four duplicates will provide five images—one for the original color RGB, one for grayscale, and one each to convert to each separate channel in the RGB, CMYK, and Lab color spaces.

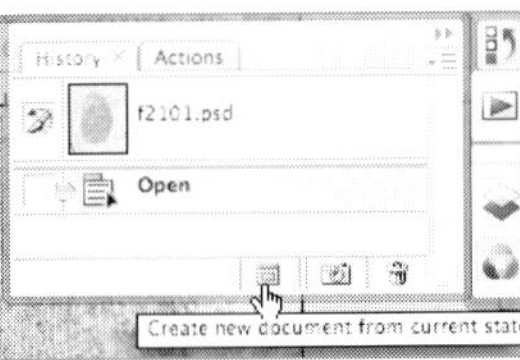

Figure 21.3 The leftmost icon on the bottom of the History palette creates a duplicate of the active document.

Once the duplicates have been created, convert one to grayscale, one to the CMYK color space, and one to the Lab color space; the other two will remain in RGB.

Choose the image intended for the CMYK conversion and choose Image > Mode > CMYK Color (see Figure 21.4). Then choose the image intended for Lab color conversion and choose Image > Mode > Lab Color, and convert one to grayscale in the same manner.

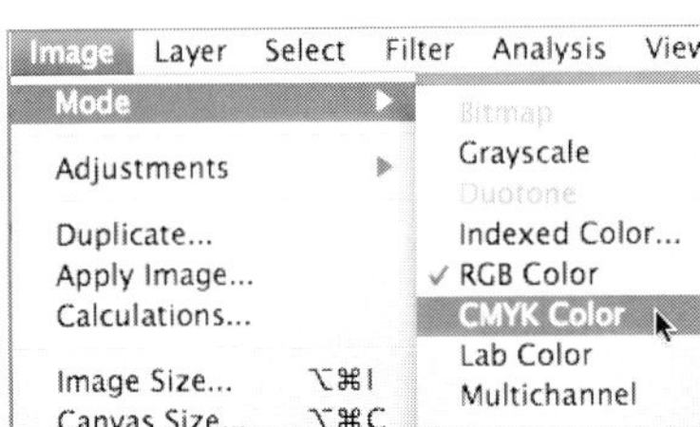

Figure 21.4 The options available for converting an image to other color spaces is under Image > Mode.

The next step is to view the separate color channels in each of these three copies of the file. One method to do this is to select each channel in the Channels palette by just clicking its thumbnail. The weakness of this approach is that it doesn't provide side-by-side comparisons. The other approach is to create separate files for each color channel by using the Split Channels command so that the files can be arranged on the monitor to compare each channel to the others.

To use the first method, select the Channels palette and click the thumbnail for each color channel, as shown in Figure 21.5, or use the keyboard shortcuts: Ctrl+1/Cmd+1 for the first channel, Ctrl+2/Cmd+2 for the second channel, and so on. As each channel is highlighted, the image will display only the values contributed by it.

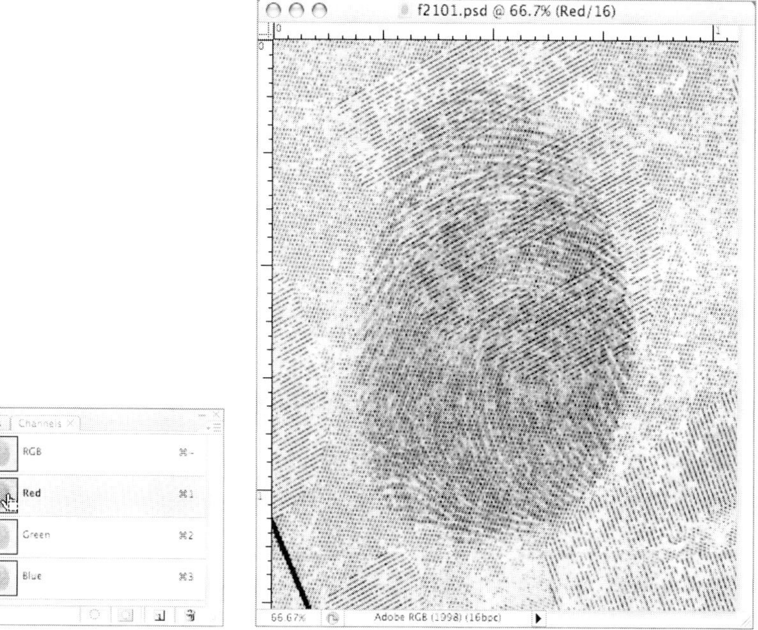

Figure 21.5 The Channels palette and one channel being displayed

The second method creates a separate image for each color channel. This is done by selecting the Split Channels command from the Channels palette flyout menu (Figure 21.6). Once that command is selected, a separate image is created for each channel. After you do this with one RGB copy of the image, the CMYK and Lab copies of the image, the 12 resulting files can be easily compared on screen (there will be one RGB image, one grayscale image, the three images for the separate red, green, and blue channels, four images for the separate cyan, magenta, yellow, and black channels, and three images for the separate Lightness, a*, and b* channels. To arrange the images on the screen as shown in Figure 21.2, choose Window > Arrange > Tile Horizontally or Window > Arrange > Tile Vertically; with 12 images, both choices will produce a similar layout as shown in Figure 21.2. Pressing the tab key prior to tiling the images will hide the toolbar, tool options bar and palettes—allowing the images to be larger. To bring back the toolbar, toolbar options bar, and palettes, press the tab key again.

If one or more of the images shows an improvement over the original, it can be saved and additional processing performed, if necessary. In this example, I selected the magenta-channel-based image and followed the color isolation technique with a Levels adjustment layer. If none of the images fully isolate the subject of interest, but one or more show improvements, use these to determine the best color space and color channels to work with using the Channel Mixer as described in the next section.

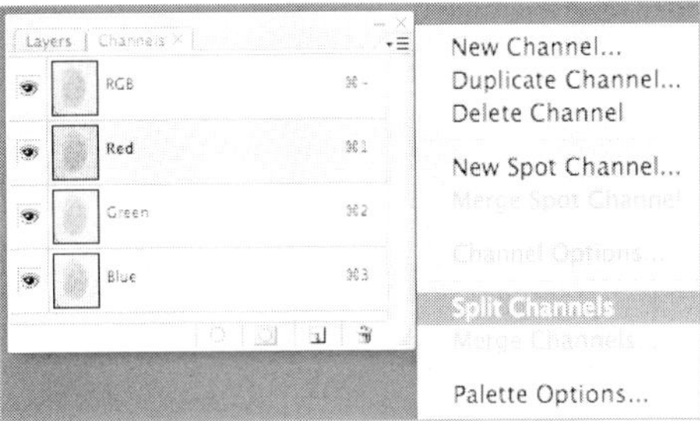

Figure 21.6 The Split Channels command from the Channels palette flyout menu

Channel Mixer

In some cases, there is important color information that can be utilized to improve the clarity of an image, but the color channels technique doesn't do an adequate job. This may be because the color is made up of a combination of two or more colors or because the color differences are too subtle for that technique to work well. In either case, using the Channel Mixer may work to improve clarity and separate color values in an image. This feature is commonly used by photographers to convert their color images to grayscale images while controlling the tonal range of each color separately—for instance to make blue skies dark gray and green foliage light in landscape photography.

The Channel Mixer can be invoked as an adjustment layer, making it a nondestructive process. The original pixel values will remain unchanged on the background layer.

In Figure 21.7, selecting the separate color channels in each of the color spaces did not significantly reduce the purple endorsement stamp. This is because there is not enough of a color contrast between the blue ink and the purple stamp. To isolate the handwriting, the Channel Mixer can be used to adjust the amount that each color channel contributes to the image and thus clarify the signature.

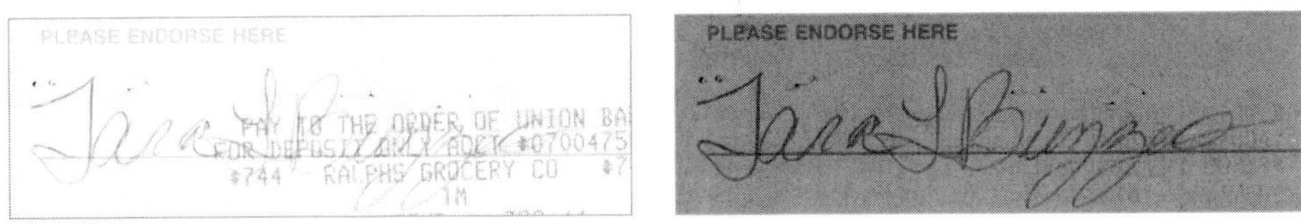

Figure 21.7 The original scan of the signature and endorsement stamp on the left, and the enhanced version on the right

The steps to use the Channel Mixer are relatively simple, although the specific settings are not intuitive. As part of my standard workflow, I view the image at

100 percent, convert to 16 bit, and convert to a Smart Object as described in Chapter 7. The process is to then create a Channel Mixer adjustment layer and adjust the color and constant sliders within the Channel Mixer dialog box. To begin, choose the Channel Mixer from the Layers palette Adjustment Layers flyout menu. This will create a new adjustment layer and open the Channel Mixer dialog box (see Figure 21.8).

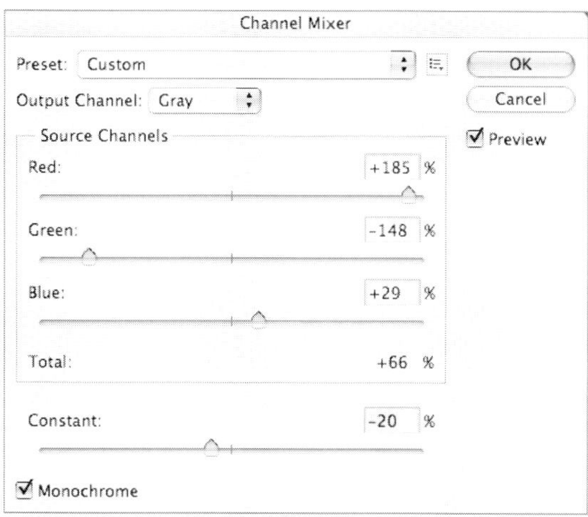

Figure 21.8 The Channel Mixer dialog box. Note that the Monochrome box must be checked for this process to work properly.

First, check the Monochrome check box at the bottom of the dialog box. Once that is checked, the Output Channel pop-up menu will read Gray and the Source Channel and Constant sliders can be adjusted to provide the needed color isolation. If the image is in the RGB color space, move the Channel sliders to the right for colors that should be lightened in value and to the left for colors that should be darkened. The Constant slider will adjust overall brightness.

In this image, red and blue contributed to the purple of the endorsement stamp, so those needed to be brightened. Yet blue and green contributed to the blue ink. Increasing red and decreasing green was the obvious starting place to separate the color values between these two features. From that point, the blue can be adjusted to determine the best combination of the three sliders. With the Preview box checked, the image is updated as each slider is adjusted. If the overall image is too light or too dark after making initial adjustments, the Constant slider can be moved to lighten or darken the image.

If good results cannot be obtained in the RGB color space, try converting the image to the CMYK color space. As with the color channels, the technique is the opposite when working in CMYK—that is, moving a color slider to the right will darken the value of that channel rather than lighten it.

Once an adjustment is made, click OK to close the dialog box and commit the changes to the adjustment layer.

This layer can then be turned on or off by clicking its visibility icon. When the visibility is off, the Background layer is displayed, showing the original image. Double-clicking the thumbnail for that layer will reopen the Channel Mixer dialog box and display the settings made to the image. I also like to rename the adjustment layer to reflect the adjustment settings I made to the image. In this example (Figure 21.9), I renamed the layer CM 185 –148 29 –20 M.

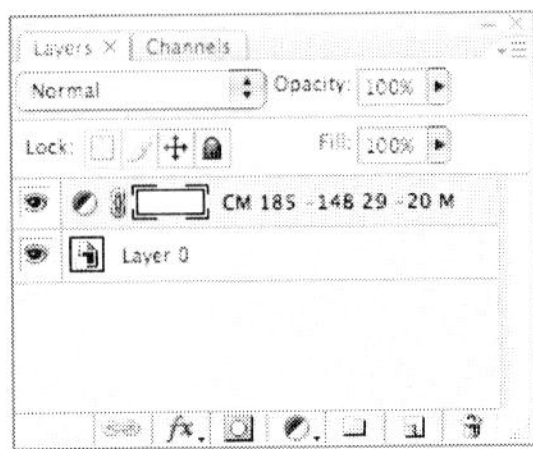

Figure 21.9 The leftmost icon on the bottom of the History palette creates a duplicate of the active document.

As a final step for this image, a Levels adjustment layer can be added to increase the contrast of the image to better clarify the signature.

Summary

The technique of isolating colors to clarify detail in images is a powerful tool. It is possible to eliminate distracting background information or to increase the visibility of important features in images. This technique can be beneficial with questioned documents, fingerprints, tool marks, paint transfer, security video, blood stains, and so on.

In addition, in areas where color is valuable and consistent, this technique can be used as an action, saving considerable time in processing images. For more information on actions, see Chapter 8 on batch printing. Because the purple stain of ninhydrin is fairly consistent, converting the image to CMYK and isolating the magenta channel works well as a standard approach to ninhydrin fingerprints.

Pattern Removal

In Chapter 21 we looked at methods for removing distracting elements of an image based on color values. Sometimes patterns exist in images that may not have color value, preventing a color isolation technique from working. Examples of patterns that may be removed with a Fast Fourier Transform (FFT) include an interference pattern in a video, a security pattern behind a fingerprint, and the cloth weave pattern behind a bloody footprint. If the pattern is consistent, it may be possible to remove the pattern while retaining the remaining valuable information in the image using an FFT filter.

There is no FFT filter built directly into Photoshop, so in this chapter we'll use a plug-in from Ocean Systems called ClearID and also a separate program called ImageJ from the National Institutes of Health. I'll show you how to get both of these tools.

22

Chapter Contents

Using the ClearID Pattern Remover

ClearID, from Ocean Systems, consists of several plug-in filters and JavaScript scripts that expand on the built-in functionality of Photoshop. These include filters and features for deblurring, noise reduction, frame averaging, an FFT filter, and others. A demo version of ClearID is included on this book's companion CD.

These tools can all be accessed directly from the Filter menu, but they can also be accessed by using scripts from the File > Scripts menu. When these filters are used with the scripts, they will convert your image to 16 bit if it isn't already. They will also warn you if the visibility is off for any layer; they will stamp all visible layers to a new layer and perform the function on that new layer, and after making adjustments, they will rename the layer to represent the settings used.

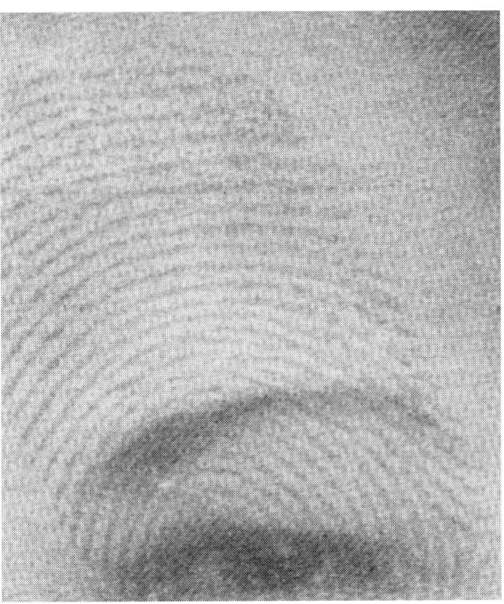

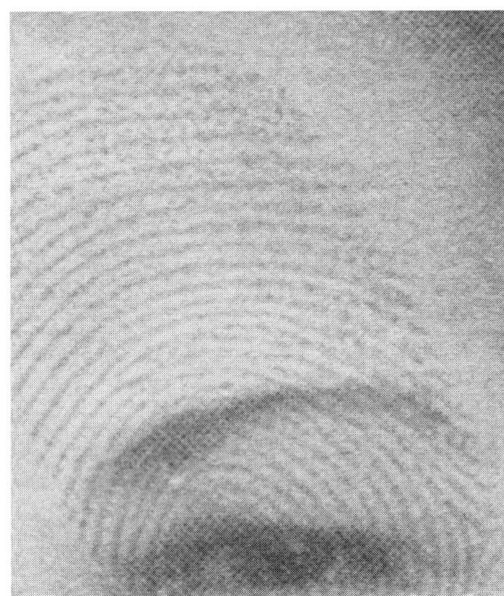

Figure 22.1 The fingerprint on the left is difficult to see because of the halftone pattern that interferes with the ridge detail. The image on the right shows this image after removing the pattern with the ClearID Pattern Remover.

To use this filter and enable the features in ClearID that automatically convert the file to 16 bit, create a new layer, and rename it, choose File > Scripts > dT Fourier Freq - Pattern Remover (see Figure 22.2).

This will convert the image to 16 bit, stamp visible layers to a new layer, and open the Pattern Remover dialog box (see Figure 22.3).

The Pattern Remover dialog box is divided into three sections. On the left is the Preview image, which shows what the image will look like after the adjustment is made. The power spectrum is at the top of the window. The light spots represent the repeating patterns in the image. The three sliders on the bottom of the image control the parameters of the filter.

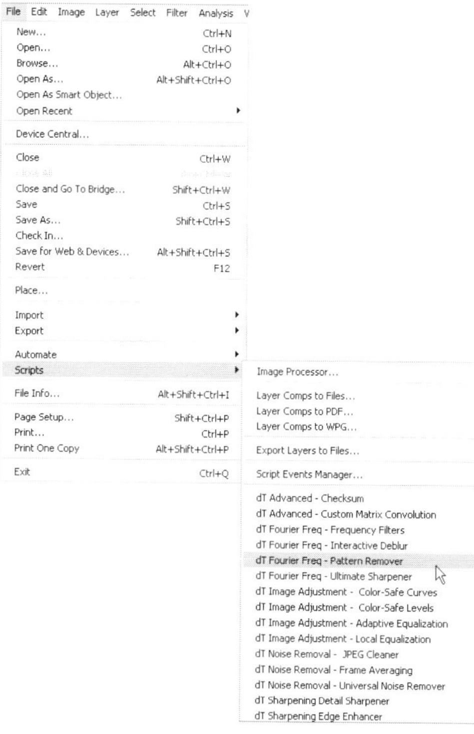

Figure 22.2 The Pattern Remover script is located in the File > Scripts submenu.

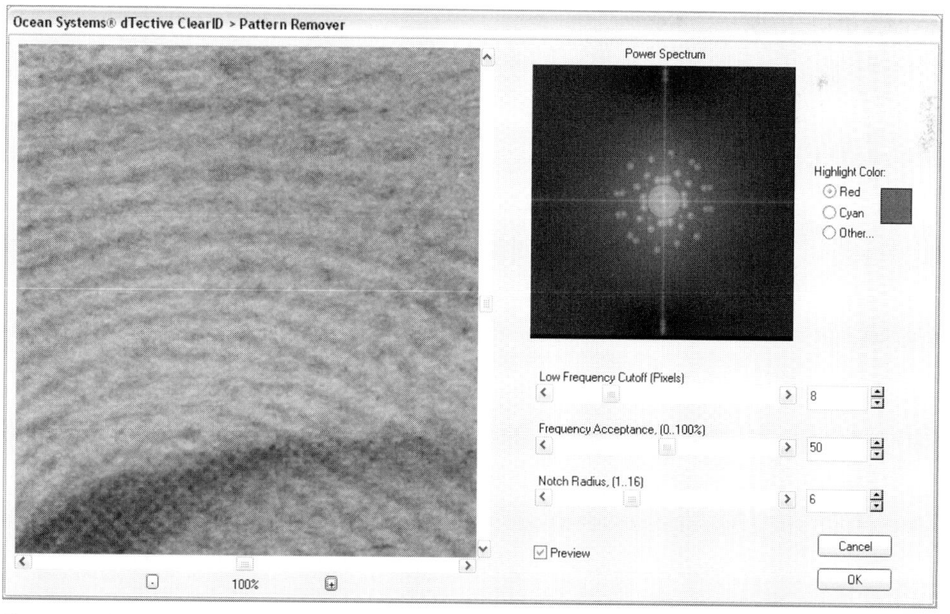

Figure 22.3 The Pattern Remover dialog box has a preview image on the left, the Power Spectrum window on the top right, and the three adjustment sliders on the bottom right.

The highlight color for the mask used to remove the repeating pattern(s) can be set to red, cyan, or another color—this simply displays the dots that represent our mask in a color that is easy to see.

The Low Frequency Cutoff slider controls the size of the area to ignore in the center of the power spectrum. Much of the subtle detail in an image is represented in this central area, so this slider should be set large enough to protect it from being a part of the areas selected by the Frequency Acceptance slider.

The Frequency Acceptance slider will select the spots in the power spectrum that potentially represent the repeating patterns. This slider should be of a high enough value to select the larger spots in the power spectrum.

The Notch Radius slider sets the radius for the spots that are placed in the power spectrum. The radius should be set large enough to completely cover the largest spots, but not much more than this.

The goal is to remove the repeating pattern without removing other information of value. The key to using this filter effectively is to watch the Preview image while making each adjustment. Avoid overprocessing the image by making the radius too large or by including too many spots.

When this filter has been adjusted, clicking the OK button will apply the settings to the layer and rename that layer with the filter name and the parameters used, as shown in Figure 22.4.

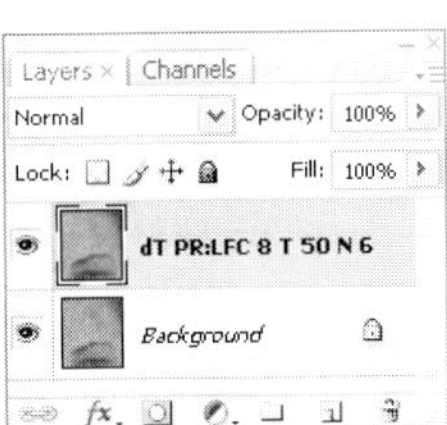

Figure 22.4 The Layers palette with the Pattern Remover layer automatically renamed

Using the ImageJ FFT Filter

ImageJ is an image processing application that was originally developed by the National Institutes of Health. It is available from http://rsb.info.nih.gov/ij free of charge for both the Macintosh and Windows platforms. ImageJ includes an FFT filter that works well but requires a bit more work than the ClearID plug-in.

To use the FFT filter in ImageJ, launch the application and open the image.

The first step is to display the power spectrum by choosing Process > FFT > FFT (see Figure 22.5).

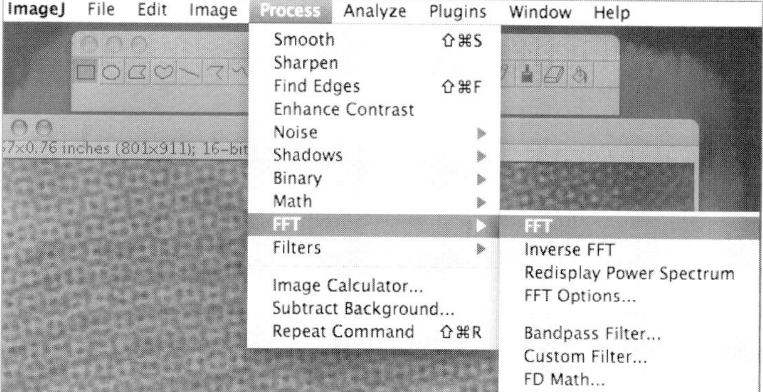

Figure 22.5 To use the FFT, first choose Process > FFT > FFT.

The power spectrum opens as a new window (Figure 22.6). It can be saved, if desired, to show how the power spectrum looked before processing. The white dots represent areas on the image that have a pattern (generally high-contrast changes that are equally spaced in the image).

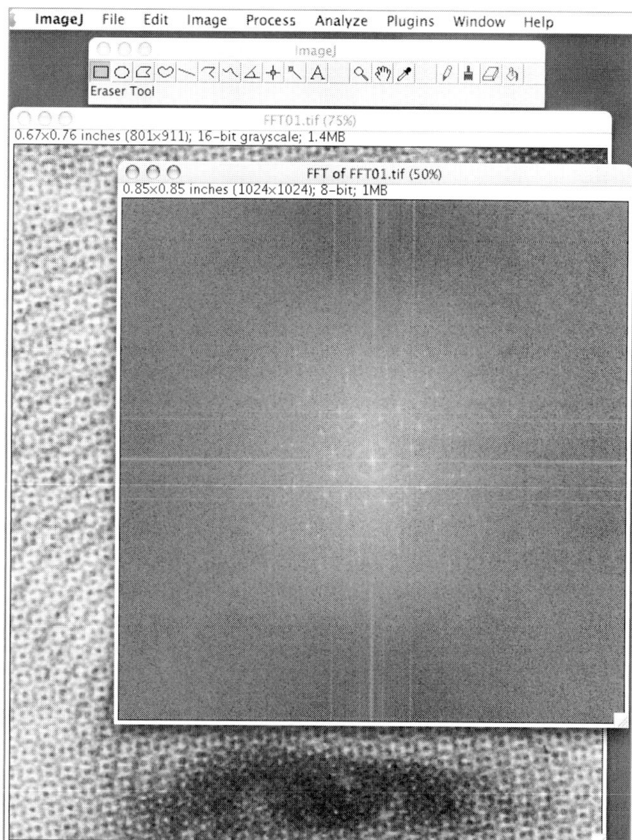

Figure 22.6 The power spectrum opens as a new window in ImageJ.

The key to using this filter is to select the paintbrush and place black dots on the white spots in the power spectrum that represent the repeating pattern, as shown in Figure 22.7. These dots are masks that will represent the features to be filtered when the process is run. It is important to never place dots on the center area of the image because this area contains a lot of the low frequency in the image that we want to retain. You will also notice that the spots are mirrored in diagonally opposing quadrants—that is, the top-right and bottom-left quadrants are mirrored as are the top left and bottom right. Be sure that if you place a black dot on a spot in one quadrant, you place one in the mirrored quadrant as well.

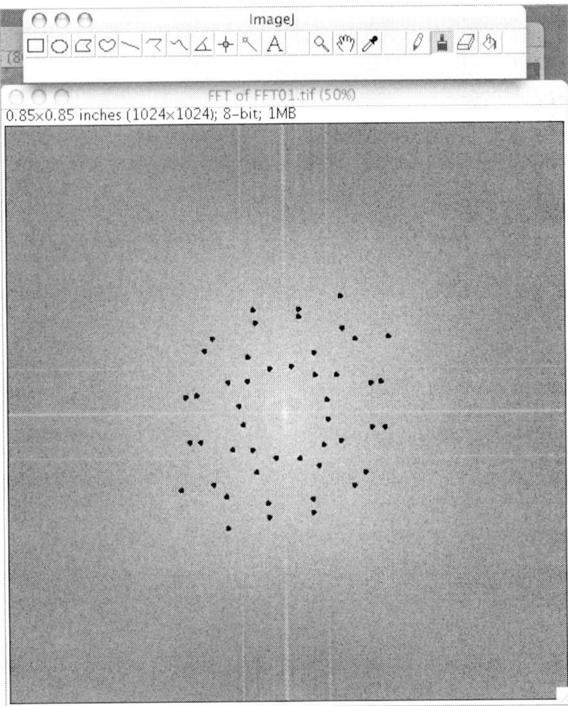

Figure 22.7 The power spectrum and Paint Brush tool with black dots placed

After placing the dots, choose Process > FFT > Inverse FFT and a new image will be opened that is the processed image, as shown in Figure 22.8.

Each file can now be saved to show four images:

- The original image
- The power spectrum
- The power spectrum with the mask created with the black dots
- The processed image

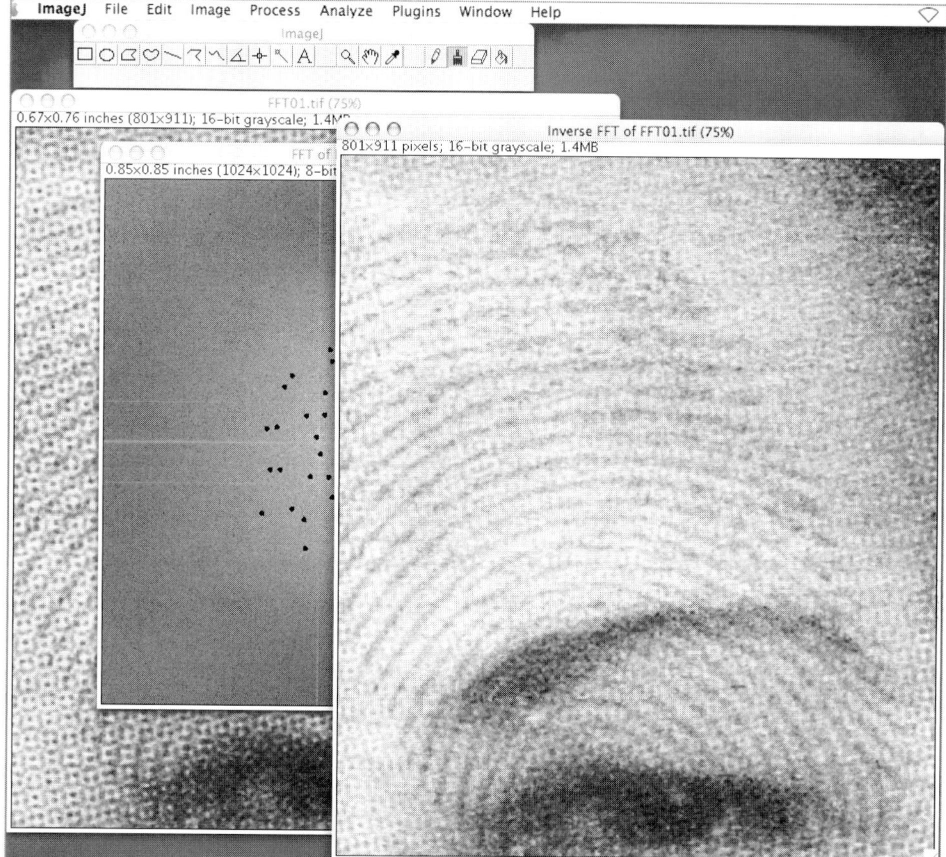

Figure 22.8 ImageJ creates a new image for each step in this process, as shown here.

Summary

The FFT filter can be used to remove repeating patterns from an image while retaining image detail. This proves beneficial when a fingerprint, signature, or other evidence is on the security portion of a check or envelope, a halftone pattern, heavily textured paper, fabric, or other surfaces with a printed or textured pattern. It can also be used to remove the electrical interference pattern on a video image.

The keys to success with the FFT filter are to recognize what types of patterns can be successfully removed and to learn to recognize them in the frequency domain.

Forensic Video Analysis

Although Photoshop is not a video editing application, there are several unique aspects to video images that can be addressed with Photoshop and Bridge.

Bridge can be used as a manual demultiplexer to sort multiple camera views and isolate the camera views of interest.

Photoshop can be used to deinterlace video, correct pixel aspect ratio, and perform frame averaging for noise reduction of image sequences. In addition to these capabilities, Photoshop CS3 Extended has the ability to import several movie formats and apply most filters and adjustments to entire sequences.

23

Chapter Contents

Demultiplexing in Bridge

Multiplexed video is common from security camera systems. The process of multiplexing is to record several cameras onto a single videotape or hard drive. Systems that record to hard drives should have demultiplexing capabilities in their software, so the need to demultiplex video in Photoshop is restricted to video from analog systems. I find that Bridge is an excellent place to demultiplex video when there are 1,000 frames or fewer. When there are more frames, the nonlinear systems that offer demultiplexing features, such as Ocean Systems's dPlex Pro, are more efficient.

Once you have exported the still image sequence from your nonlinear editing system, the process is to simply navigate to the folder of images in Bridge and sort the relevant camera views into new folders. Each folder is a single camera view, and it is easy to verify that only the relevant images are used and that no relevant frames were missed.

Figure 23.1 displays the individual frames from a multiplexed system in Bridge. To sort these frames into separate folders, each camera view needs to be selected separately, then moved into a new folder that represents it. Selecting multiple, noncontiguous images can be done by Ctrl+clicking/Cmd+clicking each relevant image or by giving each image a rating or label.

Figure 23.1 The Bridge window with frames from a multiplexed system

In the Bridge Labels preferences, you can set a preference to allow ranking without a modifier key (see Figure 23.2). This enables one to press a single key when an image is selected in Bridge to assign a star rating or a color label. I prefer ranking with no modifier key so that I can quickly navigate through the images with the arrow keys on my keyboard and rank the files with a single keystroke.

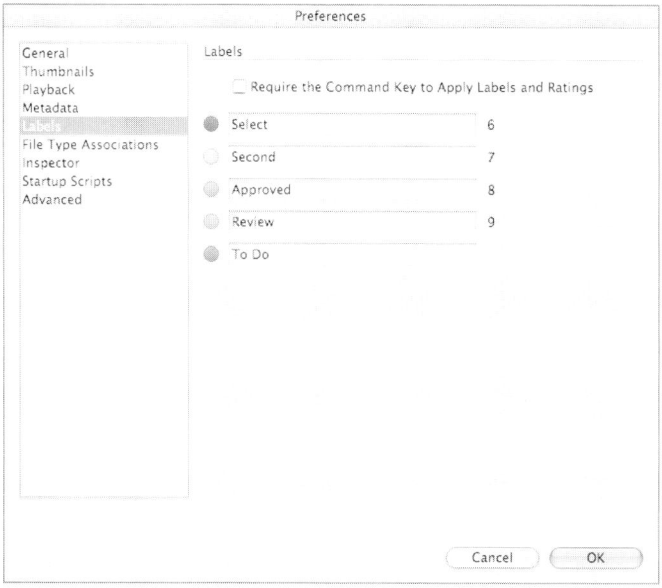

Figure 23.2 The Labels preferences in Bridge

Before sorting the first camera view, create a new folder in Bridge by choosing File > New Folder or using the keyboard shortcut Shift+Ctrl+N/Shift+Cmd+N. Rename the new folder to indicate the camera view, such as Camera 01 as in Figure 23.3. This prepares a location to place the images after they have been selected or sorted.

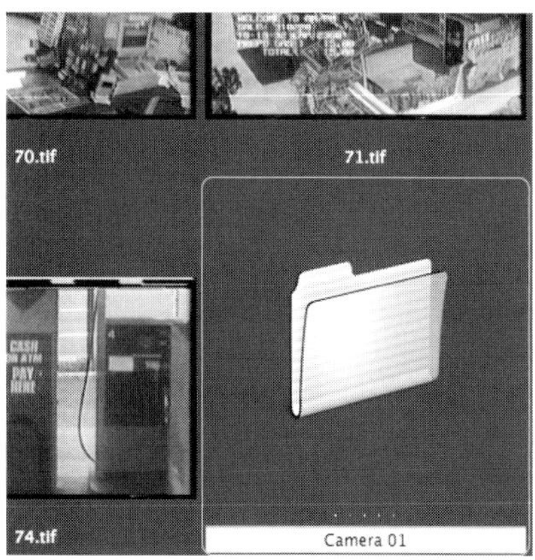

Figure 23.3 After creating a new folder in Bridge, rename it with an appropriate name.

To sort the images, click the first image of the camera view of interest. Press the number 1 on your keyboard to give it a rating of one star. Use the arrow keys on your keyboard to navigate to the next image from that sequence and press the 1 key to give it the one star rating. Continue until all images from that camera view have this rating. Figure 23.4 shows a partially completed set of images.

Figure 23.4 Rating all images from the same camera view

Once all the images from a single camera view have been given a rating, Bridge can be set to either only show the images with one or more stars (or one of several other options) or sort the files by rating. Either option will make it easy to select these images and move them into the folder created in the first step. To sort the files, choose View > Sort > By Rating. This will show all of the files, with the images having a rating at the bottom of the window. To only display the files that have a specific rating (one or more stars, a label, etc.), select that criteria in the Filter panel in Bridge and only those images plus folders will be displayed. If you're using Bridge 1 (from Photoshop CS2), there is a Filter drop-down menu at the top of Bridge's window that can be set to view only images with one or more stars, with specific labels, and so on—this will provide the same results as the Filter panel in Bridge CS3. Figure 23.5 shows both options in Bridge.

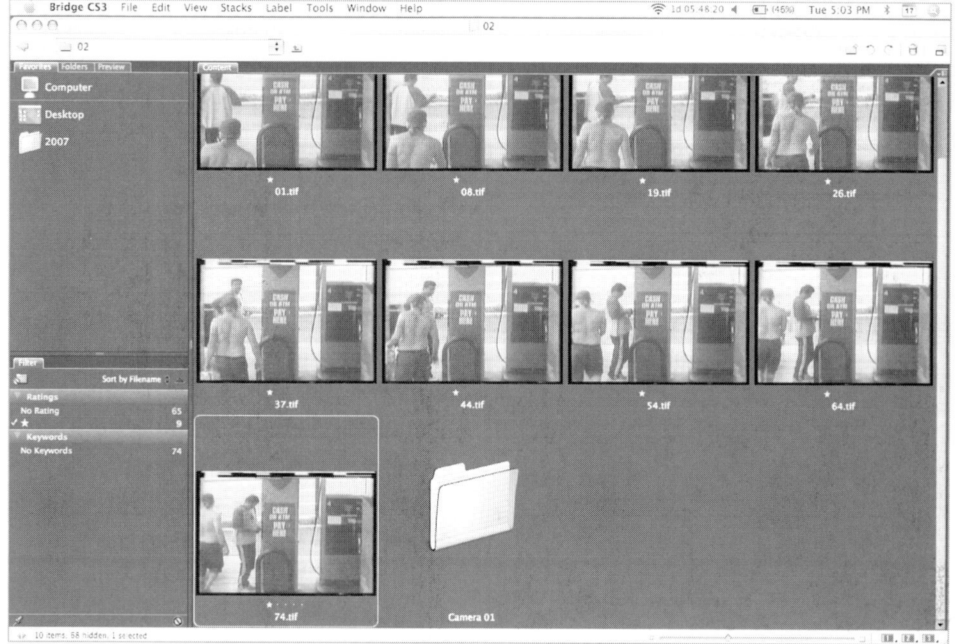

Figure 23.5 Sorting with the Filter panel to display only images with one star.

Now it's just a matter of selecting the first image in this sequence by clicking it once, then pressing the Shift key and clicking the last image in the sequence, and then dragging the images onto the folder (see Figure 23.6). This places the images into that folder and they are ready for any additional processing, for putting back into a movie sequence, for making into a contact sheet (see Chapter 10) or a PDF presentation (see Chapter 11), and so on. If additional images are to be sorted, turn off any filtering and repeat this process for each camera of interest.

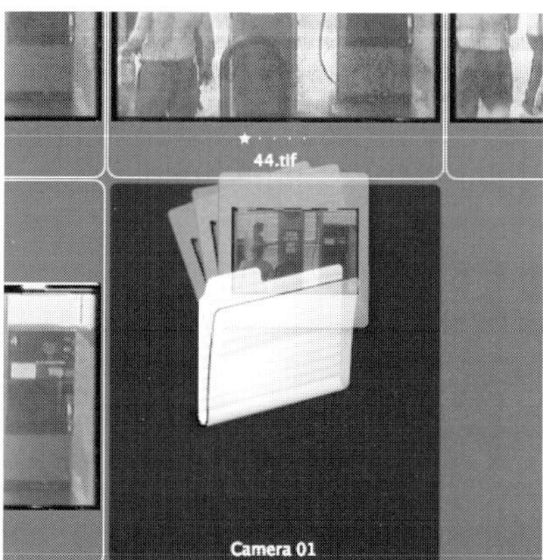

Figure 23.6 Dragging the selected images into the camera folder

This process is very efficient when you're working with up to 1,000 images, but it becomes less and less efficient when there are more images. Regardless of the number of images in the sequence, this method does enable you to verify that every image is accounted for, that any camera view contains only frames from that camera, and that no images were missed. It also may work better at sorting images from a pan-tilt-zoom camera or from cameras with very similar image content.

Deinterlacing Video

All analog video is interlaced, and digital video may be recorded in an interlaced or a progressive mode. When video is interlaced, each frame consists of two fields. One field contains the odd lines (every other horizontal row) of the frame, and the other field contains the even lines. If the two fields are of the same camera view, there may be movement between these fields causing the video to look as though a comb was dragged through it (see Figure 23.7). If the fields are from two different camera views, then the frame is a mix of the two fields.

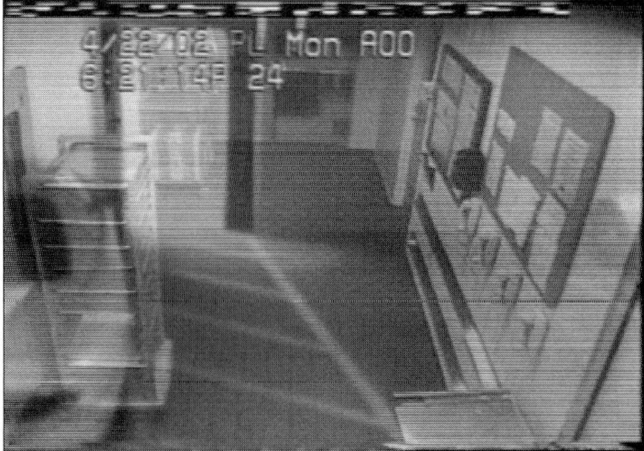

Figure 23.7 On the top is a frame of video in which movement occurred between the two fields. On the bottom is a frame of video that has a different camera view recorded to each field.

Since each frame is made up of two fields, each frame needs to be deinterlaced twice—once to show only the odd field and once to show only the even field. This can be done very efficiently using actions (see Chapter 9 for more on actions, including an action for deinterlacing). There are two different ways to deinterlace images in Photoshop for each field, plus the two fields can be aligned instead of deinterlacing (see the next section) to correct for misaligned heads or subject movement in some instances. This section will look at the methods for deinterlacing video using Photoshop's De-Interlace filter, and the next section will cover field alignment.

As in previous chapters, the first step is to convert the file to 16 bit and to a Smart Object. Because there are several options available when deinterlacing, the second step is to create three copies of the image so that there are a total of four copies open. To create duplicate copies, select Image > Duplicate, then click OK in the resulting dialog box, or click the bottom-left icon in the History palette (see Figure 23.8).

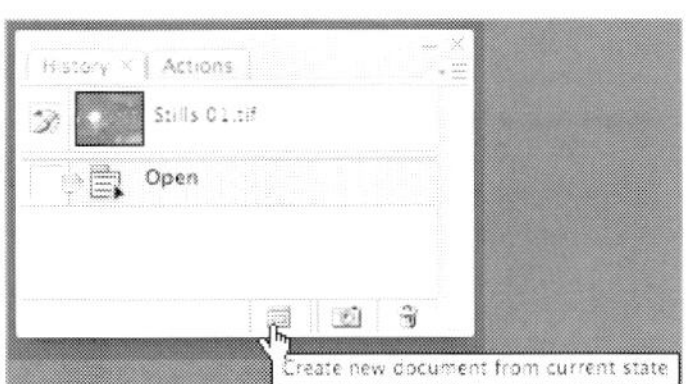

Figure 23.8 The "Create new document from current state" icon is the leftmost icon at the bottom of the History palette.

If you haven't previously done so, choose the Zoom All Windows option for the Zoom tool and the Scroll All Windows option for the Hand tool. Press the Tab key to hide the toolbar and all open palettes. Choose Window > Arrange > Tile Horizontally. If the images are not at 100 percent magnification, zoom them until they are. These three steps provide a workspace for comparing the results of the interlacing methods to help determine which method provides the best results.

Select the top-left image and choose Filter > Video > De-Interlace. In the dialog box, choose Eliminate: Even Fields and Create New Fields By: Duplication, as shown in Figure 23.9. This deinterlaces the top-left copy by keeping the odd lines in the image (lines 1, 3, 5, etc.) and replacing the even lines in the image by duplicating the odd lines, making the resulting image consist of lines 1, 1, 3, 3, 5, 5, and so on.

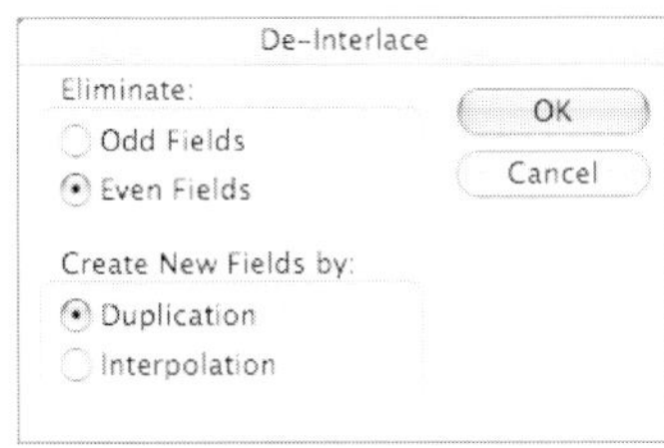

Figure 23.9 The De-Interlace filter can eliminate the odd or even field and replace that field through duplication or interpolation.

Next, select the top-right image and choose Filter > Video > De-Interlace. In the dialog box, choose Eliminate: Even Fields and Create New Fields By: Interpolation. This deinterlaces the top-right copy by keeping the odd lines in the image (lines 1, 3, 5, etc.) and replacing the even lines in the image by interpolating the values of odd lines.

For the bottom-left image, open the De-Interlace filter and eliminate the odd fields, creating the new fields by duplication. For the bottom right, eliminate the even fields, creating the new fields by interpolation.

Now the four images can be compared (Figure 23.10). It's possible that the information in each field is important, so the entire sequence may need two copies of each frame to represent each separate field. The images with field duplication will have more aliasing (jagged edges) but sharper contrast along edges. Those with interpolation will have smoother edges but less contrast on the edges. Once the preferred method is chosen, the deinterlacing can be done as an action to all of the frames in the sequence.

Figure 23.10 The four windows after applying the De-Interlace filter as described in the text

Field Alignment

Interlaced video can have two fields that are out of alignment due to mechanical issues or positional movement of the subject or camera between two fields on the same frame. In these instances, it may be better to nudge one field to align it with the other than to deinterlace the video. Deinterlacing always discards half of the data in the image, greatly reducing the potential image quality, so field alignment will be a better choice when it is appropriate.

The first step in aligning the fields is to select one of the fields (every other line) in the image. There are four Marquee tools—the Rectangular Marquee, Elliptical Marquee, Single Row Marquee, and Single Column Marquee. Potentially, a single field can be selected by selecting every other row using the Single Row Marquee tool, but this would be very time consuming. A more efficient way to make this selection is to load it from another image that already has a field selected. On the companion CD, open the file titled `Fields.psd`. With the image that needs field alignment as the active document, choose Select > Load Selection. From this dialog box, choose `Fields.psd` for the source image and select either Odd Field or Even Field for the channel and New Selection for the operation (Figure 23.11). Click the OK button and the field entered will be selected.

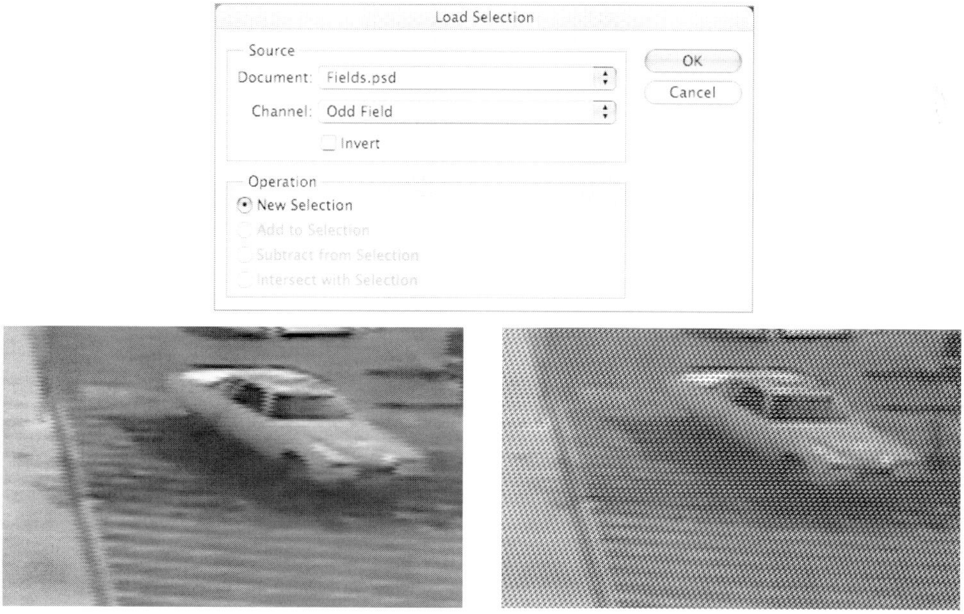

Original image

Selected field

Figure 23.11 The Load Selection dialog box, with a magnified portion showing the original image and the selected field.

You can hide the selection (the blinking lines) by choosing Select > Hide Selection or pressing Ctrl+H/Cmd+H. With the selection hidden, it is still active but the screen of blinking lines isn't preventing the image from being seen.

To nudge the selected field one pixel at a time, choose the Move tool and press the arrow keys on your keyboard. In Figure 23.12, the odd layer was nudged two pixels to the left.

Figure 23.12 The image after nudging the odd field two pixels to the left

Field Level Advance in Photoshop

As mentioned previously in this chapter, it is not uncommon for analog-based security video to be multiplexed at the field level. In these cases, each field of video needs to be viewed so that no significant images are missed. Some nonlinear editors, including all of the Avid non-linear editing software, have the ability to view video field by field. However, this capability is not present in many nonlinear editors.

There are two methods for providing this capability in Photoshop:

- Deinterlace two copies of each frame and view them in Bridge.
- Import the movie file directly into Photoshop CS3 and run the Field Advance script from the companion CD.

The technique for doing the first method is covered in the Deinterlacing section, earlier in this chapter. The deinterlacing can be done as a batch action as described in Chapter 9. In Bridge, the images can be viewed in the Filmstrip workspace and the arrow keys can be used to navigate from frame to frame. The set of images can also be grouped into a stack in Bridge and played as though it were a movie file (see Chapter 4).

The second technique is new to the Extended version of Photoshop CS3. The Extended version adds new support for video that isn't in the Standard version or in earlier versions. Movie files can now be opened directly in Photoshop. To open a movie file in Photoshop, choose File > Import > Video Frames To Layers, navigate to your movie file, and click the Load button. In the next dialog box (see Figure 23.13), choose the range of frames to import and check the Make Frame Animation box. Choosing Make Frame Animation will preload each video frame into the Animation palette, but it doesn't open the Animation palette.

To open the Animation palette, choose Window > Animation. Figure 23.14 shows the movie file open, the Animation palette across the bottom of the screen, and the Layers palette. Importing this file with the Make Frame Animation option created a separate layer for each frame and created a sequence in the Animation palette. You can navigate to each frame in the Animation palette by using the Play, Select Next Frame, and Select Previous Frame icons.

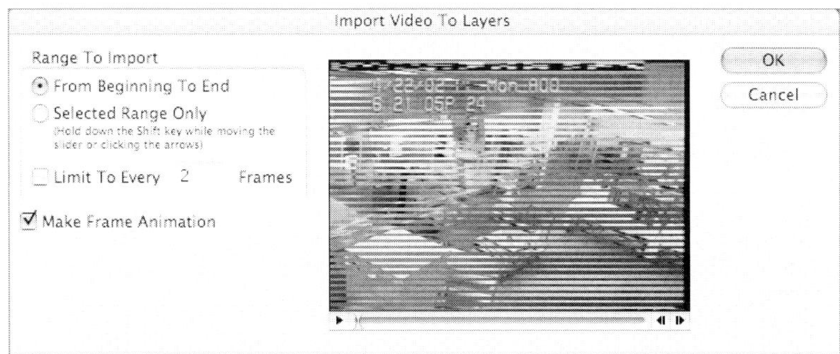

Figure 23.13 The Import Video To Layers dialog box

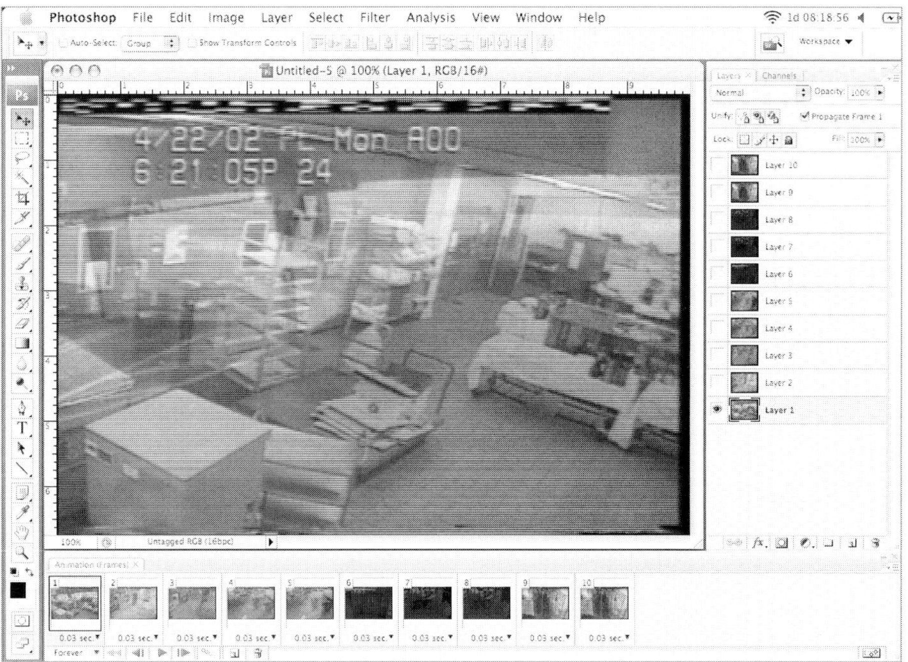

Figure 23.14 The Layers palette displays each frame as a separate layer and the Animation palette displays each frame in a sequence.

To deinterlace this sequence so that you can have field level advance in the Animation palette, each layer needs to be duplicated and then deinterlaced in order so that every other layer eliminates the odd field and the remaining layers eliminate the even field; then the Animation palette needs to be updated. This can be a tedious task, but there is a pair of scripts on the companion CD that automates this. If you have loaded this script into your scripts folder, then choose File > Scripts > Field Advance (see Figure 23.15). Otherwise choose File > Scripts > Browse and navigate to the script on the companion CD.

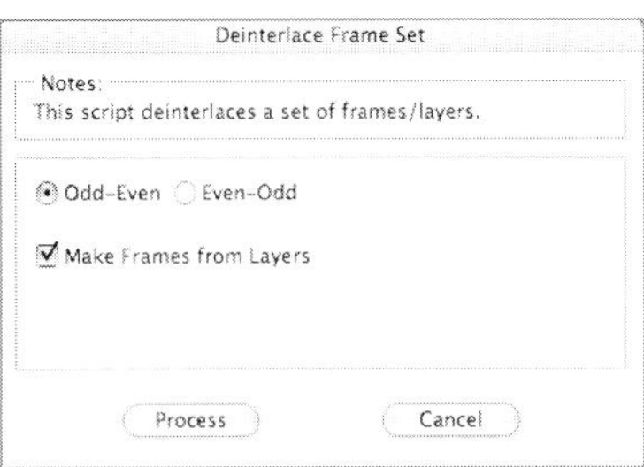

Figure 23.15 The dialog box for the Field Advance script

Choosing Even-Odd or Odd-Even determines the order that the deinterlacing will be performed. Choosing Make Frames From Layers will update the Animation palette. After you click the Process button, each layer will be duplicated and a field duplication method of deinterlacing will be done on each layer, alternating between replacing the even and odd fields and then updating the Animation palette as shown in Figure 23.16.

Figure 23.16 After this script is run, the Animation palette is updated to show each field as a separate frame, and the Layers palette shows each field as a separate layer.

If the field order is incorrect, there is a second script called Swap Layers that will reset the order of the layers and update the Animation palette to display the sequence in the opposite field order. As with all scripts, it can be run from the File > Scripts menu. If the Animation palette already has image content, the Update Animation option should be checked.

Frame Averaging

Reducing image noise almost always results in a loss of image sharpness, as discussed in Chapter 18. Frame averaging is a method of combining multiple images together to reduce noise, and it does not cause a loss of image sharpness; instead there will be greater apparent sharpness and more tones in the images. This method averages the value in a given pixel position in a stack of images; if the stack has several images and a specific pixel position has noise on only one of them, the effect of that noise is reduced to an almost insignificant amount. Because most noise is random, this method works to reduce most image noise when there is no camera or subject movement in multiple frames.

This technique is not limited to video; multiple photos can be taken of any subject and frame averaging can be applied to remove noise. This technique can also remove other objects or artifacts. For instance, multiple photos can be taken of a scene with people walking through; if the people are in different places in each frame, the mean value can show the scene without the people.

The process of frame averaging can be done in older versions of Photoshop by using multiple layers and adjusting the opacity of each layer. However, the Extended version of Photoshop CS3 has a feature called image stacks that provides greater functionality for this process. In the following sections, I will first cover the method that works with the Standard version of Photoshop CS3 and earlier versions; then I'll cover the method using stacks.

The companion CD includes a JavaScript (JS-FrameAverage.jsx) for automating frame averaging in Photoshop CS3 Standard and earlier versions. (It also works with CS3 Extended, however, the method using image stacks is my preferred method with that version of Photoshop.) The script was written by Jimmy Schroering (of the North Carolina State Bureau of Investigation; jschroering@gmail.com). The method for using this script is outlined in the next section.

Bridge Stacks vs. Photoshop Stacks

Adobe uses the word *stacks* differently in Bridge than it does in Photoshop.

In Bridge, *stack* refers to grouping a selection of images together in the same way you might put a group of slides into a stack. This stack can be easily moved from one location to another, and it can be viewed as an animation within Bridge.

In Photoshop, *stack* refers to grouping multiple layers into a single Smart Object and applying mathematical formulas to this object. The two formulas that are significant in forensics are median and mean. In a stack of images, choosing median will provide an image that displays the median value for each pixel position, and choosing mean will display the mean value in the same manner.

Frame Averaging Using Layers

Open several images (between 2 and 200) of the same subject with no camera movement or subject movement between frames. This may be a still image sequence or it may be multiple still photos. There is a script on the companion CD to do the rest of the process automatically, but I'll first describe the process to do this manually to explain how this works.

The manual process is to choose one image as the base and copy all the other images to that image file. This will result in an image with as many layers as the number of images opened. Each image can be closed after copying to the base image.

The next step is to change the opacity of each layer. Leave the bottom layer at 100 percent. Set the opacity of the next layer up (the second from the bottom) to 50 percent. This allows each pixel in the bottom two layers to be averaged. The third layer up gets set to 33 percent opacity, which provides one-third of the values from it averaged with two-thirds of the values from the layers below it. Continue this for each layer, using the formula that opacity equals 100 divided by the layer position, as shown in Table 23.1. The bottom layer is in layer position 1, the layer above it is in layer position 2, and so on. Figure 23.17 shows an image with 10 layers after frame averaging, with the Layers palette and the opacity of the top layer set to 10 percent.

To perform a frame average in a more automated manner, after opening the images, navigate to the JS Frame Average script from the companion CD. Jimmy Schroering (of the North Carolina State Bureau of Investigation) wrote this script to automate this process. The script has an interface that directs it to run on open files or a folder of images and has options to convert each image to 16-bit, use Auto Levels, or use Auto Contrast as part of the process. The script makes very fast work of frame averaging.

Table 23.1 Opacity Settings for Frame Averaging

Layer Name	Layer Position (from bottom)	Calculation	Opacity
Layer 9	Layer 10	100% / 10	10%
Layer 8	Layer 9	100% / 9	11%
Layer 7	Layer 8	100% / 8	13%
Layer 6	Layer 7	100% / 7	14%
Layer 5	Layer 6	100% / 6	17%
Layer 4	Layer 5	100% / 5	20%
Layer 3	Layer 4	100% / 4	25%
Layer 2	Layer 3	100% / 3	33%
Layer 1	Layer 2	100% / 2	50%
Background	Layer 1	100% / 1	100%

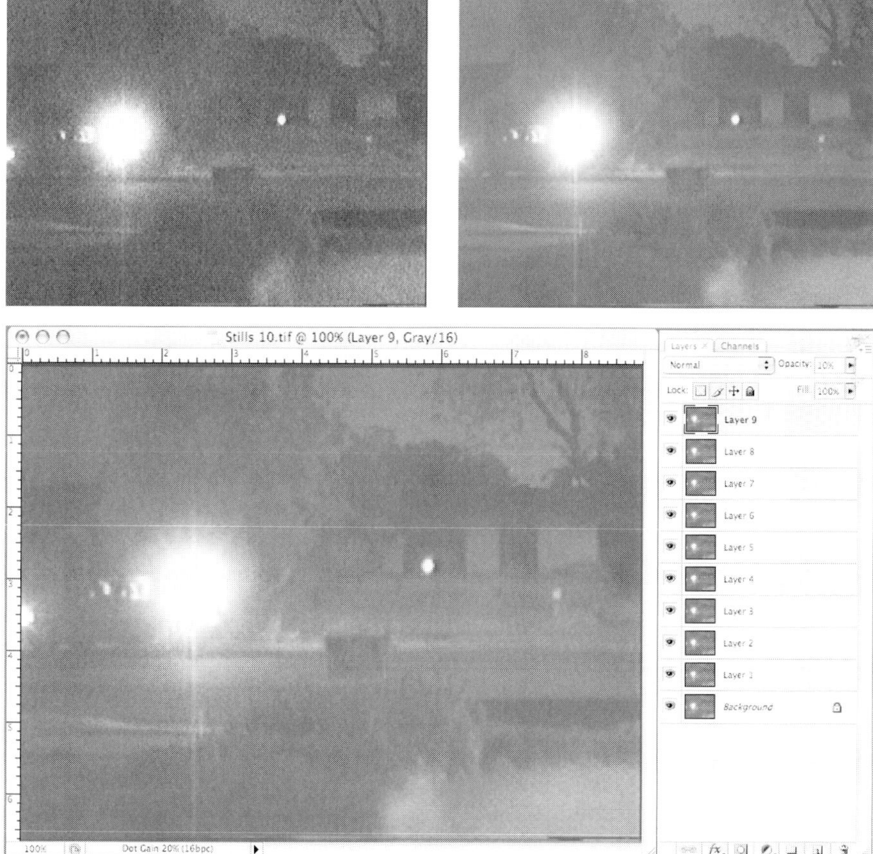

Figure 23.17 One of the original images on the left and a 10-layer frame average showing the opacity setting for the top layer

Whether performing frame averaging manually or using the Frame Average script, the results are somewhat limited because the layer opacity can only use integer values. In spite of this minor limitation, the results can be quite impressive, as shown in Figure 23.17.

Frame Averaging Using Image Stacks

In Photoshop CS3 Extended, the process is simpler than the manual method just described and does not have the same limitation of integer values as the layers method.

To begin, open the set of images into Photoshop and choose File > Scripts > Load Files Into Stack. In this dialog box (Figure 23.18), click the Add Open Files button to select all the open files. Check the Create Smart Object After Loading Layers box, which will copy all the open files to multiple layers and then group all the layers into a Smart Object. Click OK to run this script.

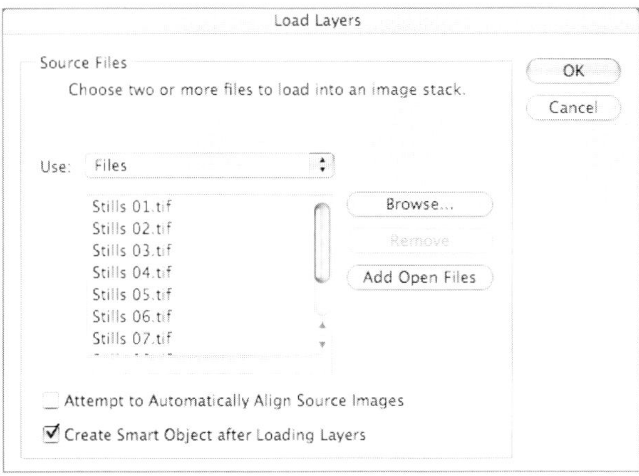

Figure 23.18 The Load Layers Files dialog box opens after selecting File > Scripts > Load Files Into Stack.

The second and final step is to select Layer > Smart Objects > Stack Mode > Mean to perform a frame average. There are several choices available, and the two that will work best for noise removal are Mean and Median. The resulting image and the Layers palette are shown in Figure 23.19.

Pixel Aspect Ratio Correction

Analog video is intended to be viewed on an NTSC or television monitor. These monitors display the video signal with the pixels closer together horizontally than vertically (what is commonly referred to as non-square pixels). Computer monitors, however, display pixels evenly spaced in both directions, or as square pixels. The difference between these two methods of display is known as the pixel aspect ratio. Because of the difference,

Figure 23.19 The frame averaged image with the final Layers palette

it is common for a video that is digitized for maximum quality to have dimensions that will properly display on a television monitor but will appear stretched on a computer monitor. This is the case with video files that are digitized at 720×486 pixels. This section addresses standard 4:3 pixel aspect ratio images that are digitized at the ITU-601 standard of 720×486 pixels. See the sidebar later in this chapter for information regarding pixel aspect ratio for digital video systems.

I recommend exporting images with the same pixel dimensions at which the files were captured. This section will assume that files were captured at 720×486 pixels. I also recommend doing all image processing at this native resolution and not correcting the pixel aspect ratio until the last step of image processing. Correcting the pixel aspect ratio will always require that the image is resampled, and this will always cause some level of image degradation (although it may be very slight).

If the image needs to be viewed at the correct pixel aspect ratio while you're working on it, this can be done by choosing Image > Pixel Aspect Ratio > D1/DV NTSC (0.9). The image still contains all of the original pixels but appears on the monitor as though the pixel aspect ratio has been adjusted. The filename in the image title bar will be appended with the word *(Stretched)*. It is important to note that this image will still print as though the pixel aspect ratio has not been corrected—this method is only for viewing on the computer monitor.

To correct the pixel aspect ratio, you must resample the image at a different rate horizontally than vertically. Some suggest that reducing the horizontal resolution to 648 pixels, making the image 648×486 pixels, is sufficient. However, this reduces the image by 10 percent of its pixels. A 720×486 pixel image has 349,920 pixels. A 648×486 pixel image has 314,928 pixels—34, 992 fewer pixels. If fine detail in the image is essential, it may be lost during this conversion.

I recommend making the pixel aspect ratio correction based on the resolution required for the output method. For instance, if the image is going to be printed 5 inches wide at 240ppi, it will be corrected based on that; if the image is going to be projected on an LCD projector with an 800×600 resolution, it will be corrected based on that resolution. The method is to determine the pixel width first, then to determine the pixel height as 75 percent of the width.

Digital Video Security Systems

Digital video systems may use "square" pixels and may not. They may have a 4:3 intended pixel aspect ratio, and may not. They may display at whatever pixel aspect ratio the window is stretched to, and they may even export at that same aspect ratio. When working with video evidence from digital video security systems, it is best to get the owner's manual for the system to determine if a non-square pixel aspect ratio is used. When this isn't possible, getting footage of a round ball from the same system will enable you to determine the correct pixel aspect ratio. A ball should have the same width and height; if the system produces an image of a ball that does not have the same width and height, it can be corrected by stretching the shorter dimension using the techniques in this section.

The first step is to open the image, convert to 16 bit, make any needed adjustments, then correct the pixel aspect ratio as part of the output process. Figure 23.20 shows the Image Size dialog box with settings to correct the pixel aspect ratio while preparing the image to be printed 5 inches wide at 240 pixels per inch.

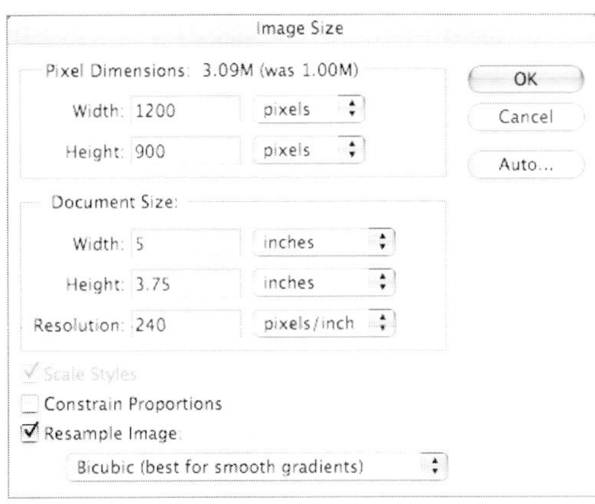

Figure 23.20 The Image Size dialog box with settings to correct pixel aspect ratio for a print output of 5 inches wide at 240ppi

To correct the pixel aspect ratio, choose Image > Image Size. In the Image Size dialog box, check the Resample Image check box and uncheck the Constrain Proportions check box. This will allow the image to be resampled at a different rate for the width and height. Next, set the image resolution based on your output—for display, the resolution is unimportant; for printing, use the resolution required by your printer (see Chapter 8 for more on printing resolution). Next, set the horizontal pixel dimension in the top of this dialog box. For printing, this will be the image resolution × the width (in this example 240ppi × 5 inches = 1200 pixels). The height is 75 percent of the width (for this example, 1200 pixels × 0.75 = 900 pixels).

The last setting is to determine the resampling method to use. Adobe recommends Bicubic Smoother for enlarging images and Bicubic Sharper for reducing images. I recommend testing all five options and using the method that provides the best results based on the image content and your equipment. The goal is to provide an output image that closely matches the image on your monitor used in your analysis.

Note: If you have a few standard sizes that you typically print, or a standard projector resolution that you use in court, it is easy to prepare an action for each to automate this process.

Summary

In many regards, working with image files from video is no different than working with any other files. All of the processes described in this book can be applied to frames from video files directly. However, there are some properties of video files that are unique, including interlacing, multiplexing, and aspect ratio intended for viewing on an NTSC monitor. Additionally, because video is often recorded at 29.97 frames per second (commonly referred to as 30 frames per second), video files are good candidates for frame averaging techniques.

Once video is exported as a still image sequence, or opened directly in Photoshop CS3 Extended, these unique issues can be addressed. Although this doesn't eliminate the need for a nonlinear editing system, it does provide a way to work with video files with Photoshop in a forensics workflow.

24 Additional Features

This book covered many of the features available in Photoshop for forensic applications. In addition to digital darkroom and image analysis tools for color, contrast, and brightness correction, it covered localized corrections, merging multiple images together, precise image sizing, measuring objects in images, using color isolation techniques, reducing image noise, and more.

When looking at the long list of Photoshop's features, it is easy to see that there is still much more to this program. Some of these features do not merit a full chapter by themselves and others are beyond the scope of this book. This chapter will provide a brief overview of these features.

Chapter Contents

Match Zoom And Location

The Match Zoom And Location feature is a capability in Photoshop CS and above that enables multiple images to be synchronized together when zooming and scrolling. When used in combination with the Tile Horizontally or Tile Vertically features, it provides a great method for comparing multiple versions of an image or doing comparative analysis.

This feature is found under Window > Arrange > Match Zoom And Location.

To use this feature, first open multiple files and choose Window > Tile Vertically or Window > Tile Vertically (or Tile Horizontally). This arranges the images on the screen so that all open images can be viewed without being covered by other images.

Choose the Zoom tool and check the Zoom All Windows box in the options bar. Choose the Hand tool and choose the Scroll All Windows box in the options bar.

Zooming or scrolling one image will now zoom or scroll all images in synchronization. Using the keyboard shortcuts to access the Zoom and Hand tools can make this very efficient ("Z" chooses the Zoom tool and "H" chooses the Hand tool). Whether comparing fingerprints, tool marks, or footwear, this feature is a great time-saver in keeping the images oriented so that you don't need to zoom each image separately.

Web Photo Gallery

We looked at the PDF Presentation feature in Chapter 11 for preparing multiple-page PDF documents of the images in a case. The Web Photo Gallery is a similar tool, except that it presents the images in a format that is viewable with a web browser such as Internet Explorer or Apple Safari. Images are copied and resized to fit into a web page window, thumbnails are created, titles can be created, and even some metadata fields can be included. This can make a very convenient method for presenting images in court or for placing images on an internal network so that those involved in a case can easily access copies of the files for review.

The Web Photo Gallery is located in File > Automate > Web Photo Gallery.

Merge To HDR

A new feature in Photoshop CS2, Merge To HDR provides support for high-dynamic-range images. This means that information from multiple images can be merged to retain detail in highlights and shadows over a wide range of tones.

It is not uncommon to photograph crime scenes that exceed the dynamic range of your camera—whether digital or film. The solution has been either to choose which values to lose (the highlights, the shadows, or some of each) or to take multiple exposures to depict the separate tonal areas. Merge To HDR allows you to take multiple images at different exposures and merge the files into a single 32-bit file, providing detail in the entire tonal range of the scene. This feature can also work well with fluorescence photography when a wide dynamic range needs to be recorded.

Vanishing Point

This tool, also new in Photoshop CS2, is primarily for retouching images on objects that are not parallel to the camera imager. However, it has some potential for measuring objects on multiple planes in a photograph. The measurement functions are not yet precise enough for most forensic applications, but it can provide quick rough estimates. Hopefully we'll see additional precision in future releases. However, two primary issues are the lack of true right angles in the real world and the lack of resolution in many images—and the software cannot control these issues.

Scripts

For several versions, Photoshop has supported some level of scripting. Photoshop CS3 supports VBScript for Windows, AppleScript for Macintosh, and JavaScript for both platforms. In this book we utilized some scripts. In several chapters we used X Bytor's script to automatically name adjustment layers, in Chapter 23 we used the frame averaging script written by Jimmy Schroering, and the ClearID filters offer scripts that add functionality by converting each image to 16 bit, stamping visible layers to a new layer and renaming the layers.

Although scripting is not intuitive, there are reasons why this is an important feature.

First, Adobe ships several scripts with Photoshop that are powerful and can be useful in forensics. The Image Processor script is an excellent tool for converting images to another format, for processing Raw files, and for resizing images for a specific purpose, such as printing. The Export Layers To Files script is perfect for creating an interactive court display or for working with multiple frames in video files and exporting them to place into a QuickTime sequence.

Second, scripts can include Boolean logic. That is, scripts can take actions based on either/or type statements. You could use a script, for example, to only rotate images that are currently in portrait orientation.

Third, many companies and individuals write scripts and make them available either free or for a modest cost. One place to find some of these scripts is at the Adobe Studio Exchange website at http://share.studio.adobe.com.

The scripts in Photoshop can be accessed in File > Scripts.

Tool Presets

Every tool in the toolbar has one or more options that can be accessed through the options bar. After using Photoshop, it is fairly common to have a few sets of options that may be used for a specific tool. The tool presets allow you to save the options and easily switch from one to another.

For example, suppose I frequently make court charts and use a specific color and font for my titles and letters but they are in two different sizes. I can set one up for the titles and save it as my Title preset and set one up for the annotations and save it as my Annotations preset. The next time I use the Text tool, if I select my Title Preset, the color, font, size, alignment, and so on will be set to my preferences.

The tool presets are located on the left edge of the options bar for each tool and also in the Tool Presets palette.

Help Menu

The help feature in Photoshop has been a valuable resource for many versions, and it has been revamped in CS3. When using any new feature or when reviewing the steps for working with a filter or other process, referring to the help menu can be a great benefit. In many cases it will provide the steps necessary to use a filter or other feature. In some cases it provides lots of information about how a process, filter, or tool works.

In addition, the bottom half of the Help menu provides many how-to references. Choose one and it brings you directly to the proper section in Photoshop Help. You can also create your own How-to menu items. This can be valuable for agencies that have a standard operating procedure for working with images as part of their documentation of these procedures.

Tonal Inversion

Fluorescing fingerprints, carbon paper, and film negatives produce images that are tonally reversed from what is "natural." It is easy to invert the tonality of any image by creating an Invert adjustment layer from the Adjustment Layer icon in the Layers palette.

This tool can also be useful in many aspects of image analysis. Our eyes tend to see detail in light objects better than in dark objects. In cases where an analysis involves working with dark features, reversing the tonality may show the subtle details better.

Layer Blend Modes

When more than one layer exists in a file, the layer blend mode can be changed and provide a variety of useful benefits in forensics.

For instance, instead of using a Levels adjustment layer to lighten or darken an image, you can duplicate the layer. Changing the blend mode to Multiply will darken the image and changing the blend mode to Screen will lighten it. The effect can be increased by adding additional layers or decreased by reducing the opacity of the layers.

Blend modes can also be used to align multiple images such as multiple frames of a video in which a car moves across the screen. In this case, one approach would be to change to opacity of the upper layer and move it into proper alignment. Another approach would be to change the upper layer to the Difference mode and align the images until the common areas appear black. Then, return the blend mode to Normal.

Summary

Digital imaging has become a part of the forensics workflow for documentation and analysis by agencies throughout the United States and the world. The use of this technology in forensics dates back to early experimentation in the 1970s and 1980s with agencies fully incorporating it in the early 1990s.

Creating a valid forensic workflow utilizing best practices is a simple procedure and involves maintaining an archive of unaltered images, only working on copies of those files, and using valid procedures that are repeatable and verifiable.

Image processing tools are available in many applications, including Adobe Photoshop and the many plug-in filters and scripts that can be used in conjunction with it, such as ClearID from Ocean Systems and the scripts included on this book's companion CD. Using these tools to provide visual evidence that depicts, for example, crime scenes and traffic accident scenes allows you to work efficiently and share the images in a variety of ways. These tools also allow corrections for image defects and clarification of details within these images.

The purpose of this book is to share information about best practices and some techniques for using Adobe Photoshop in a forensics environment. Hopefully the information contained here is beneficial to help you learn a new approach, increase efficiency, and improve your workflow or verify that you and your agency are already doing things well.

Index

Note to the Reader: Throughout this index **boldfaced** page numbers indicate primary discussions of a topic. *Italicized* page numbers indicate illustrations.

C

D

E

F

G

H

I

J

K

L

M

N

O

P

Q

R

S

T

U

V

W

X

Z